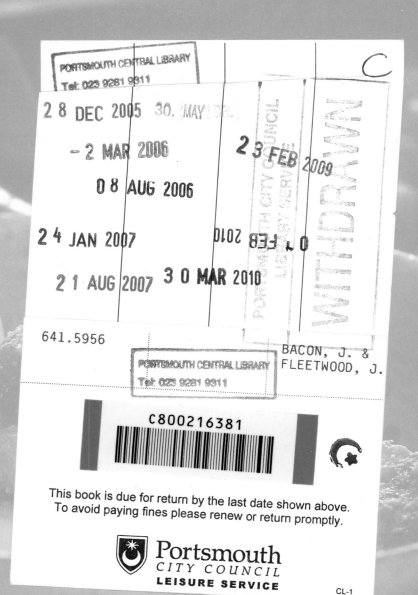

FOOD AND COOKING OF
AFRICA AND THE MIDDLE EAST

a fascinating journey through rich and diverse cuisines: the culinary history, the ingredients, the techniques and over 150 authentic dishes

JOSEPHINE BACON AND JENNI FLEETWOOD

LORENZ BOOKS

This edition is published by Lorenz Books

Lorenz Books is an imprint of Anness Publishing Ltd
Hermes House, 88-89 Blackfriars Road, London SE1 8HA
tel. 020 7401 2077; fax 020 7633 9499
www.lorenzbooks.com; info@anness.com

UK agent: The Manning Partnership Ltd, 6 The Old Dairy, Melcombe Road,
Bath BA2 3LR; tel. 01225 478444; fax 01225 478440;
sales@manning-partnership.co.uk

UK distributor: Grantham Book Services Ltd, Isaac Newton Way, Alma Park
Industrial Estate, Grantham, Lincs NG31 9SD; tel. 01476 541080;
 fax 01476 541061; orders@gbs.tbs-ltd.co.uk

North American agent/distributor: National Book Network, 4501 Forbes
Boulevard, Suite 200, Lanham, MD 20706; tel. 301 459 3366;
fax 301 429 5746; www.nbnbooks.com

Australian agent/distributor: Pan Macmillan Australia, Level 18, St Martins
Tower, 31 Market St, Sydney, NSW 2000; tel. 1300 135 113;
fax 1300 135 103; customer.service@macmillan.com.au

New Zealand agent/distributor: David Bateman Ltd, 30 Tarndale Grove,
Off Bush Road, Albany, Auckland; tel. (09) 415 7664; fax (09) 415 8892

PUBLISHER: Joanna Lorenz
EDITORIAL DIRECTOR: Helen Sudell
EXECUTIVE EDITOR: Joanne Rippin
PHOTOGRAPHS: Craig Robertson, William Adams-Lingwood, Patrick
McLeavey, Martin Brigdale
RECIPES: Ghillie Basan, Rosamund Grant, Rebekah Hassan,
Soheila Kimberley
DESIGNER: Adelle Morris
PRODUCTION CONTROLLER: Wendy Lawson
EDITORIAL READER: Jay Thundercliffe

The Publishers would like to thank the following picture libraries for
the use of their images:
Corbis pp 7, 10b, 13 all, 14 all, 15, 16b, 36, 37, 38 all, 39,
40b, 41, 42t;
Travel Ink pp 10t, 11, 12, 16t, 17t, 40t, 48t, 43bl.

NOTES
Bracketed terms are intended for American readers.
For all recipes, quantities are given in both metric and imperial measures,
and, where appropriate, measures are also given in standard cups and
spoons. Follow one set, but not a mixture, because they are not
interchangeable. Standard spoon and cup measures are level.
1 tsp = 5ml, 1 tbsp = 15 ml, 1 cup = 250ml/8fl oz. Australian standard
tablespoons are 20ml. Australian readers should use 3 tsp in place of
1 tbsp for measuring small quantities of gelatine, flour, salt, etc.
The nutritional analysis given for each recipe is calculated per portion
(i.e. serving or item), unless otherwise stated. If the recipe gives a range,
such as Serves 4–6, then the nutritional analysis will be for the smaller
portion size, i.e. 6 servings. Measurements for sodium do not include salt
added to taste. Medium (US large) eggs are used unless otherwise stated.

10 9 8 7 6 5 4 3 2 1

CONTENTS

INTRODUCTION

Eating today is an adventure in taste and discovery as we explore other cuisines and cultures through the food we enjoy. Africa and the Middle East are two vast areas that have introduced a wide range of exciting flavours for us to discover. Many of their recipes are familiar to us, but there are still many more that are less well known. In this book we take a journey through these varied cuisines.

The huge continent of Africa embraces many countries with their diverse cultures and widely differing climates. Many foods are indigenous to Africa, such as okra and melons, but many others were introduced over the centuries, and some have arrived by natural means – birds and strong sea currents. Visitors to the continent from ancient times as well as traders and colonists over the last 500 years brought their culinary heritage with them and this became absorbed into some parts of African culture. Those visitors also adapted traditional African meals to suit their own palates and took them back to their own countries.

African cooks inherit their cooking techniques by word of mouth and then develop their skills by experimenting with different ingredients and cooking methods. The resulting creations are new and interesting and it would be true to say that they cook from the heart. Dishes include staples such as rice, yams and cassava, combined with hot peppery stews, or beans, lentils, nuts, a variety of vegetables and perhaps some meat, fish or poultry.

Along part of Africa's Mediterranean coast are the countries of the Maghreb – Algeria, Morocco and Tunisia. Here we will find a distinctive cuisine using exotic spice mixtures, seafood, and couscous mixed with brightly coloured vegetables and sometimes fruit. The tagine is a traditional North African method of slow cooking using a tall funnelled pot, which gives succulent results.

Left: Chickpea Tagine, in the pot that gives the dish its name, and Egusi, Spinach and Egg in the foreground.

In the Middle East, sharing food and showing hospitality is a way of life, and many of the exciting foods enjoyed around the world today originated there, such as the well-known Tabbouleh and Stuffed Peppers. In the Middle East, as in Africa, tradition has shaped its culinary heritage: food is slaughtered according to religious laws, and pork is eaten by neither Muslims nor Jews. Festivals, too, dictate what will be eaten and when. Lamb is a popular meat, cooked with vegetables and spices, and fish will be enjoyed in a variety of delicious ways. Sweet foods, too, are an adventure in themselves with deliciously sweet cakes and pastries filled with dried fruit and nuts, as well as fresh fruit desserts and puddings.

The distinctions between African and Middle Eastern cuisine is sometimes blurred, and this is particularly true of Egypt, which is situated in North Africa but has always been seen historically as a part of the Middle East. Culturally Egypt shares much with the Middle East, from its religious beliefs – most Egyptians are Muslims – to smoking the ubiquitous hookah. Egyptian cuisine has much more of a Middle Eastern than African influence, although there is no doubt that it also shares common North African influences with its western neighbours – Libya and the countries of the Maghreb – and with its southern neighbour, the Sudan. In this book Egypt's culinary influence is discussed from both the African and Middle Eastern perspectives.

Bringing together the authentic cooking styles and classic foodstuffs of two vast and diverse regions, this book creates a colourful and enticing resource of recipes which share origins, ingredients and influences. An extensive introduction details the countries covered, their different cooking traditions and ingredients. The following six chapters provide dishes that range from appetizers and main courses to refreshing fruit desserts and delectable pastries.

Join us in a culinary tour of these exciting lands, as you discover some of the varied and enticing dishes that make up the food and cooking of Africa and the Middle East.

Below: A busy market stall selling different types of grain in Abuja, Nigeria.

AFRICA

This vast region has a rich diversity of flavours and cooking styles, an amalgam of influences from within and outside the continent. North African cooking has similar elements to Middle Eastern cuisine, while sub-Saharan and southern African cooking is more constrained by the availability of ingredients. Many dishes and styles remain unexplored by the majority of food-lovers from other cultures. Here is a chance to become familiar with the culinary heritage of this fascinating continent.

THE AFRICAN CONTINENT

Africa can be divided into three principal areas, both geographically and from a culinary point of view: North Africa, sub-Saharan Africa and the expanse of southern Africa.

NORTH AFRICA

This area is itself divided into the narrow, fertile coastal strip along the Mediterranean and on either side of the Nile, which was the hub of the ancient world, and the desert. Typically Mediterranean produce – olives, grapes, figs, dates, pomegranates and almonds – are enjoyed in the fertile areas of the north, and rich creamy milk and dairy products are provided by water buffalo in the well-watered areas. Flocks of sheep and goats that feed on the sparse vegetation of the Saharan hinterland provide most of the meat in the diet.

Egypt

The cuisine in Egypt is very similar to that of its Middle Eastern neighbours. Many dishes are made with legumes – lentils, beans and chickpeas – including two of the national dishes, ful medames and falafel. Rice and cracked wheat are both staples. Okra, that most pan-African of vegetables, is used to thicken soups and stews, as is *meloukhia*, a

Above: Men in a rowing-boat, and in a dhow in the background, use traditional methods to catch fish in the River Nile.

bright green, spinach-like leaf. *Meloukhia* soup is a universally popular dish that may be made with the fresh leaf when in season, or with dried, powdered *meloukhia*. Because most of the population is crowded between large stretches of water – the Mediterranean and the Nile – fish are of prime importance. Tilapia flourish in the

brackish waters of the Great Bitter Lake, now part of the Suez Canal, where they are also farmed. Sardines, red and grey mullet and tuna are among the fish caught in the Mediterranean. Nile perch are the favourite freshwater fish.

The Maghreb

The cuisine of the three countries of the Maghreb – Algeria, Morocco and Tunisia – is distinctive, ranging from highly sophisticated in the towns to basic in the countryside, the Atlas Mountains and the desert. Magical spice mixtures are typical of the Maghreb, including ras al hanout, in which ground cumin and hot red pepper from the Sudan, known as *filfil soudani*, predominate.

The staple of these countries is couscous, made from durum (hard) wheat or semolina. The grains are soaked in hot water and separated individually by hand, while being evenly coated with smen – clarified butter – by continuous rubbing. This is a long and monotonous task that can take up to eight hours. It is a common sight in a North African village to see women sitting outside their front doors, a large metal bowl of couscous on their knees, as they chat to their neighbours while

Left: A herd of the distinctive cattle of the Dinka people graze on the fertile lands of the Massai Mara in Kenya.

endlessly performing the lifting and rubbing movement to separate and soften the grains. In the towns, the packets of ready-made couscous – couscous *tout prêt* – show that fast food has penetrated even here, and making couscous is now a matter of minutes, rather than hours. Morocco is also famous for its *warka*, a thin dough similar to filo that is made into pies and pastries, in particular Bistilla, the famous pigeon pie. In Tunisia, the same dough is called *brik*.

THE SAHARA

The vast white expanse on the map below the countries of North Africa, and encroaching into their boundaries, is the Sahara: the world's largest desert, which can easily be seen from outer space. Here, existence has always been at subsistence level; food is hoarded and diets are meagre.

SUB-SAHARAN AFRICA

The countries of Senegal, Mali, Niger and Chad are all former French colonies, so traces of French culture remain, especially in the more fertile Senegal. The Sahara gives way here to the Sahel, a semi-arid plain where rainfall is still too low to produce crops. Protein here has added importance, but the inhabitants subsist on imported food and fermented milk, smen and dried fish from the coasts. Meat is a luxury food, eaten during festivals in the form of *mechoui*: spit-roasted lamb or goat, stuffed with rice and vegetables. Dried tomatoes and aubergines (eggplants) enliven the diets in these countries, and they are also available in Libya and, in the north the Sudan.

Despite the dryness, the countries of the Horn of Africa – eastern Sudan, Ethiopia, Somalia and the tiny state of Djibouti – have their own treasure: coffee, which is drunk at high strength. Ethiopians roast the dried, greenish beans only when they are about to drink them. The freshly roasted beans are then ground down as finely as possible and boiled in water to form the thick, syrupy drink that is familiar throughout North Africa and the Middle East.

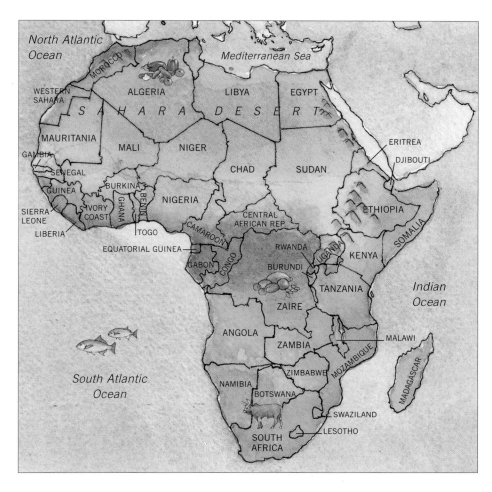

Although Ethiopians eat rice, they also have their own distinctive bread, which is made not from wheat but from a millet-like grain called teff. Unlike the tough flat breads of the Touareg and other nomads, Ethiopian bread, known as *injera*, is soft and pliable, made with a very liquid yeasty dough. It looks rather like terry towelling and has a very sour flavour because it has been leavened with wild yeasts. It is used to mop up the fiery sauces that accompany Ethiopian meat and vegetable stews.

West and Central Africa

Below the Sahara lie the thick rainforest areas of West and Central Africa, with their steamy heat, and where it is said that if you plant a stick in the ground it will take root and bear leaves like the biblical Aaron's rod. The staples here are mealies, corn cobs and cassava root, and similar large fleshy roots such as eddoes and cocoyams (colocasia). There is a profusion of vegetables, dominated by okra, squashes and beans. Most of the animal protein is in the form of fish from inland and coastal waters, as meat is in short supply.

Southern Africa

The terrain that makes up the south of Africa is a patchwork of deserts and fertile land, on which the European settlers established a strong farming tradition, allowing more intensive and productive agriculture, with pasture for cattle to graze on.

In South Africa there are strong differences between the diet of native peoples in the bush and the town-dwellers, black and white. The South Africans have developed their own distinctive foods, including dried meats – biltong – and sausages – *boerewors* – and *boboties*, a mixture of ground meat and spices.

THE AFRICAN KITCHEN

Food is scarce and precious in some areas of Africa, particularly the arid regions, and meat is rarely eaten. Dried and preserved foods are important elements in the diet, with fresh fish available only on the coast and from areas with lakes and rivers. Grains – rice, barley, wheat, maize, millet and *acha* – as well as dried beans are the backbone of the diet throughout Africa.

TRADITIONS PASSED DOWN

The North African kitchen is a sophisticated one, whose traditions date back thousands of years and whose recipes have been recorded in Arabic down through the centuries. Only in North Africa are so many cooking techniques used. Throughout the rest of the continent recipes are handed down from mother to daughter, and rarely written down. Measurements are flexible, and are usually made by handfuls, cups, calabashes and old tins, in particular Players cigarette tins, which are used in the tropics.

Throughout Africa cooking is performed almost exclusively by women, and in sub-Sarahan and southern regions the cooking techniques are slow and sometimes laborious. The pounding of mealies and yams, the fluffing of couscous grains, the peeling and shelling of beans and peas, the trimming of vegetables, the preparation of aromatic stews – these are all tasks that the average African girl learns from her mother from an early age.

Cassava, which originates from South America, contains quantities of hydrocyanic acid, making it too poisonous to be simply peeled and boiled, like a potato. In West and East Africa, it is cooked and then pounded to ensure that the acid evaporates. The sight of village women pounding cassava, using a huge pestle in a decorative wooden mortar, has been a familiar one for centuries.

Pounded yams are called *foufou*, which has a consistency similar to that of couscous. *Foufou* is a staple food of Nigeria. Rice is also an important staple, and Jollof Rice can be considered the Nigerian national dish.

Above: Women in Kenya pound cassava with a pestle in a mortar to release the poisonous hydrocyanic acid.

FOREIGN INFLUENCES

Africa has been subject to several foreign influences throughout the centuries, and this is reflected in its regional cuisine. In West Africa, it was traders – and eventually slavers – from western Europe, especially Portugal and England, and later those from the Americas, who traded with the Ashanti Empire, with its huge wealth of gold and diamonds. It is surprising how many of the African staple foods actually derive from elsewhere. Many, such as cassava, coconut, pomegranates and bananas, were brought in trading ships carried on the strong currents that run through the Indian and Atlantic Oceans between India and Africa or South America and Africa. The Arabs were early traders, bringing many spices with them, especially to East Africa.

One example of a staple ingredient introduced from outside the continent is the opuntia cactus, known in French as *figue de barbarie* (Barbary fig) – Barbary being the old name for the North African coast. However, it is not an indigenous plant, since cacti are native only to the deserts of south-western, North and Central America. It was introduced to North Africa soon after the discovery of the Americas and has flourished ever since.

Another example is the ubiquitous mint tea of Morocco. This would appear to be an ancient tradition, yet in reality it dates from as recently as 1854, when British merchants needed an alternative outlet for their wares that could not be sold in eastern Europe and Turkey owing to the Crimean War. They sold the tea cheaply in Tangiers and Essaouira (the modern name for Mogador), and the Moroccans adapted it to their own tastes, substituting milk with fresh mint leaves.

Right: Beans, grains and pulses are sold in bulk in African markets. Note the variety of measuring equipment.

EUROPEAN COLONISTS

Southern Africa, with its variety of terrains, including more temperate climates suitable for wheat cultivation, is the most heavily influenced by the foods of the former colonists. There is strong Portuguese influence in Angola and Mozambique, British influence in Zimbabwe, and British and Dutch influence in South Africa.

French influence

Not surprisingly, with its strong food culture, French food has influenced all the former French possessions, and the baguette is as universal in North and Saharan Africa as is the local flat bread. Pâté from chicken livers is another French introduction, and coffee is ground and drunk the French way. French cooking styles have had a beneficial effect on local dishes, including such delights as yam soufflé (*soufflé d'ignames*), eaten in

Below: A woman slices fish in Kayar, Senegal, where fresh fish is plentiful.

Madagascar. Vegetables from French seeds such as carrots, French (green) beans and cabbage are added to stews of local foods in Senegal, where French influence is strongest and ties to France are among the closest in Africa.

Portuguese influence

The Portuguese influence on African cooking has been extremely important, with the contribution of two basic Portuguese foods: capsicums (chilli and bell peppers) and dried cod. The peppers, originally brought from South America, have permeated the whole of Africa, with Tunisia, Saharan and West Africa being particularly fond of peppery stews spiced with large amounts of small chilli peppers. Dried fish, usually dried cod or hake, is imported into Africa in large amounts. This is an important protein element in countries in which protein is scarce and expensive. The cod is soaked in several changes of water for 24 hours, then

steamed or boiled with *foufou* and vegetables, including the ubiquitous chilli sauce (piri-piri) or chilli peppers.

Asian influence

The foods of the Republic of South Africa are also heavily influenced by the large population who came from the Indian subcontinent and very much by the "Cape Malays". These were settlers from south-east Asia, the former Malaya, Singapore and Indonesia, who arrived in the 19th century at the same time as the Indians, and who had an important influence on the national diet.

Merchants from the Indian subcontinent, whose highly spiced curries are very much in tune with the African palate, have also influenced the local cuisine. The fragrant curries of Kenya, Tanzania and South Africa, especially in cities with a large population from the subcontinent, such as Mombasa and Durban, are typical of Indian and Pakistani influence.

AFRICAN FEASTS AND FESTIVALS

Each African country enjoys its own regional dishes, sometimes influenced by their religious beliefs but more often by the ingredients that are available to them. In many parts of Africa meat is an important part of celebratory eating as it is not eaten on a daily basis.

NORTH AFRICA

Islamic traditions dictate social customs and entertaining in the countries of North Africa. For example, during the month of Ramadan, when eating and drinking are forbidden during daylight hours, each country has its own traditional food on which to break the fast in the evening. In most of North Africa, Harira, a soup made with chickpeas or lentils, will be served; however, in Egypt it will be a dish made from lentils and rice known as Mejedra.

In the Horn of Africa, Muslims celebrate both Eids (the two Muslim festivals of ul-Fitr and ul-Adha) with *sheer korma*, made with vermicelli and various nuts, including pistachio nuts, almonds and charoli nuts. The charoli nut is similar to a hazelnut and is found all over Asia and in Muslim Africa.

Whole sheep and goats are roasted for religious festivals, such as Eid, and in parts of the Maghreb, camels are also eaten. Stuffed camel stomach is a delicacy that may be served at a Moroccan feast for celebrating a special occasion such as a wedding. Naturally, there will be a dish of couscous, often a couscous royale, a massive dish where the grain is piled high in a huge metal dish, garnished with vegetables and sprinkled with rosebuds. This will be accompanied by a spicy sauce made from the stock in which the vegetables were stewed, laced with spices – ground cumin, saffron, ginger, chilli pepper and cardamom.

Choua, a dish of stewed lamb, may also be served, and the elegant pigeon pie known as Bastilla as well as other pies made with phyllo (or filo) dough. The meal will be rounded off by apricots, almonds, dates, figs and sweetmeats, such as baklava or halva. No alcohol is consumed as it is forbidden to Muslims.

SUB-SAHARAN AFRICA

In the countries of sub-Saharan Africa, which are predominantly non-Muslim, the feasts that are reserved for religious festivals and weddings may last for days. In Kenya, no wedding feast is complete without *ugali*, a kind of maize porridge, which can also be made from millet or cassava flour. *Ugali* is often accompanied by green bananas, wrapped in banana leaves and cooked on open fires. Another accompaniment to *ugali* and green bananas is *chiswa*, white ants or termites boiled and then fried. Perhaps more to European taste are the *simsim balls*: made from toasted, ground sesame seeds, which are also served with the maize porridge.

In Nigeria, a festive meal will include Chicken Suya, grilled chicken with a fragrantly spicy coating. The classic Nigerian dish, Jollof Rice, is always on offer, as well as fried plantains and bean porridge, a spicy stew of field

Above: The feast of Eid ul-Fitr marks the end of Ramadan. Here in the market of Habta in Sharqiya, Egypt, men are buying food for the celebration.

beans. Beans also feature in the snack food called Ackroes: fried bean cakes served to visitors, which are also available from street stalls all over Nigeria. Puff-puff – little puffs of fried dough – and meat pies are also served as appetizers at parties, although they can also be bought in the street. In the Cameroon, a wedding feast will certainly feature a dish called Folon, a stew of chicken and prawns (shrimp) flavoured with coconut water and folon leaf, a bitter leaf native to the Cameroon.

In sub-Saharan tropical Africa, palm wine and beer are the favourite drinks for celebrations: Star Beer in Ghana, Tusker Beer in Kenya. Local breweries can be found throughout the region, but many still prefer to drink Guinness.

SOUTHERN AFRICA

Celebrations in South Africa usually centre on the barbecue, known as a *braai* (pronounced "bry"). These barbecues originated as spit roasts in the late 17th century at celebrations held by the Dutch governor of what is now Cape Province. Later, the voortrekkers, the Dutch settlers, had to cook their meat in this way due to lack of other facilities. Cooks in different regions use different ingredients for the braai. In the Karoo, the central desert, mutton, lamb and eland are popular. In Natal, on the east coast, barracuda and yellowtail fish are wrapped in banana leaves and served with typical Zulu accompaniments such as mealies (corn on the cob), cornmeal breads and fritters. The South African lager, Castle, is popular as well as their wide range of sherries and wines.

On the island of Madagascar the wedding feast will be of fresh seafood and rice, as well as manioc flour (gari or tapioca) to accompany the Romazava: a meat and vegetable stew spiced with ginger. *Ranovola*, a watery rice drink, is

Below: Men of the Masai tribe roast a white bull for the festival of Olingsher, when boys of the village come of age.

enjoyed at celebrations, and in the north of the island there is *trembo* (fermented coconut juice).

Sweetmeats of various kinds are always served at weddings. Particular favourites include coconut and honey sticks in Mali, and *kashata na nazi* (coconut candy) in Uganda. These are the same sweets that are served for any other kind of entertaining. Pastries are

Above: In rural Africa weddings involve the entire community. Here Sudanese men participate in a wedding dance.

always popular: the Arab *sambusak* metamorphosed into the Indian samosa, and both are served throughout Africa. These small triangular pastries may be filled with either sweet or savoury mixtures before being fried.

AFRICAN INGREDIENTS

In the arid regions of Africa all foods are scarce and precious, and are carefully prepared. The favourite grains, rice and millet, maize and acha, are pounded and dried then made into a liquid porridge or couscous-like cooked grain. Dried beans, dried *meloukhia* and dried okra are sometimes the only vegetables available, supplemented during the rainy season with squashes, fresh beans and green leafy vegetables. Fermented foods – pickles, rancid clarified butter and yogurt – are important items of the diet, as are dried fish, sardines and prawns (shrimp), in areas away from lakes and the sea. Fish is an important item of diet where it is available, mainly Nile perch and tilapia.

GRAINS

A wide range of grains is eaten: various types of millet, including finger millet (*eleusine*), sorghum and teff (in the Horn of Africa). The main staples are rice in Egypt and couscous, cracked grain, usually durum wheat, in the Maghreb (Algeria, Morocco and Tunisia). Couscous is sometimes made from barley, especially among the

Kabyles of Algeria. Sesame (*simsim* or *benné*) is an African plant that is rich in oil and, like peanuts, the oil can be extracted and used for cooking.

Above: Fishermen work in the water and on traditional boats for tuna and pomfret in the Indian Ocean, off the coast of Mombasa, Kenya.

PROTEIN

Because meat is expensive and scarce in most parts of the African continent, certainly among the poor and the tribal peoples, vegetable protein is extremely important. This is provided by the native peanut and other varieties of nuts, and various types of beans and peas throughout the continent. Almonds grow in North Africa and are often added to savoury dishes, such as couscous. Kola nuts are popular because they act as a stimulant. They grow in the tropical rainforests of West Africa and are chewed fresh, or dried and ground to a powder for making into a drink. One type can be found as far south as Angola. The seeds may be white or pink, but purple is preferred. The nut is often eaten as a digestive before a

Left: Grains play a central part in the African diet, and are still farmed using traditional methods.

meal, as it is claimed that its slightly bitter flavour makes food subsequently eaten taste sweet. It is customary for a bride and groom to exchange kola nuts at a Nigerian wedding. Similar to the kola nut is the misnamed Java olive, which grows throughout Africa.

Black-eyed beans (peas) and cowpeas are typical ingredients in Africa's classic stews, which mainly consist of vegetables and dried beans, occasionally supplemented with a little fish, and even more occasionally with meat or poultry.

Fish are valuable adjuncts to the diet and both saltwater and freshwater fish are eaten all over the continent, as are prawns, shrimps and mussels.

Meat comes in the form of lamb and goat, camel (mainly for festive occasions), and game such as gazelle and cane-rat (also known as *agouti*). All over Central Africa wild game, known as "bush meat" is eaten: including kudu and eland, and, in parts of West Africa, even monkey.

In areas where dairy cattle are bred, such as among the Dinka peoples, whose territory extends across southern Sudan, Uganda and northern Kenya, the animals are a sign of wealth. As such they are far too valuable to be slaughtered. The dairy herds are, however, regularly bled from the neck and the nutrition-rich blood is mixed with *chisaka* – African spinach or amaranth – and stewed. This mixture is eaten with *ugali* (maize meal).

Below: Spices are used extensively in Africa, and are often made into mixes.

FRUIT AND VEGETABLES

A wide variety of fruits are grown in the region, many of them unknown and unavailable outside Africa. Vegetables are an important ingredient in Africa, especially leaves and greens, but also staples such as yams and plantains.

DAIRY PRODUCTS

Fermented milks of all kinds are widespread. Many peoples simply milk their flocks and pour the liquid into a gourd that is left in a tree for four or five

Below: Many varieties of nuts are cultivated in Africa, but also grow wild.

Above: Cloves are spread out to dry in the sun on the island of Zanzibar.

days until the milk has fermented. Fermented milk, yogurt and butter are often given to children.

SPICES

Spices are a favourite and essential ingredient in African cuisine. Some are produced and sold locally, but most of them are grown in East Africa on the island of Zanzibar.

Below: Giant snails and prawns, popular in Ghana, are used to flavour stews.

PRESERVED FOOD AND OILS

Refrigeration is still rare in much of Africa, but advancements in modern food preservation techniques, especially canning, have been a boon to tropical Africa. Pickled, dried and preserved food is an African tradition that continues to be as important today as it was in the past. Alongside the mounds of colourful fruits and vegetables, the open-air markets feature huge cans of condensed milk and butter or ghee (clarified butter or vegetable fat), as well as corned beef and lamb to supplement the meagre diet in the arid lands. Oils extracted from nuts and seeds are also used in different parts of the continent.

PRESERVES

Dried and puréed tomatoes are popular ingredients. It is not unusual to see women sieving and drying tomatoes on large mats in villages. Garden eggs – aubergines (eggplants) – are also dried for use when they are out of season.

Below: Various types of vegetables are pickled throughout Africa, peppers and turnips are particular favourites.

DRIED FISH

In areas of Africa away from lakes or the sea, dried fish is an important part of the diet. Many kinds are dried, including sardines, prawns and shrimps, which are used mainly in stews. However, salt cod, eaten widely in sub-Saharan Africa, is imported.

CANNED AND BOTTLED FOODS

As well as canned tomatoes and tomato purée (paste), which are imported, there are many locally produced canned and bottled foods that are used in African cooking.

Pickles

Vegetables pickled in brine are eaten throughout the continent. In North Africa, pickles (*torshi*) are made from aubergines, turnips, (bell) peppers, onions, and cucumbers, usually coloured pink with beetroot juice.

Smen

Used throughout Africa, smen is clarified butter used for cooking. It is also preserved and laid down in the

Above: Dried shrimps and anchovies are both used in African stews.

same way that Europeans lay down vintage wines. Sometimes it is preserved for many years, stored in jars and kept in cellars.

Spiced ghee and shea butter

In Ethiopia, *niter kebbeh*, or spiced ghee, is used for cooking. This is made by adding onion, garlic, ginger, turmeric, cardamom, cinnamon, clove and nutmeg to unsalted (sweet) butter.

Shea butter is a solid fat prepared from the seeds of a tree found in Ghana and Nigeria. The oval fruits contain a thin pulp and a large, oval, shiny brown seed. The pulp is allowed to rot away through exposure to the sun and the kernels are then roasted and pounded to make butter. The Hausa people of northern Nigeria prefer not to roast the nut before its butter is extracted. The fat then extracted is less odorous and more to European taste. Shea butter is also boiled in water and exported to Europe where it is added to margarine. It is also used in cosmetics.

Dairy fats

Fermented milk and butter are very important in the African diet. Buttermilks and mixtures that are a kind of intermediate stage between yogurt and clarified butter are used in cooking and added to all types of foods to enrich them. Buttermilks are often given to babies that are being weaned and to young children. In Senegal, a thick buttermilk mixture known as *nebam*

sirne is highly prized as a cooking medium. It is mostly home-made but small factories have begun producing it commercially. *Nebam sirne* may also be used fresh or, like smen, be kept for years to mature.

Coconut

Coconut milk is available in cans and can be stored indefinitely. A favourite cooking medium, creamed coconut is used for many types of fried snacks sold as street food in tropical Africa.

OILS

As well as smen, there are several varieties of oils that are used for cooking throughout Africa.

Palm oil

Also known as palm kernel oil, palm oil is reddish in colour, due to its high vitamin A content. It is made from the kernel of a palm tree native to West and Central Africa, from Benin to the Congo Valley, and is a valuable export. The nut produced by this palm is the dendé nut. This is a rare example of an African food travelling to South America. It was probably taken to Brazil by Portuguese slave traders; at any event it is now popular there, especially in the province of Salvador, whose inhabitants are largely of African origin. The fibrous pulp of the dendé nut is very oily, and the stone (pit), which is the size of a

Below: Shea butter, bottom, and coconut cream, top, are highly nutritious fats used African cooking.

Above: A selection of oils used in African cooking: in front is coconut oil, palm oil on the left and olive oil on the

right. The oils at the back are corn oil on the right and the lighter groundnut oil on the left.

walnut, has a white, oily kernel. In the 19th century, Europeans realized the potential of palm oil for making margarine, as it solidifies much more quickly than other vegetable oils. Palm oil is exported from tropical Africa.

Nut oils

Other oils used in African cooking include peanut, sesame seed and corn, which are all crushed and their oil extracted. Sesame oil has a strong flavour and fragrance and is used in dishes that can withstand it.

Bush butter is derived from a tropical tree that is known as the African pear, native pear, *safu* or *eben*. The purplish

plum-sized fruit grows in tropical Africa and is added to stews and curries. It has a high protein content.

Other oils

Cotton oil is an important oil for cooking in the dry areas of the continent that produce the finest cotton. The biggest African producers, and also exporters, of cotton oil are Egypt and the Sudan.

Sunflower oil is a lighter oil, which is used in Kenyan and Nigerian cooking, especially for frying.

Olive oil is also used, especially in North African countries, although less extensively than elsewhere in the Mediterranean region.

GRAINS, BEANS AND SEEDS

Africa has a variety of staple foods, filling starches for a continent where famine is not uncommon. To complement the grains are many different beans and lentils, another important form of protein.

GRAINS

In the more temperate climates of North Africa – Egypt, Algeria, Morocco and Tunisia – where the climate allows for as many as three wheat or barley harvests a year, the staple grains are coarsely ground to make couscous. Millet and sorghum are grains that are used for animal feed outside Africa, but here they are important ingredients in the human diet.

Wheat

The wheat used to make couscous is a hard wheat: durum wheat. Wheat is also made into bread: the flat breads of North Africa or the thick, porous *injera* of Ethiopia, which is used as much as an eating implement as a food, for mopping up the rich, thick sauces of Ethiopian stews known as *wat*.

Rice

Another staple eaten in all parts of the continent is rice, which is grown in Egypt, along the Nile, and other river valleys in Africa. The so-called Carolina rice was introduced into the United States from Africa by the slave ships, which carried it to feed their human cargo. This rice variety is still cultivated and eaten throughout tropical Africa and in Egypt.

Right: Green (top) and grey, or Puy lentils (bottom) grow wild around the Mediterranean and are a valuable vegetable protein.

Cornmeal

The other universal grain is cornmeal or maize, originally imported from the Americas in the 16th century. Maize is dried and served as cornmeal for use as a thickener for stews, such as *kenkey* and *banku*, both eaten in the Congo with spicy vegetable stews.

Millet

Also known as *acha*, *giro*, hungry rice and *fonio*, millet has been long used in western Europe as birdseed but is gaining popularity as a healthy, wholegrain food. It is another popular staple in Africa. The nutty, slightly bitter flavour combines well with stews. It is native to Africa, looks a little like maize,

Left: Two African varieties of grain, Carolina rice (top) and millet or acha (bottom), and sesame seeds (middle).

and grows about 4m/13ft tall, like corn on the cob. It is a fast-growing crop that needs little water, so it flourishes in the dryer parts of the continent. It stores well without deteriorating, which is another reason for its popularity in the Horn of Africa, where drought and famine are not unknown.

Millet is mixed with other food in some countries: in Nigeria, for example, it is mixed with baobab grain or the dry pulp of the baobab fruit.

Sorghum

Also known as *dawa* or guinea corn, sorghum is related to millet and is native to the drier uplands, and has been cultivated in Ethiopia for thousands of years. It is also especially popular in West Africa. Two varieties, black African and white pearl, are popular for grinding into a porridge, but because the grain contains no gluten it cannot be made into bread. Certain cultivars have sap in their thick stems that can be turned into syrup. It will not crystallize into grains because it does not have enough sucrose. Sorghum syrup is dark brown and sticky and tastes a little like molasses, but it has a milder flavour.

Teff

The teff seed is an important grain in Ethiopia. It is the smallest grain seed: 150 grains being equal in size to one grain of wheat. It is low in gluten and high in protein and carbohydrates, a good source of calcium and iron, and high in fibre, and consequently has become the latest fashionable wholegrain in the United States and western Europe and is now available from health food stores.

Cassava

Known by various names, including *gari*, cassava flour may be made in the home, but it is also produced commercially. It is cooked with water and eaten as a filling staple.

Above: Cassava flour (top) and cornmeal are staples of sub-Saharan Africa and come from South America. They are eaten with stews.

DRIED BEANS

All types of bean are valuable additions to the diet in Africa. The field bean, the forerunner of the broad (fava) bean, is a staple in the Egyptian diet, as are lentils – both the puy and the green.

Chickpeas

Native to North Africa, chickpeas feature in stews and all savoury dishes, although they are also coated with icing sugar and eaten as candies in the

Below: The peanut (groundnut) is native to Africa, and is a legume or pulse, like a pea or bean. The pods develop underground, hence its name.

winter. Chickpeas are almost always found dried, but they are in season in May, and fresh green chickpeas are a delicious snack eaten in Egypt and throughout North Africa. The Indian influence is apparent where chickpeas are split after drying and made into channa dhal. This is then fried as chickpea fritters. These fritters are popular all along the coasts of West and East Africa and in South Africa.

Field beans

In Egypt, the day usually begins with a bowl of ful medames – field beans stewed in water, with olive oil, lemon juice, cumin, onion and garlic, sometimes with the addition of a quartered hard-boiled egg.

Pigeon peas

Like all varieties of peas, pigeon peas are native to Africa. They may be eaten fresh or dried and, if very young, boiled in the pod. When dried, they are added to soups and stews.

Peanuts

Known for their high protein and fat content, peanuts are native to Africa and an important ingredient where animal protein is scarce. Mainly known as groundnuts, peanuts are cooked in stews. They also yield valuable groundnut oil. Groundnut stew is the national dish of Ghana, a stew that includes meat and aubergines as well as roasted peanuts. It is served with rice and small side dishes of raw onion rings, banana slices sprinkled with cayenne pepper, chutney, grated coconut and more toasted peanuts. Peanuts are grown in large plantations and are exported, dried, roasted or as oil, to Europe. Peanut flour is mixed with other flours to enrich the diet.

SEEDS

Benné, or sesame seed, is another highly nutritious native African plant. The seeds may be toasted and ground,

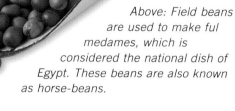

Above: Field beans are used to make ful medames, which is considered the national dish of Egypt. These beans are also known as horse-beans.

and served with honey or sugar as cakes, or sprinkled on savoury rice or other starches to enrich the main meal. The oil from the seed is also used for adding flavour to cooking.

The oil-yielding niger seed is from the same family as the sunflower but is native to East Africa, and is cultivated in Ethiopia. Niger seeds are eaten fried, in pickles or in cakes. The oil the seeds yield has a nutty flavour, and is sometimes used as a substitute for ghee or smen.

Below: Blackeyed peas or beans (top) and pigeon peas (bottom) take the place of the field bean in sub-Saharan Africa as a source of protein.

SPICES AND HERBS

One feature that is typical of African food throughout the continent is the love of spices and, in particular, hot peppery sauces. Fresh herbs are less widely used, and are mainly lemongrass, mint, basil and rocket.

SPICES

Many of the spices used in African cooking were imported by the Arab traders, but are now grown locally or come from East Africa, the Sudan, Ethiopia and, especially, Zanzibar. The climate and growing conditions in the picturesque island of Zanzibar, with its strongly Arab-influenced culture and lifestyle, are similar to those of the original Spice Islands: the Dutch East Indies. In the early 18th century, the Arabs brought spices to Zanzibar, now also known as Spice Island, for cultivation, and the island still supplies much of Africa with these essential cooking ingredients.

The island is still the prime source of the world's supply of cloves, and, unsurprisingly, cloves are used extensively in the cookery of the region. Other spices grown in Zanzibar are pepper, cardamom, ginger and nutmeg. These spices are important in the local cuisine, which is heavily influenced by the large population from the Indian subcontinent. Curry powder, also known as *mchusi*, has become a much-used ingredient in the African kitchen, thanks

to the Asian influence from traders and settlers. As well as these cultivated and exported spices, there are also spices that are native to Africa, and which still grow wild throughout the region. These include dried baobab leaves and fruits, and grains of selim (also known as African nutmeg). Okra, when dried, is also used as a spice. Potash, from the Bitter Lakes, is used as a substitute for salt and as a raising agent. Egusi seeds, the seeds of certain varieties of watermelon, are used to flavour soups, and are beneficial to the diet owing to their oil content.

Saffron

The classic spice of North Africa is saffron. Once grown even as far north as the United Kingdom (as in Saffron Walden), the saffron crocus is now mainly grown in Morocco, and is exported around the world. In North

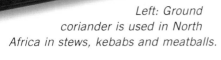

Left: Ground coriander is used in North Africa in stews, kebabs and meatballs.

African cooking it is an important ingredient in a variety of stews and is used to flavour and colour rice with its subtle fragrance and bright yellow hue. Another spice that is used in African cooking for its rich yellow colour, as well as its flavour, is turmeric.

Cloves

Cloves were originally imported from the Spice Islands by the Arabs, who traded extensively along the East Coast of Africa. They are grown throughout northern and eastern Africa and used lavishly in cooking. In Zanzibar, cloves are chewed to sweeten the breath.

Ginger

Ginger, like cloves, is used in many African dishes, and is a particularly favourite spice for flavouring stews.

Nutmeg

The fruit seed is about the size of an apricot. It has a lacy covering known as mace, which tastes similar to the nut and is also used as a spice. Nutmeg is used in sweet and savoury dishes.

Below: Saffron, the most prized and rare of all spices, has a subtle taste and imparts a golden colour to food.

Below: Turmeric, also known as the poor man's saffron, has a stronger flavour and is extensively used in Indian-influenced dishes.

Below: Ginger root can be used fresh, but more often is dried and used in its powdered form.

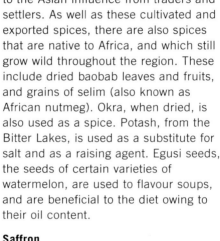

Above: Scotch bonnets are colourful African varieties of chilli pepper that are also grown in the West Indies.

Chillies

The hot peppers used to make the dipping sauces and pastes are almost certainly an import from South America from the days of the early traders in the 17th century, although this applies to many foods in Africa, because the climates of both continents are similar. In fact, there was a local pepper that was used in quantity before chillies became available. It is known as *melegueta* pepper or, more poetically, as grains of paradise. The plant is a tall reed that has elongated red and orange

Below: Chilli powder is a preservative, which kills bacteria on fresh food, an added benefit in hot countries where food quickly becomes bad.

fruits. These fruits contain as many as 100 seeds, which are the "grains of paradise" themselves. Melegueta pepper became popular in Europe soon after West Africa was discovered by explorers, and was shipped in large quantities, but its popularity declined and it is now hard to find outside its native area.

SPICE MIXES

These include the ras el hanout of Algeria and Morocco, the harissa of Tunisia, the berbere of Ethiopia and the pilpil of Angola and Mozambique. In North Africa, Tunisian dishes are the most fiery, with Algeria and Morocco tending to favour more subtle flavours. Tunisian harissa, usually the famous Le Phare du Cap Bon variety, can now be found in food stores all over the world in its distinctive yellow "toothpaste" tube.

Berbere
This is an Ethiopian blend of spices added to many local dishes, from baked fish to chicken stews.

8 white cardamoms
10 dried red chillies
5ml/1 tsp cumin seeds
5ml/1 tsp coriander seeds
5ml/1 tsp fenugreek seeds
8 cloves
5ml/1 tsp allspice berries
10ml/2 tsp black peppercorns
5ml/1 tsp ajowan seeds
5ml/1 tsp ground ginger
2.5ml/½ tsp ground nutmeg
15ml/1 tbsp salt

Heat a heavy frying pan. Bruise the cardamom pods and add to the pan with the chillies, cumin, coriander, fenugreek, cloves, allspice, peppercorns and ajowan seeds. Toast the spices until they give off a rich aroma. Remove the seeds from the cardamoms and discard the husks. Grind all the spices to a fine powder. Mix in the ginger, nutmeg and salt. You can use the mix at once or store it in a jar.

All three countries of the Maghreb make extensive use of a mixture called ras el hanout (meaning "head of the shop") consisting of as many as twenty spices dominated by cumin and hot red pepper, although the mixture varies depending on where it is made. In Ethiopia, bitter spices and herbs, such as fenugreek and ajwan, are included in spice mixtures and added to stews.

In Egypt, the classic spice mixture is a dried one known as duqqa (which derives from an Arabic word meaning "pounded"). The ingredients in duqqa, and their proportions, vary from one family to another but generally include sesame and coriander seeds, dried crushed mint, salt and pepper. It may also include chickpea flour and crushed millet. It is usually sprinkled on bread dipped in olive oil.

HERBS

Fresh herbs are used less than spices in African cooking. Lemongrass is used in Kenya, strongly influenced as it is by its Asian population. Lemongrass can be dried, whole or shaved, powdered or distilled into a fragrant oil. It has a fragrant citrus flavour and aroma.

Basil was known in ancient Egypt and is still used in many Egyptian dishes. Mint is an essential ingredient for mint tea in the Maghreb, and flat leaf parsley is used lavishly in many soup and salad recipes as an ingredient in its own right.

Below: Lemon grass is used extensively in the cooking of Kenya. It can be shaved and dried, as here.

FRESH VEGETABLES

African cooking has always placed great reliance on locally grown fresh vegetables, and in spite of imported or canned foods, this is still the case.

Green leafy vegetables

A winter luxury in the arid lands, green leafy vegetables are available only when the summer sun does not shrivel the leaves. *Meloukhia* is a green, spinach-like vegetable with a slightly slimy consistency that is used to make soup and added to stews in Egypt and Saharan Africa. Spinach is used in stews and fritters. Bitterleaf is another variety of green vegetable available in East and West Africa. The leaves of bean plants and pumpkins are eaten as green vegetables. Cassava leaves are also eaten.

Amaranth, also known as African spinach, is another popular green vegetable. Marrow greens and cowpea leaves are enjoyed, as are sweet potato tops, which, unlike the tops of ordinary potato, are not poisonous.

Above: Turnips and their tops are an essential ingredient in the stew that accompanies couscous in North Africa.

The leaves of other root vegetables are also added to soups and stews in Africa. No part of the plant is wasted; turnip tops and mustard greens (still eaten in the southern states of the USA by people of African origin) and the green leaves of okra (a type of hibiscus) are all added to soups and stews. The tough, fibrous leaves of the banana and plantain are used as disposable plates and to package foods, such as gari (cassava or tapioca flour) for steaming and boiling. In West Africa, a favourite way to use green

vegetables is in palaver sauce. Whatever green leaves are available are used to make this sauce, although it should always contain bitterleaf. A little meat, including offal (variety meats), and shellfish are added, as well as watermelon, or egusi, seeds. The mixture is then sprinkled with palm oil. The dish is known as *plassas* in Sierra Leone and *ban flo* in Ghana.

The green leaves of the manioc plant are the main ingredients in *kpwem*, a soup from southern Cameroon. The leaves should be as young and tender as possible. They are stewed with ground peanuts and a little palm oil.

Squashes

Pumpkins, squashes and gourds all flourish in the heat, and many varieties of these are eaten, even the liffa, the gourd from which loofahs are made. Squashes and pumpkins are particularly popular, finding their way into most stews. Gourds are not only eaten but are also used as containers (calabashes), utensils (cut in half and used as ladles) and as drinking vessels.

Aubergines

In Kenya, aubergine is known as eggplant or *brinjal*, the latter being the

Below: From top to bottom, cocoyam, cassava yam, guinea yam (left) and soft yam (right).

Above: Pumpkin is an important food all over Africa, mainly as an ingredient for stew. In Libya, it is pickled and mashed and eaten with couscous.

Above: Okra is valued for the gelatinous texture it gives to stews and soups. It is also known as gumbo.

Right: Ackee is usually sold in cans.

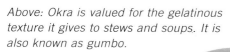

Indian name. Garden eggs are a white or greenish-yellow variety of aubergine, which are eaten mainly in West Africa. A favourite Nigerian dish is chicken gumbo, for which chicken is stewed with garden eggs.

Okra

Gumbo is also another name for okra, the vegetable that is perhaps most closely associated with Africa. In North Africa, okra is deep-fried in oil, which eliminates any trace of sliminess. However, the slimy texture is valued elsewhere in Africa, for the bulk it gives to stews.

Peppers

Chilli peppers and sweet (bell) peppers, known as bell chillies, are eaten all over the continent. They vary in size and shape from tiny red birdseye chillies and so-called cherry peppers to larger, elongated, milder green (bell) peppers.

Yams

The cocoyam and Guinea soff yam are varieties of yam that are probably indigenous to West Africa. The Guinea

Above: Plantains are members of the banana family. They are eaten green or ripe, baked or boiled or fried.

soff yam is known locally as *allato*; it may be white or yellow. Yellow yams should not be confused with the sweet potato, which is often known as yellow yam in the United States.

Ackee

Now associated principally with Jamaica, the ackee was originally introduced there from West Africa in the

Below: Bell peppers or capsicums, originally from central and South America, are popular in North African cooking.

Above: Garlic, the pungent Mediterranean plant, is used extensively as a flavouring all over Africa.

18th century. The fruit is fluffy and yellow like scrambled egg, but the centre is poisonous, so ackee is always sold canned outside its native habitat.

Plantains

A member of the banana family, plantains are inedible raw, and are cooked extensively in Africa in many different ways.

OTHER VEGETABLES

Colocassia is a root eaten since antiquity, when it was Europe's equivalent of the potato. Colocassia is still eaten widely in Africa, as are eddoes, a taproot related to colocassia. Tomatoes, potatoes and carrots were introduced by the Europeans. The onion, garlic, and other members of the allium family are grown throughout northern Africa.

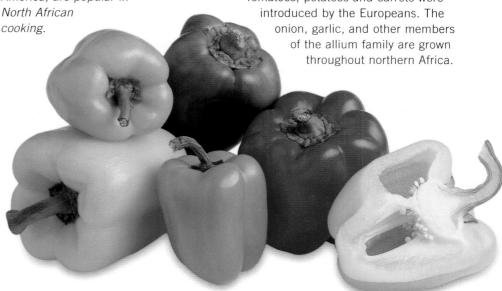

FRESH FRUIT

Africa is famous for its fruits, although many of the native fruits are rarely seen outside the continent, baobab fruits being one example. The baobab is a huge tree that grows all over tropical Africa, from Senegal to Zimbabwe, and can live to be 3,000 years old. It is very strange looking in that the branches look more like roots, as if it were growing upside down. The fruit, which grows up to 30cm/1ft long, contains tartaric acid and vitamin C, and can either be sucked or soaked in water to make a refreshing drink. The fruits are also dried and roasted then ground up to make a coffee-like drink or used as a flavouring and spice.

Other wild fruits, which grow in Kenya, are *muratina*, *burarakambi*, *chufutu* and *busemwa*. Many fruits that are considered to be indigenous are, in fact, not native to the continent, such as orange, tangerine, coconut, banana, mango and papaya.

Surinam cherry

The acerola, or Surinam cherry, originally from the Caribbean, has become very popular in the Horn of Africa. It cannot be eaten fresh as it is too acidic, but makes wonderful jams, jellies and preserves.

Citrus fruit

Imported via India, most citrus fruits probably originally came from China. They have taken to the African climate and are available throughout the year, which makes them widely used. They have largely been spread not by human plantations but by birds, especially

Right: Tangerines are cultivated in Algeria, and are harvested between the months of November and April.

parrots, and grow wild in the forests of Kenya and Zimbabwe. Of course, they are carefully cultivated in North Africa, and Algeria has produced its own varieties, such as the clementine and the tangerine, which are an important Christmas export.

Banana

It is surprising to think that bananas, which are an African staple, are not native to the continent, but originally came from India. In addition to the fruit itself, which is eaten ripe, as a fruit, or unripe, as a vegetable, the leaves make wrappers for food, and disposable plates. Green

Right: Prickly pears come from the opuntia cactus. The flesh inside is sweet, though full of seeds.

bananas are certain unripe varieties that are used as a vegetable. They are boiled, with or without their skins.

African horned melon

Also known by the name of kiwano, this extraordinary fruit is bright orange and covered with small bumps or protrusions. The flesh is green and it has small crunchy pips similar to passion fruit.

Dates and figs

Luscious dates and figs are native to coastal regions of North Africa. They are dried and exported southwards to Saharan and sub-Saharan Africa. Dates are important in the practice of Islam, as the prophet Mohammed

Below: Jackfruit or jakfruit are large fruits with nutritious seeds that must be boiled before being eaten.

Below: Dates are ideal food for hot regions as in their dried form they keep for months.

Below: The kiwano, or African horned melon, is spectacular with its bright orange skin, thick spines, green flesh and black seeds.

advocated breaking the Ramadan fast by eating dates and drinking water. Figs are mainly found in North Africa, and are used in desserts, as well as eaten fresh and dried.

Locust bean

Also known as carob, this bean grows in the drier parts of North Africa on a large, handsome tree. The long brown beans have a sweet pulp, which is enjoyed by children and also fed to domestic animals. The beans are also fermented and then cooked with the *meloukhia* leaf, especially in Saharan Africa, where the resulting dish is known as *crain crain*.

Below right: Physalis is grown in, and exported widely from, Cape Province, hence its other name of Cape gooseberry.

Physalis

Also known as a Cape gooseberry, the physalis looks like an orange cherry, encased in a papery calyx, and is rich in vitamin C. It is often used for decoration because of its attractive appearance. Despite the profusion in which it grows around the Cape of Good Hope in South Africa, it is really a native fruit of Peru.

Jackfruit

Another fruit originally from the Indian continent is the jackfruit, the largest of the tree-born fruits. It can weigh as much as 41kg/90lb. The fruit growing on the tree is a strange sight because it grows directly out of the trunk on a short stem. Inside the fruit, the thick, warty flesh is yellow, very sweet, and firm rather than fibrous. The large seeds, known as jacknuts, are also edible but are eaten boiled.

The jackfruit has an unpleasant smell, but this does not permeate the flesh. The flesh must be eaten as soon as it is ripe because the fruit will continue to ripen after the flesh is cut.

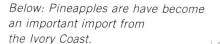

Below: Pineapples are have become an important import from the Ivory Coast.

Cactus fruit

Also known as prickly pear, this small greenish-orange fruit is from the opuntia cactus, the cactus fruit is native to the Americas, and possibly China, and was introduced into the Middle East and North Africa by merchant traders in the 16th century.

Pineapple

Just as Kenya is famous for its exports of vegetables, most of which were originally from the Americas, so the Ivory Coast and Malawi are exporters of another South American fruit, the

Right: Watermelon is an African native fruit that has spread all over the world.

pineapple. Miniature pineapples, grown more for their beauty than their usefulness, are also exported.

Grapes

Vines are indigenous to North Africa and there has always been a flourishing wine trade there. Algeria, Morocco and Tunisia also all produce table grapes, and raisins, for export

Watermelon

The watermelon has been grown in Africa for centuries and is depicted on Egyptian wall paintings, although earlier varieties were small and probably bitter. They are now universally sweet and very large and are grown throughout Africa. The two main varieties of watermelon are round with a dark-green skin and deep-red flesh, or elongated with a pale green skin or a skin striped with darker green. Watermelons were taken to the Americas via the slave trade.

FISH AND SHELLFISH

Fresh fish and shellfish are found all along the coasts. Fishing methods in Africa (except for South Africa) remain traditional: fish are speared or caught in nets by fishermen in boats working as a team, and lake fish are often netted by a single fisherman. Fish forms a vital part of the African diet, even inland, although the problem of keeping fish fresh is a serious one where refrigeration is still a luxury.

Thébouidienne is a classic fish stew from Senegal, in which any white fish is stewed slowly in a casserole with cabbage, sweet potato, bell chillies, pimentos and chilli peppers. The stew is served on a bed of rice. In the Ivory Coast, the fish is casseroled similarly, but the flavourings are pumpkin, marrow and fresh coconut, strips of which are laid over the fish. To this is added rice, fried onions and seasoning, it is then simmered in coconut water until tender.

FRESH FISH

The following fish are to be found in the rivers or seas of the African continent, but they can all be substituted with similar-sized white fish that may be more easily available.

Below: The brightly coloured parrot fish is popular in West Africa.

Nile perch and tilapia

Both these freshwater fish are eaten in Egypt and the Sudan, with the Nile perch the most frequently consumed. They are usually fried in oil.

Jobfish

A member of the snapper family, the jobfish lives in the waters of the Indian Ocean and is sold along the coast in Kenya, Tanzania and Mozambique. It is an attractive orange or lavender colour.

Above: Red mullet is an important catch in the Mediterranean and is used for a variety of North African dishes.

Red mullet

Among the finest of all sea fish, the flesh of red mullet is lean and firm, and its flavour is robust and distinctive. Because of this, red mullet is a favourite in North African countries, where it is used in a wide variety of dishes. It is caught in the Mediterranean, so does not feature in the more southern areas of Africa.

Parrotfish

The parrotfish is a colourful fish that lives on coral reefs, and is popular in the fish stews of West Africa. In Liberia, it is often cooked with coconut cream and served with *foufou* (mashed cassava or yam). The fish are sautéed in butter or ghee, seasoned with salt and pepper and fried. They are then stewed in coconut milk in a covered pan. The cover is then removed and the sauce reduced until it is creamy.

Other species

In West and South Africa, it is the fish of the southern Atlantic that are caught, including grey mullet and albacore, swordfish and marlin as well as species

Cape Kedgeree

Although originally a curry, Cape kedgeree from South Africa is no longer a spicy dish, owing to the influence of the British and Dutch. Fish that has been precooked – usually red mullet or snoek – is mixed with cooked rice (there should be twice as much fish as rice) and chopped egg whites. It is then seasoned with salt and pepper and simmered in evaporated milk or single cream. The yolks of hardboiled eggs are then pushed through a sieve and used to garnish the dish before it is served.

of shark and snoek. In East Africa, the best ocean catch is considered to be shark, known as *papa*, which is mainly cut into strips, dried and sent inland. The snoek is an oily fish and as such is particularly delicious dried or smoked. Other varieties used are yellowtail, steenbrass and Hottentot fish.

DRIED FISH

A highly prized ingredient in Africa, many different types of small fish are dried and used extensively for flavouring foods. Particular favourites are dried anchovies, which are sold in great piles

Below: Oysters are often eaten as an appetizer in the restaurants of Kenya.

Above: Salt cod before soaking.

in all African markets, and used in meat dishes as well as fish-based recipes such as the stews of Senegal and Mali, Uganda, Kenya and Tanzania. In the western Cape province, fatty fish including mullet and herring are strung up in bunches to dry in the sun, to make a dried fish called *hardums*.

Fish calulu is an Angolan fish stew, which is made from a mixture of dried and fresh fish. The dried fish are softened in hot water then stewed with the fresh fish, seasoned with garlic, salt, vinegar and lemon. Alternate layers of the dried and fresh fish are then placed in a large pan with sliced onion, tomatoes, spinach or sweet potato leaves and sliced okra. This is then simmered in palm oil until cooked. The rich stew is usually served with a manioc flour porridge known as *funge*.

Salt fish

Also known as stockfish, salted cod is an important ingredient in cooking throughout sub-Saharan Africa. The fish is imported from countries bordering the North Atlantic, such as Portugal. It is rock hard when purchased, and needs soaking for at least 24 hours in several changes of water before it is ready for cooking.

In Tanzania, the cod is made into a stew called *dagaa*, which is made with tomatoes, onions, chilli and coconut milk.

SHELLFISH

Seafood is a particular favourite of South Africans, where freshly caught lobsters and scallops are widely available. Throughout the rest of Africa shrimps or prawns are dried, and used as flavourings.

Oysters

The oysters of the East African coast are said to be the most delicious in the world. They are regularly served as an appetizer in Kenyan restaurants, European-style with rose-marie sauce and wedges of lemon.

Prawns and shrimps

In Egypt, fresh prawns (shrimp) are a favourite appetizer. In Nigeria they are made into pancakes, using a batter made from ground white haricot beans, tomatoes, onions, cooked prawns and eggs. The pancakes are deep fried, and are often available as street food.

The Indian influence in South Africa is obvious from the fish curries that are often made with prawns. The curries are served with rice and a variety of raitas, such as onion rings, bananas, sliced cucumbers, chutney and shredded coconut. A similar curry is made in East Africa, with small shrimps.

Below: Fresh prawns (shrimp) are a popular ingredient, and when dried they are used extensively throughout Africa.

MEAT AND POULTRY

Red meat is a luxury, especially in central Africa, but poultry, such as the guinea fowl, a bird native to Africa and probably domesticated here as long as five thousand years ago, is an important source of meat. In Africa, meat and fish are often cooked together in the same dish, especially in the former Portuguese colonies of Angola and Mozambique, in a dish known as *futu*, which should have twice as much meat as fish.

Above: Beef is a luxury food throughout Africa, except in South Africa, where cattle are bred for meat.

RED MEAT

The most popular red meats in the Maghreb (Algeria, Morocco and Tunisia) and Saharan Africa, where the animals are raised for milk and meat as well as for their skins or fleece, are that of sheep and goats. The meat is ground, or it might be cut into small pieces or ground with spices and spit-roasted. It may also be added to stews. Only kid is roasted, as older goat is too tough and so it is usually boiled or stewed. Curried goat is a popular dish in Nigeria, and *nyama choma* is very popular in Kenya. This dish consists of goat kebabs served with cooked green banana mash.

Below: Goat is popular in Kenya and Nigeria; it is a tough meat that needs long, slow cooking.

Above: Lamb, in chunks or minced, is the favourite meat of North African cuisine.

In those parts of Kenya and the Sudan where herders count their wealth in cattle, the animals are too valuable to be eaten, so beef is not commonly eaten in East Africa. The Masai, for

Below: Buffalo is one of the game meats that is hunted and eaten in Africa.

example, would never eat cattle. However, it is extremely popular in South Africa, where it is used is many different ways, including curries and barbecues. In the Cameroon it is stewed in a fragrant curry with coconut and pineapple. Hump-backed cattle, or zebu, of the type found in India, are also bred in Africa, although more for their milk than meat.

Although pork is forbidden by Islamic law, and not eaten in Muslim countries, it is popular among non-Muslims in West and South Africa in the form of stews and barbecued spare ribs.

GAME

The cane-rat or grasscutter (known as *agouti* in French-speaking Africa) is a rodent that may be as much as 60cm/24in long, not including the tail. It is widely eaten in sub-Saharan Africa. The bush-pig is related to the wart-hog and is eaten in tropical Africa. It has a gamey flavour, tasting more like wild boar. In Central Africa, even monkey and bat are eaten. Gazelle, kudu, eland and other game animals are also eaten in the savannah and in the Sahel, where they roam. Ostrich has lately gained in popularity, as the red meat is lean and flavoursome. The Cape buffalo is hunted and eaten in Africa. The meat from most of these game animals can be airdried and smoked to make biltong.

INSECTS

In Africa, insects are widely eaten, and are a good source of free protein, including grubs, white ants, termites and especially locusts. Plagues of locusts were once common, and eating them was a good way of getting animal protein and helping to protect the crops at the same time, as they were caught before they could damage the crops. Those who have eaten locusts describe them as delicious: crunchy on the outside and creamy within.

Other insects that are eaten include crickets, grasshoppers and flying ants. Even worms and caterpillars are sold as

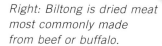

Right: Biltong is dried meat most commonly made from beef or buffalo.

fried snacks, in towns and cities as well as in more isolated rural areas.

BILTONG

In Southern Africa, and South Africa in particular, beef and other lean meats can be seasoned and dried to make biltong. Game is often preserved this way, including animals such as eland, zebra and ostrich, A long piece of muscle is trimmed into an oval shape and then rubbed with salt, pepper, coriander and fennel. The meat is soaked in vinegar and left to marinate for a few days. It is then hung up in the open air to dry in the wind. When dried out, it is smoked.

If made from game, the biltong is so hard that it can be grated. In South Africa it is often eaten this way as a snack, on top of buttered bread.

CHICKEN

Eggs and chicken are important items in the diet of the those who live in the cities, and those who can afford it put chicken in their stews. Chicken eaten in town or cities in Africa may be the plump, domesticated fowl or even broiler fowl, but in the villages all over Africa chickens roam freely and are consequently lean and tough.

Broiling chicken is known in French West Africa as *poulet bicyclette* (bicycle chicken). No one quite knows why this term is used, perhaps because they are as lean as if they had kept fit by riding a bicycle, but more probably because they are kept for laying and eaten only if they are unfortunate enough to be "road kill". These chickens need long, slow cooking in stews such as Ashanti Chicken from Ghana, where the chicken is slow-cooked with yams, tomatoes and mint leaves, and Yassa Chicken, a traditional recipe from the Camance region of Senegal. Here the chicken is first fried in peanut oil, then slowly stewed in

water with spices, including mustard and chilli peppers, lemon juice, vinegar, cabbage and carrots for at least six hours. It is served with *foufou*, cooked and mashed green banana, or rice. Rabbit and guinea fowl can be treated in the same way.

In Angola, chicken is often barbecued (grilled), such as peri-peri chicken, where the bird is first marinated in paprika, hot chilli powder, lemon juice, cloves and ginger.

In North Africa, rich omelettes similar to those eaten in Iran are popular. Chicken irio, a Kikuyu dish from Kenya, is made from eggs, puréed beans, maize and potatoes or cassava, and served with curried chicken.

PIGEON

In the Maghreb and Egypt, pigeon is also an important food item. Pigeons are raised in special towers and their meat is used in roast pigeon with pine nuts and honey or in Bastilla, the famous Moroccan pie.

GUINEA FOWL

There are four species of guinea fowl, all of which are native to Africa, and their ranges extend from the north to south of the Sahara. Guinea fowl were probably domesticated by the ancient Egyptians, but they are expensive and eaten mainly on feast days.

Above: Pigeon is a great delicacy in Egypt and Morocco, where the birds are bred for the table.

Below: Guinea fowl is a domesticated bird that is native to Africa. The flesh is well flavoured and gamey.

BREADS AND BEVERAGES

Africa is the home of bread, for it is here that the ancient Egyptians first mixed flour with water and left it in the sun. The natural yeasts in the air did the rest. Similarly, most beverages are based on fermentation, including the so-called palm wines of Central Africa.

BREADS AND PASTRIES

In Africa breads are generally flat breads made from wheat. The Ethiopians have two main forms of bread. One is *hambasha*, a firm dough kneaded like a European bread and flavoured with black onion seed or nigella, ground cumin and ground coriander. *Injera* is made with a loose dough, usually made with teff, an indigenous grain grown in the Ethiopian highlands. *Injera* is eaten as a bread, but it is also laid flat on the table and used like the trencher of the Middle Ages – a kind of edible plate on which stew is poured, allowing the bread to soak up the juices as the meal progresses. Diners also use the bread to scoop up meat and vegetable stews. For this purpose, it is cut into long strips.

Phyllo or brik dough is a thin pastry dough, almost identical to filo pastry or strudel dough. One of its uses is to make a pastry from Tunisia that has a filling of egg, vegetables and tuna.

BEVERAGES

Two of the most universally drunk beverages in the world, coffee and beer, were given to the world by Africa.

Above: Phyllo*, the pastry dough that is the trademark of Moroccan cooking.*

Coffee and tea

The coffee shrub grows wild in Ethiopia, and the beans are harvested both from the wild plant and from cultivated varieties. The Ethiopians prefer to dry the beans just until they are still green, then roast and grind them as needed. The coffee drunk all over North and Saharan Africa is prepared in the same way as in the Middle East: ground to a powder, then added to water and boiled over an open fire. Sometimes cardamom or cinnamon is added. In southern Africa coffee is made by percolating rather than boiling, and in South Africa it is drunk with milk.

Below: Flat bread, baked on stones or on the floor of the oven, is probably similar to ancient Egyptian bread.

Tea, both black and green varieties is grown in East and West Africa. In the Maghreb it is taken with a form of spearmint, which is particularly aromatic, rather than milk. Copious amounts of tea are drunk throughout Africa, with meals and on its own. Like coffee, it is the drink of hospitality. Red tea, or Rooibos is a herbal tea that is a favourite drink in South Africa

Milk

Fresh milk is a luxury in hot climates without refrigeration, but goat's milk and fermented milks (yogurt and kefir-type drinks) are drunk in tropical Africa. Camel milk is also drunk in the Sahara.

Beer

Originally, beer was invented by the ancient Egyptians, who baked cakes of barley then let them ferment in water to produce a rich yeast, beer being an accidental by-product of the process. Thus, beer was developed before people discovered what an improvement yeast made when added to the baked paste of water and flour that came to be eaten as bread. Africans now consume much less beer than people on other continents: about 9 litres/16 pints per capita per year, compared to 21 litres/37 pints as a world average.

Tusker beer is the national drink of Kenya: a light, refreshing beer that

Below: Castle lager, South Africa's most popular beer. All non-Muslim African countries brew their own brands.

Above: Tusker beer, Kenya's own brand, is exported widely, and very much appreciated by Kenyan expatriates.

Above: Coconut water, left, is often drunk in a cocktail. Van der Hum, right, is South Africa's coffee liqueur.

should be drunk ice cold. There are also breweries producing alcohol-free beers, including ABC in Egypt. In South Africa, apart from the popular lagers and ales, such as Castle lager, beer is also brewed illegally and sold at unlicensed bars, known by the Irish name of "shebeens".

Spirits and liqueurs

In Madagascar, rum and fermented coconut water are popular drinks, especially in the north of the island. Africans also brew and distil alcohol from millet. Palm wine is made in tropical Africa. Van der Hum is a liqueur made from brandy and rum steeped in orange peel, orange blossoms, cloves, nutmeg, cinnamon and cardamom. It was originally made by the Dutch settlers, and was named after the Dutch admiral who liked it.

WINES OF AFRICA

Grape-growing began in Algeria in ancient times, and wines were even exported to Rome. Viticulture was revived in 1830, with the arrival of French colonists. In the 1870s, vineyards in France were ravaged by the insect pest phylloxera, and many wine-makers moved to Algeria, where they planted the best French vine

stocks. The vineyards are concentrated in three regions: Oran, Constantine and Algiers. The grape varieties grown are mainly Cinsault, Carignan and Grenache, but in some regions Cabernet, Syrah and Merlot are also used. Although the wines of Algeria have suffered from a poor reputation in the past, they are improving. Red wines account for 65 per cent of production, owing to the southern climate, although there are some good whites, especially Coteaux du Zaccar and Médéa. In Oran, Oued-Imbert wines are red, white and rosé. The red wines are generally heavy, coarse and dark, with a high alcohol content and low acidity. They are mainly exported to France, to be blended with wines of the Midi to increase their low alcohol content and add colour and body.

Tunisian vines grow mainly around Cap Bon. Many are dessert wines of the muscat variety, and some of the reds are mixed with rectified spirit to produce a drink called mistelle. The rosé wines are considered among the best in North Africa. Moroccan wines

Right: Fairview Pinotage, on the right, is made with a grape created in South Africa. Danie de Wet Chardonnay is a white wine that has won great praise.

come mainly from the region around Meknès, although vines are grown in Rabat, Casablanca, Fez, Oujda and Marrakech. There are white and red grapes, one variety of which, the Rafsai white grape of the Rif mountain region, is now being vinified. North-eastern Morocco produces rosé wines of comparable quality to Algeria's.

The wines of South Africa have a well established reputation. The first vine cuttings were brought there in 1654, probably from the Rhineland. Wine was made in the Cape by the Dutch colonists for the first time in 1659. The French Huguenots, who first arrived in 1688 and settled in the Franschek Valley, extended the vineyards and improved the quality of the vines. Today, the two vine-growing areas are the Coastal Belt and the Little Karoo. Harvesting is between February and April, before autumn. Many of the vineyards grow in beautiful countryside, presided over by period Dutch plantation houses, some still owned by the original families.

THE MIDDLE EAST

For centuries the Middle East has had an unrivalled reputation for hospitality. The Persian saying, Mehmân Hediyeh Khodâst ~ a guest is God's gift ~ is true of the entire region, where sharing what food you have is regarded not simply as a duty, but as an honour. Many of the world's favourite foods originated in the Middle East. The style of cooking varies from the deceptively simple to the sumptuous and sophisticated recipes that are the legacy of the Ottoman Empire. Herbs and spices ~ often little known in the West ~ are used with consummate care and even the most ordinary meals can be magical.

HISTORICAL BACKGROUND

Exactly what constitutes the Middle East varies, depending upon which authority you consult. Some include the Maghreb – Algeria, Morocco and Tunisia – on the basis that these predominantly Muslim African countries share so much common ground with their eastern neighbours; some exclude Israel but include Afghanistan and some cling doggedly to the older term Near East, which used to comprise the Balkan States and the area of the Ottoman Empire. In this book we include Egypt's Middle Eastern culinary tradition. Therefore, the Middle East, the "belly of the Orient", includes Egypt, Iran, Iraq, Israel and the Palestinian Territories, Jordan, Lebanon, Saudi Arabia, Syria, Turkey, Yemen and the Gulf States of Kuwait, Bahrain, Qatar, the United Arab Emirates and Oman.

All these countries, with the exception of Israel, are strongly Islamic. In Iran, for example, 99 per cent of its population are Muslim; in Jordan the figure is around 96 per cent and in Kuwait around 85 per cent. Lebanon has a 60:40 Muslim:Christian split.

Iranians speak Persian (Farsi), Israelis Hebrew and Turks Turkish, but elsewhere the first language is Arabic. English is also widely spoken.

A FERTILE BEGINNING

Two mighty civilizations set the stage for the Middle Eastern story. Both developed in lush valleys and both owed their early stimulus to agriculture. The first of these was in ancient Egypt, in the extraordinarily fertile Nile Valley. The river flooded every year with predictable regularity. This laid down rich deposits of silt, which enabled wheat and other crops to be grown with ease. Beyond the river, irrigation made farming possible even in the surrounding desert, and the co-operation this required was one of the aspects that led to an ordered society.

In what is now Iraq, there was another mighty river valley. This was Mesopotamia, the land between the Tigris and Euphrates rivers. It formed part of a larger area known as the Fertile Crescent, which stretched in an arc from Israel to the Persian Gulf.

Here, as in Egypt, irrigation made large-scale agriculture possible. Nomadic hunter-gatherers became farmers, cultivating wheat, barley, figs, dates and pomegranates in the rich alluvial soil. There were marsh fowl and fish in the Delta, and these were incorporated into a diet that was not so very different from modern Iraqi fare.

FOOD FIT FOR PHAROAHS

The daily diet for most inhabitants of ancient Egypt was bread, vegetables and fruit, with perhaps a little fresh or dried fish. *Meloukhia*, a green vegetable that resembles spinach, was used for soup. The wealthier inhabitants might also have meat – duck, goose or maybe gazelle. Dried beans and lentils were widely eaten, just as they are today, and sweetmeats were popular. The earliest recorded Egyptian recipe is for a sweetmeat, a mixture of dates, walnuts and cinnamon, rolled into balls and coated with honey and ground nuts.

Below: Bedouin shepherds in Syria tend to their sheep.

A PATTERN OF CONQUEST

Egypt fell to Rome in 34 BC. Food played a role even in this event, for the conquest was prompted in part by Rome's desire for Egypt's vast grain reserves. In Mesopotamia, the Sumerians had long since been vanquished by the Akkadians, and a succession of new rulers took their place. Eventually, Mesopotamia, too, became a province of Rome. This pattern of events continued throughout the Middle East – with different principal characters – for centuries. Countries were invaded, bitter battles were fought and then there followed a period of relative calm and stability. The invading armies brought with them their favourite dishes and learned to like the local food as well, and when they swept on, as they inevitably did, they took with them the ingredients and cooking methods they had acquired.

This helps to explain why, wherever you go in the Middle East, you will encounter the same recipes. The names will be different and there will be subtle local nuances, but each will be recognizable. Of course, there are individual specialities, too. Iran (formerly Persia), for example, has a rich repertoire of rice dishes and a reputation for subtle spicing. The country was at one time on the famous Silk Route, so Persians had access to exotic ingredients to augment a diet that was already rich and varied.

Recipes of Arab origin, like Tabbouleh, and stuffed lamb with baba ganoush, were disseminated during the Arab Conquest, which began in the 7th century AD, when an army of the Prophet Muhammad's followers conquered all the lands that comprise present-day Syria, Lebanon, Israel, Iraq, Iran, Jordan and Egypt.

THE OTTOMAN EMPIRE

The cuisine of the Middle East may have been shaped by these disparate influences, but it was the Turkish Ottomans who refined it. They came to power at the beginning of the 14th century. Within 150 years they had conquered Constantinople (now

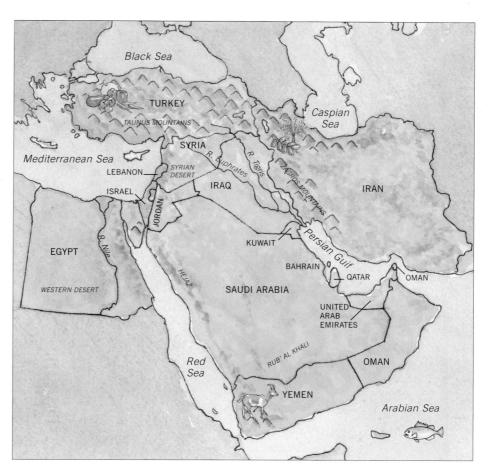

Istanbul), the former Byzantine capital, and built the fabulous Topkapi Palace. Banquets at the palace became legendary. Food was prepared by a team of cooks, including butchers, bakers, pastry cooks, confectioners, yogurt and cheese makers and experts in pickling and preserving vegetables and fruit. Only the finest ingredients were used. The empire that eventually stretched from Cairo to Budapest, and from Tripoli to Baghdad, provided plenty of ingredients and inspiration.

FOREIGN INFLUENCES

After the First World War, which signalled the end of the Ottoman Empire, Britain administered Palestine, Transjordan, Iraq and Egypt, whereas France took control of Lebanon and Syria. France had the greater impact, not so much in the way of introducing typical French dishes, but rather in refining the cooking and presentation of local specialities.

Omani cuisine reveals several foreign influences. Between the 17th and 19th centuries, Oman was a powerful seafaring nation that rivalled Portugal and England in the Gulf, the Indian Ocean and the coasts of India and East Africa. Returning sailors introduced spices from Zanzibar and curries from India. The food in Yemen has an Indian flavour, too, thanks to interaction with Indian merchants. Chillies are used more widely in Yemen than anywhere else in the Middle East.

Israel has a dynamic and very varied cuisine. Since the establishment of the State of Israel in 1948, hundreds of thousands of Jews from many countries have emigrated there, each national group bringing their traditional dishes to add to the Kosher tradition. Chopped liver from Alsace, polenta fritters from Italy, cherry soup from Hungary, *pierogi* from Poland – all these plus a host of typically Middle Eastern dishes are to be found on the menu.

A Cuisine Steeped in Tradition

Social mores and religious observance play a large role in the way food is prepared, cooked and served in the Middle East. Muslims and Jews both abstain from eating pork, and there are strict laws governing the way permitted animals are slaughtered. Custom dictates how food is served and to whom, and there are largely unspoken but firmly entrenched traditions surrounding the role of the host and the offering of hospitality.

MUSLIM RELIGIOUS OBSERVANCE

Islamic doctrine is enshrined in the Koran, or Qur'an. The word literally means "recitation" and is held to be the word of God (Allah) as dictated to the Prophet Mohammad by the Angel Jibril (Gabriel). There are five articles of faith, the first of which is the doctrine that there is only one true God and his name is Allah. The prime observances or duties Muslims must perform include public acknowledgement of Allah and of Muhammad as his prophet; praying five times a day; giving alms; making a pilgrimage to Mecca at least once in a lifetime and fasting from sunrise to sunset every day during Ramadan.

Below: A stall in the famous night-time marketplace Jema al Fnr, Marrakesh, Morocco, renowned for fabulous food.

Food that may be eaten is described as halal (lawful). This includes beef, goat, lamb and poultry slaughtered in the permitted manner. Pork is taboo. Game may be eaten in certain circumstances, provided the hunter is a Muslim or the child of a Muslim. Fish with scales are halal, provided they were alive when taken from the water. This also applies to prawns (shrimp), but lobster, crab, shellfish and fish that lack scales, such as shark, are not allowed. All alcohol and other stimulants are forbidden.

Above: Bedouin women eat after they have served the men, sitting outside their tent in the Sinai Desert.

In addition to the Koran, Muslims honour the Hadith, or Tradition, a record of the sayings of Muhammad, together with accounts by others of how the Prophet himself lived. The Hadith offers additional guidance on how adherents should conduct themselves, and has quite a bit to say on the subject of food. Some of the tenets are simply good practice; for example, Muslims are

The Laws of Kashrut

Observant Jews also adhere to strict dietary laws. Only certain meats and types of fish are permitted, and animals must be dispatched by a *shochet,* or ritual slaughterer. Blood must be removed from the animal immediately after slaughter. Dairy foods and meat must not be cooked together, and if meat has been eaten, a period of time must elapse before any type of dairy food can be consumed. Wine, beer and spirits are permitted, with some limitations. There are special observances for the Sabbath, and for festivals such as Pesach (Passover) and Purim.

advised to wash fruit thoroughly but not to peel it before eating, water should be sipped, not gulped, and no Muslim should drink from a cup with a cracked rim. Food must not be wasted. Any leftovers must be fed to animals or used in another dish. This has led to the development of some intriguing recipes, including Fattoush, a salad composed largely of stale bread and vegetables.

THE HONOURED GUEST

The offering of hospitality is deeply ingrained in the Arab psyche. As an old proverb declares: "Three things are no disgrace to man, to serve his guest, to serve his horse and to serve in his own house." In Bedouin society, this concern for the well-being of a guest is particularly marked. A traveller seeking food and accommodation will not be turned away. Even an enemy must be taken in for 48 hours if need be, and then given safe conduct as he proceeds on his journey.

In Bedouin society, as is the Arab pattern, men and women eat separately. The women prepare the food, but do not eat until after the men have finished their meal. A Western female guest will be accorded the same courtesies as her husband, however. The meal begins with the ceremonial washing of hands. Guests sit cross-legged on the carpeted floor of the tent and the meal is placed in the centre. Traditionally, this is likely to be *mansaf*, Jordan's national dish. The word means "big tray", which is an accurate description. A very large tray is covered with several sheets of flat bread. On top of this is piled rice mixed with roasted pine nuts and almonds, and over that is heaped pieces of succulent cooked lamb. The whole dish is bathed in a yogurt sauce, which is regularly replenished as the meal proceeds. No utensils are used. Instead, everyone eats with the right hand, the left being reserved for personal hygiene.

Before taking the first bite, prayers may be said. During the meal, the guest will be encouraged to eat his fill, and more than his fill. When everyone has eaten, coffee will be served and it is

accepted form for a guest to drink several small cups before signifying – with a wave of the empty cup – that he has had enough.

If there are obligations on the host, there are also expectations of the guest. He may be offered a special delicacy, like the eyes or testicles. This titbit must not be refused. It is expected that a guest will eat heartily and show appreciation. Finally, a guest should not overstay his welcome. As Muhammad said: "It is not right for a guest to stay so long as to incommode his host."

MODERN TRENDS

Although the Bedouin model of hospitality may not be encountered very often by the average visitor to the Middle East, kindness and courtesy

Above: Ancient farming methods in rural areas of the Middle East reflect the enduring social traditions of the culture.

remain a mark of even the most ordinary encounter. Meals will be prepared with elaborate care, because to take time and trouble honours the guest. Cooking will probably begin early in the day, so that there will be plenty of tasters – the mezzes – for the visitor to sample before moving on to the main course. The meal will be ample and the host will be satisfied only if waistbands are put under strain. Guests will be offered the best chairs and everything will be done to make them feel at home. In contemporary households, men and women may eat together, and serve alcohol, even in Muslim homes.

DAILY EATING PATTERNS

In the Middle East, it is invariably the women who cook, clean and care for children. This is the case even when the woman works full time, as more and more women do. In Israel, the pattern is altering somewhat, particularly among young couples where both are wage earners, but in Arab-Muslim societies in particular, women are the ones who go to market, prepare the food and, in many cases, serve their menfolk first before they and their children have their meal. Convenience foods, like finely ground or minced meat for meatballs and kebabs, ready-to-use shredded pastry and filo pastry, prepared mezzes and salads from shiny supermarkets, make women's lives easier, but many still prefer the old ways, and buy their produce from the *souk* or market.

THE DAILY DIET

In most of the Middle East, the pattern of meals is more or less the same. The day begins early for many people,

because it makes sense to get as much work done as possible before it becomes unbearably hot.

For the business person, breakfast might simply consist of a bowl of yogurt with some honey or preserves, or a couple of bite-size pastries bought from the bakery on the way to the office. Many people start the day with bread, olives, soft cheese, tomato and cucumber, but the traditional breakfast, enjoyed from Alexandria to Aqaba, is *foul*. The word can be spelled in many different ways, but the dish is always basically the same: cooked dried broad (fava) beans mashed with oil and lemon juice. The Jordanians add some chopped chilli and the Lebanese like to stir in chopped fresh coriander (cilantro). In Turkey, a favourite breakfast dish is *menemen*, which

Below: The markets of the Middle East are full of fresh fruit and vegetables, which are bought on a daily basis.

Above: Dinner in a Jordanian restaurant, where food is served from a large plate set in the centre of the table.

consists of a thick tomato sauce spiked with chilli. Hollows are made in the sauce and an egg is broken into each. When the eggs are cooked, the dish is topped with crumbled feta cheese and served with flat bread.

Lunch is eaten between 1.00 and 3.00 p.m. Rural dwellers often make this their main meal, but in the cities, people prefer a snack and will often choose two or three mezzes with some bread and perhaps a piece of fruit. Those eating at home might plump for a bowl of beef and herb soup with yogurt, or spinach and lemon soup with meatballs. There'll always be bread, even if all it accompanies is a little cheese and a few olives.

Hummus, which is chickpea purée, is popular, as is the broad bean equivalent, byesar. Office workers may choose some street food, such as Falafel served in pitta bread with onion slices and tomatoes.

The evening meal can be eaten at any time between 8.00 and 11.00 p.m. This is generally the main meal of the day for city people. It will begin in a leisurely fashion, with the serving of mezzes. The main course might be anything from grilled (broiled) fish or poultry to a meat dish. Offal (variety meats) is very popular in the Middle East, or a simple stew may be offered. If you are in Iran, this is likely to be a Khoresh, served over rice. Bread will accompany the meal and there will probably be several salads, all served with a dollop of yogurt on the side. Dessert will be fresh fruit – perhaps a slice of chilled melon – or just a single perfect peach. If it is a special occasion, a sticky pastry such as baklava or kodafa may be served, or a piece of basbousa, the coconut halva beloved of the Egyptians. Creamy rice puddings, scented with rosewater or spiced with cardamom are also popular.

Above: Street food has an important role in the Middle East, and stalls laden with vast arrays of sweetmeats are common.

RAMADAN

During the month of Ramadan, the ninth month in the Islamic calendar, Muslims fast. Most families rise very early, long before daybreak, to share a meal – *sahur*. When it is light enough (when "the white thread can be distinguished from the black thread of dawn") the fast begins and all who are able must refrain from eating or drinking until the sun goes down.

In the evening the fast is broken with another meal – *iftar*. This is very much a family time, although guests are very welcome, and the meal is often shared with others, especially those considered to be less fortunate than their hosts. Ramadan ends with the festival of Eid ul-Fitr, when gifts are exchanged and parties held.

MIDDLE EASTERN INGREDIENTS

The food of the Middle East, like that of the Mediterranean, is fundamentally healthy. There are regions where meat is the mainstay, and the diet is high in animal fats, but most people eat plenty of vegetables and fruit, fresh fish and a relatively small amount of meat, which is generally grilled (broiled) over an open fire. For energy, they rely on slow-release carbohydrates like pulses. The extra-sweet pastries for which the region is famous are eaten as treats with coffee or tea, rather than as daily desserts, so don't have the devastating impact on the diet that might be assumed.

The exciting world of Middle Eastern ingredients is encapsulated in the open-air markets throughout the regions, where the senses are stimulated by the sight of glossy purple aubergines (eggplants), bright red cherries, yellow quinces, baskets of fresh greens and sacks of lentils. The aroma of lemons, warm spices and fresh coffee fills the air. Having filled your basket, you are invited to munch on a handful of nuts or sample a few marinated olives before stepping into a shop for more mysterious items, like pomegranate molasses, *pekmez* and *zahtar*.

Below: Turkish coffee, thick, black and sweet, is served after dinner, or with a sweetmeat in the afternoon.

FAVOURITE FOODS

Wheat is the favourite grain, and bread is always on the table. There is a wide variety of breads, including leavened and unleavened loaves and flat breads. All the bread must be eaten; leftovers will be incorporated into a tasty dish. Rice, introduced from India, is also widely eaten, especially in Iran. As well as forming a main part of the meal, it is also used to make stuffings for vegetables and vine leaves and there are numerous recipes for rice mixed with vegetables or lentils. Short-grain rice is used for puddings and soups.

The most popular meat is lamb, followed closely by chicken, which is cooked in a variety of ways, perhaps spatchcocked and cooked over a brazier – to be enjoyed as a street food – or simmered in yogurt until tender. Middle Eastern cooks also specialize in the cooking of offal (variety meats). Everything from liver and kidneys to trotters and testicles is eaten, and some of the tastiest spiced dishes are made from these apparently unpromising ingredients. Fish is very popular in coastal regions, especially in Turkey and

Above: Fresh vegetables locally grown are an important part of cooking in the Middle East. Here an Egyptian farming family pick their peppers.

Below: These distinctive oval-shaped olives have been grown in the Middle East for centuries.

Oman, and freshwater or sea fish are generally preferred to shellfish. Many recipes for cooking fish include spicy sauces or herb stuffings, and nuts and fruit may also be added to complement the flavours of the fish.

Vegetables and fruits are important in their own right, but are also used in stews and ragoûts. Particularly popular are aubergines, courgettes (zucchini), spinach and green beans. There is a wide range of salads, often served with labna (white cheese) or yogurt. Salads always appear as part of mezze – a selection of small dishes served as a first course or to accompany a main dish. Garlic is popular in Mediterranean lands, but elsewhere in the Middle East it is regarded as being rather brash and is often omitted from recipes.

Luscious Middle Eastern fruits, such as melon and pomegranate, are enjoyed after a meal, and many fruits, both fresh and dried, will also be cooked with savoury foods. Deliciously sweet Middle Eastern pastries, however, are traditionally served with afternoon coffee and not as a dessert. Coffee and tea are widely drunk. Both are served without

Below: Dried fruits are used widely in the Middle East, as snacks and desserts, and as an ingredient in both sweet and savoury dishes.

Above: Dried beans and peas are staple ingredients and are used widely in many traditional dishes.

milk. Fruit drinks and drinks that are based on yogurt are on offer everywhere, but alcohol is less widely available due to the Muslim prohibition on its consumption.

The following pages introduce and explain some of the regions' raw ingredients, used for everyday cooking throughout the Middle East, as well as traditional breads, pastries and drinks.

Nations of nut lovers

Almonds, cashew nuts, pine nuts, peanuts, hazelnuts and pistachio nuts are extremely popular in the Middle East. Nuts serve as snacks, street food and as the basis for sauces like *tarator* – a lemon, garlic and pine nut mixture traditionally served with fish. Ground nuts are used, often with dried fruits, in stuffings for poultry and as fillings for sweet pastries. *Ma'amoul*, for example, can have a walnut and cinnamon filling, a pistachio and rosewater filling, a ground almond and orange flower water filling or any combination of these, with dates or other dried fruit. Nuts are often combined with seeds, as in the Egyptian snack food *dukkah*, which is a mixture of crushed roasted hazelnuts or chickpeas with sesame and coriander seeds.

Many of the ingredients featured are widely available in general stores and supermarkets; for some of the others you might need to find a specialist supplier, or make a substitute.

Below: Ras al hanout is a spice mix used throughout the Middle East.

WHEAT, RICE AND BEANS

First cultivated in Mesopotamia some ten thousand years ago, wheat is an extremely important crop in the Middle East, where some kind of bread is eaten at every meal. Rice is also widely eaten, while beans add variety and protein.

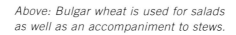

Above: Bulgar wheat is used for salads as well as an accompaniment to stews.

WHEAT

An unfussy cereal, wheat will flourish in a range of climates, although it does best in cooler conditions. In most areas of the Middle East wheat is therefore a winter crop. The main areas of cultivation are Turkey, central Iran, coastal Lebanon and Israel, northern Syria and Iraq, Jordan and the Nile Delta.

There are two main varieties: bread wheat and durum wheat, which is used for pasta and semolina. What distinguishes bread wheat is its high gluten content. This elastic protein substance is what makes leavened bread maintain its rise. It does this by strengthening the dough so that it traps the carbon dioxide produced when yeast ferments.

Bulgur wheat

Sometimes described as the world's first processed food, bulgur wheat is durum wheat that has been ground into particles after being cleaned, lightly boiled, dried and hulled. Before use, it needs only brief cooking, or can simply be soaked in boiling water. In the Middle East it is widely used in pilaffs, salads – especially Tabbouleh – and the

legendary Lebanese dish, Kibbeh. Bulgur wheat is also the basis of several sweet dishes, and is mixed with fermented yogurt and then dried to make another pelleted product, *kishk*, which is used to thicken stews.

Whole-wheat grains, called *kamh* in Egypt, are boiled in milk and water to make a porridge-like mixture, which is generally eaten with yogurt and honey.

Semolina and wheat

Also known as *smeed*, semolina is coarsely milled durum wheat. The Berbers use it to make a thick gruel, and it is also an ingredient in some desserts and cakes, especially halva. Couscous is made from semolina.

Wheat flour is used for breadmaking, and is also the basis of the thin, crisp pastry that we know as filo or phyllo. The Turkish version, yufka, comes in

Below: Fine yufka, made from semolina and used for pastries.

various thicknesses. Fine yufka is used for pastries, while the thicker type of dough is used for a stuffed bread called *gözleme*.

RICE

Long-grain rice arrived in the Middle East from northern India and Afghanistan, which helps to explain why fine varieties like basmati are generally preferred in countries like Iran and Iraq. In Egypt, where rice was traded through Alexandria's "Pepper Gate" towards the end of the first century AD, the grain was originally perceived as a medicinal

Below: Couscous is perhaps the most common ingredient in the Middle East.

Below: Semolina is used to make porridge, puddings and desserts.

Below: Long-grain rice, such as this Iranian rice, is the most popular variety.

food and used to treat stomach ailments. Today, Egyptians eat around 43kg/94lb per person annually, making them among the world's highest consumers. Despite this impressive figure, the richly fertile Nile Delta produces so much rice (three times the average yield) that Egypt is the only Middle Eastern country with a surplus. Most of this goes to its close neighbours: the Middle East is the world's third biggest importer of rice, after Europe and Brazil.

Middle Eastern cooks use rice in a wide variety of ways, but no nation is as adept at cooking it as the Iranians. Rice is grown along the Caspian coast. There are several varieties, including the much-prized *domsiah*. In Persian cooking (still called Persian, despite the name of the country being changed to Iran), light, fluffy rice with each grain separate is a speciality. Rice is so important that the stew served with it, Khoresh, is somewhat dismissively referred to as a sauce. Persians have also perfected the art of cooking rice so that a crisp crust forms on the base of the pan. This is the tahdeeg, which is broken up and served to guests.

BEANS AND LENTILS

Beans, peas and lentils have been cultivated and dried in the Middle East for centuries, and today's pulses (legumes) were developed from wild plants that originally grew in the lands bordering the Eastern Mediterranean. There are numerous mentions of pulses in the Bible, the most famous of which describes the incident when Esau sold his birthright for "a pottage of lentiles". A direct descendant from that famous bowl of lentil soup is *mujaddarah*, a lentil and rice stew that is traditionally eaten by Christian communities in Lebanon during Lent. The name means "smallpox" and it refers to the way in which the lentils stud the white rice and create a spotted appearance.

Dried beans and peas

Of the many varieties of dried bean eaten in the Middle East, broad (fava) beans are probably the most common.

A small brown variety called ful or foul is the basis of Egypt's national dish, ful medames. The soaked beans are cooked very simply, with onion skin and whole eggs, and the thick broth that results is eaten throughout the Middle East for breakfast, lunch, dinner and as a street snack.

In Israel, white haricot (navy) beans are widely used, especially in the long-simmered stew known as Cholent. Black-eyed beans (peas) are popular, too. Chickpeas are extensively used throughout the region, particularly for

Below: Dried haricot beans from Israel, where they are a particular favourite.

Above: Hummus, made from chickpeas, is a popular mezze dish.

Hummus and Falafel. Small and khaki-coloured, chickpeas look a little like pale hazelnuts. They retain their shape when cooked and are delicious in a spinach salad. Chickpea flour is frequently used as a thickener.

Lentils

Cheap, nutritious and easy to cook, lentils are widely used in the Middle East. The small red split lentil is favoured in Egypt and Syria, whereas Lebanese cooks tend to prefer the green or brown varieties.

Green shoots for Christmas

As Christmas approaches in the Lebanon, Christian children layer chickpeas, lentils and beans between pieces of cotton wool. These are placed on saucers and watered regularly until the shoots are about 15cm/6in long. When the family sets up the nativity scene, the shoots are placed in the manger and on the floor of the stable to represent hay.

HERBS AND SPICES

Judicious use of herbs and spices is the secret of many Middle Eastern dishes. Although there are some countries where fiery food is enjoyed, such as Yemen, the preference tends to be for mild, warm spices and cool, fresh herbs such as mint and parsley.

The Middle East is also home to some fascinating spice blends. Until recently these were little known outside their countries of origin, but the universal demand for new taste sensations has led to their being packaged and marketed worldwide.

Mint

Mint is an essential fresh herb in Middle Eastern cooking. It is used with lamb dishes, as an ingredient in salads and vegetable dishes, as a flavouring for yogurt sauces and with fruit. A sprig of fresh mint is often added to a glass of the sweet black tea that is such a feature of Middle Eastern life.

Parsley

You are unlikely to find curly parsley in the Middle East, but the flatleaf variety is extremely popular. This is particularly true in Lebanon, where cooks add extravagant handfuls of chopped parsley to dishes like Tabbouleh. In Iran, flat leaf parsley is one of the herbs used in *kuku sabzi*, a baked egg dish, rather like a large omelette, which is served to celebrate the New Year.

Coriander

This herb, also known as cilantro, is a member of the parsley family native to the Middle East and Mediterranean. In Middle Eastern cooking it is the leaves

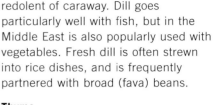

Above: Mint is used in enormous quantities in Turkey, for tea and salads.

and seeds that are most commonly used. Fresh coriander has a spicy citrus and ginger flavour, quite different from that of flat leaf parsley, which it resembles. The small, round seeds look like pale, creamy peppercorns; they are used whole in pickles, but are more often roasted and ground. Freshly ground coriander has a mild, warm flavour that is discernible in many Middle Eastern dishes, especially meatballs and stews.

Dill

Although most people associate dill with Scandinavia, the herb is actually native to western Asia and is hugely popular in the Middle East. The feathery, fern-like leaves and seeds have a flavour

redolent of caraway. Dill goes particularly well with fish, but in the Middle East is also popularly used with vegetables. Fresh dill is often strewn into rice dishes, and is frequently partnered with broad (fava) beans.

Thyme

The aroma of wild thyme is familiar to anyone who has journeyed to the Eastern Mediterranean. In the Middle East, the herb is known by its Arabic name of *zahtar*. Confusingly, the same name is also used to describe a popular spice mix based on thyme.

Cardamom

Ancient Egyptians chewed cardamom pods to whiten their teeth and sweeten their breath. The spice grows mainly in India, and reached the Middle East via Iran. It consists of small fleshy pods, which reveal tiny seeds when split. Green, white (bleached) and black cardamoms are grown, the former being the most popular. The seeds have a warm, slightly citrus flavour. Coffee flavoured with cardamom – *gahwa* – is a favourite drink among Arabs, and is served with considerable ceremony.

Cumin

A native of Upper Egypt and the Mediterranean, cumin has been a favourite spice in the Middle East for centuries. The ancient Egyptians were reputedly very fond of it, and cumin seeds have been found in the tombs of the pharaohs. Today, cumin is widely cultivated throughout the Middle East. Turkey and Iran are particularly important producers of cumin seeds,

Below: Flatleaf parsley is used generously in dishes such as tabbouleh.

Below: Thyme is a woody herb that retains much of its flavour when dried.

Below: Dill is used in fish and vegetable dishes and goes well with broad beans.

Above: Ground cinnamon

Above: White cumin

Above: Black cumin seeds

Above: Ground sumac

with Iran being a source of black cumin as well as the more familiar brownish-yellow variety.

Paprika

Made from a mild red sweet pepper, this sweet, pungent spice is more popular in Turkey than other parts of the Middle East.

Saffron

Used sparingly, this costly spice imparts a delicate flavour and yellow colour to foods, but it can taste musty if overdone. The familiar thin red threads are the stigmas of a crocus that grows well in Iran and Turkey. The threads are usually steeped in a liquid before being used. Ground saffron is also available.

Cinnamon

The rolled bark of an evergreen tree related to the laurel, cinnamon is a sweet, warm spice. It was known to the ancient Egyptians, who used it in religious ritual as well as in the kitchen.

Below: Harissa, a Tunisian spice mix, is also used in the Middle East.

Modern Middle Eastern cooks enjoy its mellow fragrance in both sweet and savoury dishes. In Turkey it is used to flavour tea, while in Azerbaijan it is an important ingredient in beef soup. Cinnamon is also mixed with ground nuts to make a variety of sweet pastries.

Other spices

Sumac is derived from the red berries of a bush that grows throughout the Middle East. The dried berries can be used whole, but are more often ground or cracked, then soaked in water. The liquid that results has a slightly sour, fruity flavour, which gives a pleasing astringency to stews. The berries can be ground and used as a rub for chicken, steaks or kebabs, and is also sprinkled over salads.

Hawaij

This earthy spice blend comes from Yemen. It tastes great in stews, soups and sauces and is also good sprinkled on vegetables before they are roasted. Try it as a rub for lamb chops that are to be grilled (broiled) or barbecued. You can buy ready mixed hawaij in packets, but it is easy to make:

Place 30ml/2 tbsp black peppercorns in a mortar and add 15ml/1 tbsp caraway seeds, 5ml/1 tsp cardamom seeds and several pinches of saffron threads. Use a pestle to grind the mixture.

Add 10ml/2 tsp each of ground cumin and turmeric. Mix together. Use as indicated in recipes. Surplus hawaij should be kept in a sealed jar in a cool, dark place.

Tamarind is another souring agent. It is not as widely used in the Middle East as it is in India, but a drink made from it is popular. Mahlebi is a ground spice, made from the kernel found inside the stone of a small black cherry that grows in Turkey and elsewhere in the Middle East. It has a nutty flavour, suggestive of almonds and cherries, and is used in cakes, breads and pastries.

Spice mixes

The Middle East is a source of some excellent spice mixes, many of which are now available in the West. Harissa, actually a North African mix, is used in couscous, and is widely available. Try baharat, a warm blend of paprika, nutmeg and cardamom that tastes good in meat and vegetable dishes. Kabsa, from Saudi Arabia, is a fiery mixture that typically contains cayenne pepper, cinnamon, cumin, black peppercorns, nutmeg, cardamom, lime rind, cloves and coriander. Zahtar is a blend of sesame seeds, thyme and sumac.

Below: Zahtar is a dry spice mix often used to flavour an olive oil dip.

OLIVES AND OLIVE OILS

There's something miraculous about a tree that can live for hundreds of years on poor soil, baked by the sun and denied regular rainfall, yet still produce fruits that are not only delicious in their own right, but also yield an exquisite oil. Perhaps this explains why olives have always had such cultural and spiritual significance. The olive branch is an ancient symbol of peace and the oil is used to anoint adherents of several religions. Olive oil was used in ancient Egypt as part of the embalming process and is central to the ritual of Christian baptism. Jars of cured olives have been found in the tombs of the Pharaohs, presumably placed there to give them sustenance in the afterlife. Muhammad advised his followers to eat the olive's oil and massage it over their bodies.

The olive tree has been cultivated for more than six thousand years. Whether it originated in Syria or Crete is a matter of constant conjecture (and heated argument) but there is ample evidence of its being traded in both these places by 2500 BC. The Minoans introduced olives and olive oil to mainland Greece. Soon, thanks to Phoenician traders, the fruit and oil were both widely known throughout the Mediterranean region.

Freshly picked olives are extremely bitter and have a metallic taste. When it was discovered that preserving them made them infinitely more palatable, their popularity was assured. The oil,

meanwhile, had myriad uses: in lamps, it burned beautifully without smoking; when perfumed, it made a fine medium for massage; it had proven medicinal qualities and could even be used to lubricate chariot axles (and was reputed to have made it easier to manoeuvre the huge stones into position when the pyramids were built). And, of course, it could be used as a marinade, as a cooking medium and as a preservative.

The Roman empire played an important role in disseminating the olive, introducing it to countries it had conquered, and expanding olive cultivation in lands where it was already well known, such as Palestine. It was

Above: Market stalls all over the Middle East sell a wide variety of olives

the Romans who developed the screw press, used for the efficient extraction of olive oil. Meanwhile, in more remote Arab lands, farmers continued to tend their trees as they had done for generations, harvesting the olives in due season, preserving them or pressing them to remove the oil.

Olive oil was not the only cooking medium in ancient times. Arabs also favoured oils derived from nuts of various types and used sesame, sunflower and corn oil. In many areas, especially among nomadic tribes,

Below: Black olives have been left on the tree to ripen the longest.

Below: These distinctive brown olives are very popular in the Middle East.

Below: Fresh olives have to be preserved before they are edible.

animal fats such as sheep tail fat and butter were preferred, since these could be extracted or churned from the milk of their herd animals.

Today, however, olive oil is the main type of oil used for cooking and as a condiment in much of the Middle East, especially in Syria, Turkey, Jordan and Lebanon. Syria and Turkey are both important oil producers – not in the same league as Spain, Italy and Greece, but still in the top ten of producers.

TYPES OF OLIVE

There's always a crowd around the olive stall in a Middle Eastern market. Everyone has a favourite fruit, and there will often be intense discussion as to the virtues of this glossy black olive or that smaller green one, or whether olives in brine taste better than those that have been cured in salt. The colours of the olives are an indication not of the variety, but rather of ripeness. Immature olives are green, and at this stage the flavour is quite acrid. The fruit must be treated with lye before being preserved. As the olives ripen, the colour changes to khaki, brown, red, purple and finally black. The longer the olives stay on the tree, the sweeter they become. Black olives also yield more oil than green ones.

Table olives – as distinct from olives grown specifically for their oil – are generally preserved in brine, although

Above: Virgin olive oil is prized for its distinctive flavour.

some will be packed in oil, cured in salt or merely packed in water. Graded by size, the smallest weigh around 3.2g/$\frac{1}{16}$ oz whereas the largest, aptly described as "supercolossal", tip the scales at around 15g/$\frac{1}{4}$oz.

OLIVE OIL

Increasingly, olive oils are being appreciated for their individual flavours. Some are mild and buttery; others are fruity or have a distinctly peppery flavour. Colours range from palest yellow to deep, intense green. Some oils come from a single type of fruit, others are blends. Middle Eastern oils are now attracting the attention of discriminating

Above: Various types of oil, from very dark green virgin olive oil at the front, is. flanked by sesame oil to the left, and a lighter olive oil to the right.

buyers. Highly regarded extra virgin oils are Mishelanu from Galilee in Israel and Rashaya from Lebanon. Sadoun is an interesting oil from Jordan.

Grades of oil

Olive oil is graded in terms of its acidity level and how many pressings it has had. In addition to the categories below, there are blended oils and oils flavoured with aromatics and herbs.
• Extra virgin olive oil, which comes from the first pressing of the olives, has low acidity and a superior flavour. It is not recommended for frying, but is the perfect choice for salad dressings.
• Virgin olive oil has a slightly higher level of acidity than extra virgin and is also a first-pressed oil.
• Pure olive oil has been refined and blended and has a lighter, more subtle flavour than virgin olive oil. It is suitable for all types of cooking and can also be used as a dressing.

Marinated olives

For a tasty snack or mezze, try marinated olives. Tip 450g/1lb black olives into a bowl. Pour over 30ml/2 tbsp red wine vinegar, then add 1 garlic clove, cut into slivers, with 2 whole red chillies and 3–4 slices of lemon. Mix well, then spoon the olives into a large jar or several smaller jars, and pour in enough olive oil to cover them. Cover tightly and leave for 2–3 weeks at room temperature.

FISH, MEAT AND POULTRY

The diet of the average man or woman in the Middle East, unless he or she lives in a modern city, is likely to be limited to what is fished, raised or grown in the immediate vicinity. Fish is a valuable addition to the diet and is often more affordable than meat, which is saved for special occasions. Lamb is widely enjoyed in many different forms. Chicken is also popular; it is common to buy live birds from market, which are dispatched and prepared at home.

FISH

Most of the countries in the Middle East have extensive coastlines. In many parts a fisherman can still make a decent living and those who fish the eastern Mediterranean have better hauls than their counterparts to the west. The Arabian Sea also yields a rich harvest, whereas the Red Sea is the source of colourful reef fish, as well as king prawns (jumbo shrimp) and tasty flat lobsters. Oman has some of the finest fishing territories in the Middle East, and shark, tuna and grouper, are landed in its waters. From the Black

Below: Grey mullet, a favourite Middle Eastern fish, are often cooked with dill.

Sea come delicious fresh anchovies, while the Caspian is home to the sturgeon, from which comes the expensive delicacy, caviar.

Shellfish are not as widely eaten as sea fish or freshwater fish. This is largely because Jews who observe the dietary laws of Kashrut must abstain from eating any kind of shellfish and crustaceans, as well as squid, octopus and certain types of fish. Muslims may not eat lobster or crab, although prawns are permissible if taken from the water alive. The Koran also forbids the eating of fish that do not have scales, such as shark or catfish. The following are some of the more popular varieties of fish available and eaten in the Middle East.

Red mullet

Common in Mediterranean waters, red mullet are considered to be among the best tasting sea fish. Perhaps that's one reason why they are given the grand title of Sultan Ibrahim in the Middle East. Red mullet are often cooked whole, either in the pan or – more often – on the barbecue (grill) where they may be wrapped in vine leaves to protect the flesh. Egyptians like to serve red mullet with a sauce made from chopped hazelnuts and pine nuts.

Grey mullet

A favourite way of cooking this fish is to stuff it with dill – a herb that is extremely popular in the Middle East – and grill (broil) it, dousing it with arak or raki (both spirits) from time to time.

Red snapper

Around the Arabian Sea, these handsome fish are often called job or jobfish. Red snapper are generally pan fried or baked. The flesh is robust enough to compete with quite strong flavours, and Egyptians like to bake red snapper in a lightly spiced tomato sauce.

Tilapia

The succulent white flesh of tilapia is quite sweet, and goes well with fruity flavours. In Egypt and Israel the fish is sometimes marketed as St Peter's fish, which can be confusing, as John Dory has the same nickname.

Trout

This is a popular fish, especially in Turkey and Iran, where the rivers and lakes of the Alborz mountains north of Tehran are well stocked with trout, and fishing is a popular pastime.

Below: Brown trout and rainbow trout are both farmed extensively throughout the Middle East.

Caviar and bottarga

The finest caviar is said to be beluga, from the large Caspian sturgeon; oseotre comes from the Danube sturgeon (also found in the Caspian) while sevruga comes from the small Caspian sturgeon. Sadly, all these fish are now endangered species, with beluga on the critical list. Many people now prefer to buy bottarga (shown below), the salted and dried roe of the grey mullet.

MEAT

The quality of meat available varies considerably, but Middle Eastern cooks have devised numerous ways of making even the least promising cuts taste good. All parts of the animal are eaten, and some offal (variety meats) is considered to be a delicacy.

Lamb is the meat of choice throughout the Middle East. Very little pork is consumed, since neither observant Jews nor Muslims may eat it, and beef's availability is limited, largely because there is not enough suitable grazing for the best beef animals, nor is the climate ideal. Goat (kid) is eaten, as is – on occasion – young camel. Game is also served, particularly in Iran, which has wild deer, and some of the biggest wild boar in the world.

Beef

There has been a gradual shift towards more beef consumption, particularly in larger, more cosmopolitan cities, and in Iran and Iraq, where beef and lamb are often used interchangeably. This is particularly true in the case of Koftas (meatballs). Beef is also eaten in stews, such as the Persian Khoresh.

Lamb

Used in a variety of recipes, lamb is roasted, chargrilled, baked, braised, stewed and used as a filling. Ground or minced lamb is baked as a loaf or transformed into meatballs, which are

Below: Shin of beef is an ideal cut for slow stewing in a casserole.

Above: Lamb is used in a great variety of dishes throughout the region.

cooked in a rich tomato sauce or threaded on to skewers and cooked on an open fire. Very finely ground or pounded lamb, mixed with bulgur wheat, is the basis for the famous Lebanese and Syrian dish Kibbeh. Lamb kidneys are enjoyed skewered or sautéed, and lambs liver, often cooked with paprika and garlic, is a favourite dish in Turkey.

POULTRY

Spatchcocked chickens are a favourite street food basted with oil and lemon juice, with herbs or a sprinkling of sumac. Roast chicken is popular, too, and is often stuffed with spiced dried fruit and nuts. Chicken is cooked in yogurt for the Persian dish Tah Chin, which makes it beautifully tender. Perhaps the Middle East's most famous chicken dish is Khoresh Fesenjan, from Iran – a colourful mixture of chicken,

Below: Jointed chicken is used in many different Middle Eastern dishes.

Roast pigeon, Egyptian-style

Pigeon is always popular in Egypt. This dish, Hamam Mashwi, is one of the simplest ways of cooking young birds, the marinade makes the flesh and keeps it moist.

4 plump young pigeons
1 large onion, finely chopped
juice and zest of 2 lemons
30ml/2 tbsp olive oil
salt

Preheat the oven to 180°C/ 350°F/Gas 4. Clean the pigeons, and rinse them under cold water. Drain and pat dry with kitchen paper. Place side by side in a shallow dish and strew with the chopped onion. Grate the zest of the lemons over the birds, then use your hands to work the onion and lemon rind into the skin. Mix the juice from the lemons with the olive oil and pour over the pigeons. Cover and leave to marinate in a cool place for 4–6 hours.

Place the pigeons, with the marinade, in the roasting pan, sprinkle with salt and roast for 45–55 minutes, or until the birds are fully cooked, basting frequently.

pomegranates and walnuts. Also popular, especially in Egypt, is pigeon. In the Nile Delta pigeons are plump and of a good size. Egyptians like them roasted or grilled (broiled).

Below: Pigeon is farmed in the Nile Delta and is enjoyed roasted or grillled.

FRESH FRUIT AND VEGETABLES

Middle Eastern markets are a kaleidoscope of colour. Baskets of tomatoes, piles of dusky purple aubergines (eggplants), scented lemons, fat peaches, exotic pomegranates and okra pods are all there for the buying. Shopping for ingredients, especially fruit and vegetables, is a serious business for the Middle Eastern cook. First a circuit must be made of the market to locate the finest produce, and then the niceties must be observed – an inquiry as to the health of the stallholder's sister, perhaps, or a remark about the weather. After this, honour is satisfied and the purchase is completed.

FRUIT

It is traditional throughout the Middle East for a meal to conclude with fresh fruit. A slice of chilled melon, perhaps, a bowl of cherries or just a perfect peach. In winter, such fresh fruit as is available may be added to a dried fruit compote, or a rice pudding topped with berries picked earlier in the year and preserved for just such an occasion. Fresh fruit is used in salads, as when pomegranate arils are mixed with fresh greens, or added to stews. Lemon is the linchpin of Middle Eastern cooking, but other types of citrus are important, too. From Israel, one of the world's most important citrus producers, come Jaffa oranges, white and pink grapefruit and kumquats. Lebanon is famous for soft fruits, Iran for cherries and melons and

Above: Apricots are a particular favourite in the Middle East.

Turkey for superb figs. Baalbek, the former Phoenician city close to Beirut, is known for its magnificent apricots. It is said that their flesh is so fine that when the fruit is held up to the light, the stone can be seen inside. Apples are grown in the more temperate areas; bananas, pineapples and mangoes grow in coastal regions with good irrigation.

Figs

Turkey is one of the world's leading exporters of this delicious fruit. Smyrna figs are sweet and succulent, with golden flesh, while Mission figs are deep purple, with red flesh. Figs are delicious on their own, but can also be split and opened out to hold a nut filling, baked with honey or served with white cheese.

Below: Quinces have a delectable fragrance and mild, sweet flesh.

Quinces

These are fabulous fruit that originated in Turkestan and Persia. In colder climes, they do not achieve their full potential, but when they are placed in the heat they fill the air with their exquisite perfume.

Quinces make delicious jams and jellies, but are also good in meat dishes, and stuffed quince – *dolmeh beh* – is excellent. This Persian dish involves coring the fruit, packing it with a meat and split pea mixture and cooking it in a sweet-and-sour sauce.

Pomegranates

On the tree, pomegranates look like polished cricket balls, but cut them and you find jewelled treasure. Inside the fruit, each seed is encased in a translucent sac of pulp. These arils, as they are called, are deliciously refreshing, but getting at them is no mean feat. It is important to avoid the bitter pith, so the arils must either be picked out individually, using a pin, or pressed into a bowl and then picked over by hand. Middle Eastern cooks use pomegranate seeds in salads, in savoury dishes and in desserts. They are inordinately fond of pomegranate juice, which they sweeten and serve very cold. Juicing a pomegranate is easy – just press it down very gently on a citrus squeezer.

Below: The jewel-like seeds of the pomegranate are sharp and refreshing.

Below: Figs are eaten fresh, or cooked in a variety of delicious desserts.

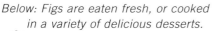

Above: This flavoursome, ridged tomato is grown in the Lebanon.

VEGETABLES

There's something almost decadent about the vegetables of the Middle East. No prissy broccoli or prudish peas here, but instead voluptuous violet aubergines (eggplants), perky (bell) peppers, courgettes (zucchini) – so prolific as to be positively indecent – and shiny round tomatoes, exquisitely sweet, thanks to being grown in bright sunshine in unpolluted desert air. Also on the menu are artichokes, fresh broad (fava) beans, long thin cucumbers, leafy spinach and glossy pumpkin, which is served as a vegetable and also transformed into a candied sweet. Okra, with its mucilaginous texture, isn't to everyone's taste, but the pods are delicious in a chickpea stir-fry or a tomato stew. Peppers are widely used, and are just one of the vegetables that Middle Eastern cooks like to stuff with rice and herbs or a savoury meat mixture. And let's not forget salads: these are universally popular and, thanks to modern farming methods, even the driest desert regions are now capable of producing crisp, fresh greens. A salad will often be delivered to the restaurant table along with the menu, so that diners can take the edge off their appetites while they make their meal choices. Salads form part of

Desert truffles

Oil is not the only treasure to lie beneath desert sands. From Egypt to Iraq, a rich harvest of truffles is gathered each year. Called *terfas* by the Bedouin of the Western Desert, and *kamaa* in Syria, they are not so strongly flavoured as European truffles, but are still delicious – and much more affordable.

every mezze spread, often with yogurt dressings, and are also served as separate courses in their own right. Most of the vegetables that feature in Middle Eastern cooking will be familiar to cooks everywhere, but the following warrant a little more explanation.

Artichokes

As soon as globe artichokes are in season they are seized upon by cooks eager to use them for mezze or in main-course dishes. When very young, before the choke has formed, the entire artichoke is edible.

Okra

Also called ladies' fingers, or *baamieh* in Arabic, okra pods are shaped like slim, tapering lanterns. If the pods are cooked whole, as in a stir-fry, they stay crisp, with no trace of slime, but cut them and cook them in a stew, and the

Below: Aubergines come in several shapes and sizes, and can also be white or purple and white in colour.

Above: Artichokes are used extensively in Middle Eastern mezzes and salads.

rows of seeds release a sticky liquid. This has the effect of thickening the sauce, but in a glutinous way that is not to everyone's taste. Okra goes well with tomatoes, chillies and ginger.

Aubergines

Known as eggplants in America and *brinjals* in India, these tasty vegetables come in several different shapes and sizes. They are especially appreciated in Turkey, a nation that is said to have more than two hundred recipes for preparing them.

Middle Eastern recipes often recommend salting aubergines to draw out some of their bitter juices, but this is seldom necessary in the West, where the vegetables available are usually young and tender.

DRIED FRUIT AND FLAVOURINGS

Most Arabs have a sweet tooth, which is hardly surprising when you consider that sweet, succulent dates have been part of their diet since childhood. Dried fruits and nuts are favourite snacks, and the penchant for mixing sweet with savoury flavours means that dried fruits are a feature of both meat dishes and desserts. Fruit syrups are highly concentrated and can be overwhelming. For more subtlety, select one of those signature Middle Eastern flavours: rosewater or orange flower water.

POPULAR VARIETIES OF DRIED FRUIT

Middle Eastern cooks often use dried fruit to add a touch of sweetness to a savoury dish. A mixture of nuts and dried cherries, apricots and barberries might be used to stuff a chicken, for example, or meatballs might be studded with the tiny black currants referred to as bird grapes. In

Above: Sun-dried apricots.

are produced in the Mediterranean region, especially in Turkey.

Dates

Plump and succulent, dates are among the most delicious of fruit, whether you enjoy them fresh from the tree or dried. The date palm is extensively cultivated throughout the Middle East. Iraq leads the world in date production, closely followed by Iran and Saudi Arabia. For centuries, dates have been an important food for Arab tribesmen and traders. An excellent energy source, they are easily portable and provide valuable minerals, making them a good match for the fermented milk and occasional meat meals that are standard desert fare.

There are more than three hundred date varieties, classified by how much moisture they contain.

Soft dates are deliciously sweet and juicy. Arabs like to eat them before they are fully ripe, when the flesh is still crunchy and the flavour has a tart undertone. Ripe dates of this type taste like toffee and are almost as sticky. Popular varieties include the Khadrawi, which comes from Iraq, and the Bahri, from Israel and Egypt. Another date that is widely grown in Egypt is the Halawi, which is soft fleshed and slightly chewy. The

queen among soft dates is, however, the Medjool, a Moroccan variety that is now cultivated in the Middle East, California and South Africa. Plump and voluptuous, this deep red-coloured date has little fibre and a superb flavour.

Semi-dry dates are firmer than soft varieties and have a lower moisture content. Deglet Noor, Dayri and Zahidi fall into this category. These dates are often sold in boxes, with what look like plastic twigs for winkling them out.

Dry dates are hard and fibrous, almost nutty in texture. These are the dates traditionally eaten

Clockwise from top left: sultanas, currants, and raisins.

by nomadic Arabs, who refer to them as bread dates. The dryness is natural, but they are sometimes dried even more so that they can be ground to a powder.

Below: Two different sizes of dried figs.

Above: Once dried and packed, dates will last for months.

Azerbaijan, dried fruit is the basis of a beef soup flavoured with mint and cinnamon, whereas in Israel dried apricots and prunes are cooked with vegetables to make *tzimmes*. Raisins, sultanas (golden raisins) and currants

Compressed dates are dried fruit that have been tightly packed together in blocks. Very high in sugar, they are largely intended for baking, and are often softened in water before use.

Dried figs

Turkey is the world's major producer of dried figs. Smyrna figs from Izmir are particularly prized, but the purple Mission figs are popular too. Travellers to Turkey will often see the flattened fruit, suspended in loops from reeds or spread on hurdles to dry in the sun. Drying concentrates the natural sugars, which in turn helps to preserve the fruit. Tiny dried figs are eaten like sweets in the Middle East; larger fruits are stuffed and baked, or stewed in water scented with rosewater to make a compote.

Dried apricots

Called *zard-alu* or "yellow plum" by the Persians and *mishmish* in Arabic, apricots have been sun-dried for centuries in the Middle East. In addition to being dried individually, apricots are compressed to make *qamar el-deen*, thin sheets of fruit leather that make a drink when dissolved in boiling water. During Ramadan, serving this drink often signals the end of the daily fast.

Dried barberries and sour cherries

An Iranian speciality, dried barberries are often sprinkled over pilaffs or added to stews. The berries themselves are a small, wild, red fruit, about the size of redcurrants. They are too bitter to eat fresh but become sweeter dried. Dried sour cherries are used to flavour stews in Turkey, Iran and Syria.

Below: Dried sour cherries.

Above: Flower waters: on the left orange flower water, on the right rosewater.

Dried pomegranate seeds

When dried, the arils, or seeds, of pomegranates can be used in place of raisins in desserts and also to flavour vegetables and lentil dishes in Iran and Iraq. The pomegranates from which the arils are extracted are a sour variety, not suitable for eating raw.

FRUIT SYRUPS

Popular throughout the Middle East, fruit syrups are used in marinades, meat dishes and desserts, but their primary function is as a flavouring for long, cold drinks. A small amount of syrup, topped up with iced water or soda (carbonated) water makes a sweet but refreshing beverage.

Also known as *visne*, cherry syrup is the sweetened juice of sour cherries. It is sold by street sellers and makes a pretty drink when diluted over ice.

Made from concentrated grape juice, *pekmez* is remarkably sweet, despite the fact that the only sugar comes from the grapes themselves. Used sparingly, pekmez can add an interesting flavour to chicken and also works well in a dried fruit compote. Also known as *halek*, *dibis* is a concentrated date syrup. Popular in Israel, it is widely sold

in jars, but can also be made at home by soaking dried dates in water until plump, then boiling them in water until soft. After being puréed, the date mixture is then cooked again until it reduces to a thick, syrupy paste to be diluted with water. Also called pomegranate molasses, this syrup is a delicious product with the consistency of treacle. It goes well in dressings and has long been an important ingredient in Persian cooking.

FLOWER WATERS

Rosewater has a unique flavour, delicate yet always clearly discernible. Distilled from the petals of the pink damask rose, it is used throughout the Middle East, in cakes, desserts and ice creams. Perhaps best known for its role in *lokum* (Turkish delight), rosewater is the perfect partner for iced melon.

Orange flower water is made from bitter orange blossoms. It is used to flavour pastries and cakes, and is the basis for the well-known Lebanese "café blanc", which is actually a beverage made by boiling the essence with water.

Below: Clockwise from bottom right: date syrup, sour grape juice, pomegranate paste, rosehip syrup and sour cherry juice.

BREADS, PASTRIES AND CAKES

The expression "daily bread" is nowhere more accurate than in the Middle East, where peasant workers eat over 1kg/2¼lb a day and it is enjoyed at every meal. Cakes and pastries, for which the region is equally famous, are as lavish as the loaves of bread are plain. Many of them are extremely sweet: the perfect accompaniment to a cup of strong, black Turkish coffee.

BREADS

Although bread is of enormous value merely as sustenance, it also plays a role in religious observance throughout the Middle East. The baking and buying of bread is a social event, too. Many Middle Eastern housewives work together to bake for themselves and the community, or take their risen dough to the village baker.

Above: Pide.
Below: Simits.

Below: Ekmek.

Muslims are enjoined to treat bread with respect. It should be torn, not cut with a knife, which would show disrespect to what they regard as a gift from Allah. When it is brought to the table it should be eaten immediately, taking precedence over other foods. Any bread remaining at the end of a meal must be used, perhaps in the delicious salad known as Fattoush. Even crumbs must be gathered up and either eaten by those present or fed to animals. This rule – that no food must be wasted – is fundamental to the teachings of Islam.

The royal bakers who prepared food for the pharaohs are known to have made more than 30 different types of bread. Across the whole of the Middle East today, the number is much higher. Flat breads, such as *lavash*, plump loaves such as *hashas*, sheets, crusty bread rings, puffy individual breads that reveal pockets when split – the range of both leavened and unleavened loaves is vast. What they have in common is that they must be eaten fresh. Bread stales rapidly in the Middle East, but this is not a problem since bread is baked at home or in a bakery at least once a day.

Right: A pile of lavash, *the flat bread used to scoop up food at mealtimes.*

Above: A selection of the bread sold each day all over the Middle East.

Pide

This is the Turkish version of the bread the Greeks call pitta. It can be shaped in rounds or be slipper-shaped. When baked in a very hot oven, the dough puffs up so that the centre remains hollow, making each individual bread the perfect receptacle for a salad, some cheese or a few chunks of grilled (broiled) lamb slid from a skewer. *Pide* is often served with mezzes.

Aiysh

This is similar to *pide*, but smaller and thicker. This Egyptian bread, which has been made in the same way for thousands of years, is found throughout the Middle East. It is generally made with wholemeal (whole-wheat) flour and ranges in shape from 15cm/6in rounds to ovals of up to 38cm/15in. In Yemen the bread is known as *saluf*; in Jordan and Palestine as *shrak*; and in Syria as *aiysh shami*.

Ekmek

The word simply means "bread" in Turkey, but usually refers to a large round or oval leavened bread made simply from a plain white or wholemeal dough. *Sutlu Ekmek*, for example, is made by arranging a circle of round rolls around a central roll in a baking pan so that they rise and stick together to form a single loaf.

Khoubz

Virtually identical to *aiysh*, this flat, slightly leavened bread is popular in the Levant and Arabian peninsula. Originally made with finely ground wholemeal flour similar to chapati flour, it is now more often made using white flour.

Simits

Shaped in golden bread rings, *simits* are traditionally coated with sesame seeds, and are sold in the streets. They look like bagels and are made in the same way, being first poached in water and then baked.

Barbari

These flattish white breads from Iran come in various sizes and shapes, and are dimpled or slashed to give the surface a fretwork effect. They may be brushed with oil before being baked, and spiced versions are often topped with cumin or caraway seeds.

Lavash

This pancake-thin bread originated in Armenia, but is now popular throughout the Middle East. It can be round, oval or square, and is made in various sizes, the largest sheets measuring up to

60cm/24in across. A large *lavash*, placed in the centre of the table, will serve the entire party. Guests tear off as much as they need and use the bread as a wrap or for scooping up sauce.

Challah

Traditionally made for the Jewish Sabbath or for religious festivals, this braided bread has a deep brown crust. The dough is made using eggs and vegetable oil, which gives the baked bread a texture somewhere between that of a brioche and a soft white loaf.

PASTRIES AND CAKES

Middle Eastern pastries are the stuff of dreams. Whisper-thin pastry, cooked to crisp perfection, is filled with some of the most delicious concoctions imaginable. Ground pistachio nuts and cardamom, dates and almonds, candied apricots, coconut and semolina custard – these are just some of the many possibilities. Further flavouring comes from lemon or lime rind, warm spices or the subtle yet pervasive taste of flower waters. Syrup or honey is often poured over the hot pastries as they emerge from the oven, soaking in to become sensationally sticky. Eat something like this at the end of a large meal and it seems over-sweet, over-indulgent and

Above: Briouates are one of the many varieties of sweet pastries available.

decidedly over the top. But cut a small portion and enjoy it in the middle of the afternoon with a cup of strong, black Turkish coffee, as people in the Middle East do, and its appeal becomes immediately obvious.

Pastries are popular street foods and it is not unusual to see a vendor performing a seemingly impossible balancing act as he hurries to his pitch with a large tray of pastries on his head. Among the most popular treats is *kodafa*, a rich cheesecake made with an unusual shredded pastry called *kadaif*. The *kodafa* is strewn with pistachio nuts and served with a honey and saffron syrup scented with orange flower water.

It is in Israel and other communities with large Jewish populations that the largest variety of cakes are to be found. Almond cakes, Russian poppy seed cake, Polish apple cake and honey cake are the legacy of those who left the lands of their birth to settle in Israel. Many of them are made without flour; groundnuts and matzo meal are used instead, with beaten egg whites as the raising agent. This allows them to be eaten during Pesach, when leavened foods are forbidden.

COFFEE, TEA AND SOCIAL DRINKING

Aside from water, coffee and tea are the most widely drunk beverages in the Middle East. Each has its own rituals regarding preparation and serving. Tea and coffee ease introductions, cement friendships and oil the wheels of commerce. Anyone contemplating making a major purchase is liable to be offered a cup of coffee or glass of tea to ease the pain of parting with money. Muslims may not drink alcohol, so fresh fruit drinks and beverages made from fruit syrups are freely available, as are several milk- or yogurt-based beverages.

COFFEE

There's some disagreement about whether the coffee plant originated in Ethiopia or the Middle East, but Yemen can certainly lay claim to being one of the first countries to cultivate coffee on a large scale. The southern part of the country is suited to coffee production, and the terraced slopes of the mountains are criss-crossed with coffee plants, each row protected from the harsh sun by a row of poplar trees. The arabica coffee from the south-western tip of the Arabian Peninsula is rich and mellow, with underlying acidity and a chocolate aftertaste. It was originally

Below: Turkish coffee will have a froth on the top if it has been made correctly.

exported through the port of Mocha. This not only gave it its name – Yemen Mocha – but also led to the word "mocha" being used to describe any chocolate-coffee flavour.

The coffee trade in Yemen reached its peak in the 17th and 18th centuries. Today it is in decline, due in part to increased demand for *qat*. This leafy narcotic, a source of a natural amphetamine, is regularly chewed by a large percentage of the population, and coffee bushes are constantly being grubbed up so that more *qat* (*Catha edulis*) trees can be planted.

None of this has diminished the popularity of coffee, however. Arabs, particularly those who live in Yemen and Saudi Arabia, brew the beverage without sugar, in kettles or pots called *dallahs*. The coffee is then poured into tall pots, many of which are exquisitely crafted, before being served in cups.

Turkish coffee

This thick, sweet beverage is not a specific type of coffee, but rather a method of preparation that was developed in the Middle East in the early 16th century. Traders introduced it to the Ottoman court, and the proper preparation of Turkish coffee soon became a vital skill. Women in the harem were instructed in the art, and

Above: Mint tea is a refreshing drink in the heat of the summer.

young girls had to become expert if they hoped to find suitable husbands.

A small open pot with a long handle is used for brewing Turkish coffee. Generally made of tin-lined brass, it is called an *ibrik* or *cezve*. Legend has it that the desert sands become so hot during the day that coffee can be brewed directly on them as evening falls, but the more usual method is for the pot to be placed on the stove or in the embers of a fire. Any arabica coffee can be used, but it must be ground very finely, so that it resembles a powder. Ground cardamom or ginger can be added, giving a distinctive flavour.

When making Turkish coffee, the aim is to allow the brew to bubble up several times without boiling over, so that a thick froth forms on top of the liquid. When the coffee is poured out, it should be left to stand briefly so that the ground coffee sinks. It forms a sludge on the bottom of the cup, which should not be drunk.

The amount of sugar in the coffee varies. Technically there are six levels of sweetness, but in practice most people ask for *sekerli* (very sweet), *orta sekerli* (with a little sugar) or *sekersiz* (without sugar). These are Turkish terms; elsewhere in the Middle East different classifications are used. Arabic or Bedouin coffee, on the other hand, is

Above: Fruit juices (clockwise from front) rosehip, pomegranate and peach.

Above: Sugar cane juice is a very sweet drink served in the Middle East.

Above: Aryan is made of yoghurt that has been diluted with water.

drunk without sugar. This green or grey liquid, with its slightly bitter taste, is enjoyed in Syria and Jordan.

TEA

Although coffee is widely drunk, especially in Lebanon, tea, or *chai,* is the favourite drink in many parts of the Middle East. Like coffee, it is served with considerable ceremony, and – again like coffee – it is drunk without milk and with sugar. It is the custom in some areas for the recipient to place a cube of sugar between their front teeth, and sip the tea through it. Tea is often flavoured with mint or with spices such as ginger or cinnamon. In Turkey, herb and fruit teas made from sage, rose hips and apples are on sale.

SOFT DRINKS

Fresh fruit juices are widely available from stand-up juice bars, but long, cold drinks made from concentrated fruit syrups topped up with iced water are even more popular. In Egypt, hibiscus juice – often called "red tea" – is a favourite drink, along with apricot juice, tamarind juice and a drink made from dates. Cherry juice is popular in Iran, whereas orange and tamarind juice, either separately or as a mixture, are enjoyed in Israel. Liquorice juice is a more unusual choice, found in Egypt

and Jordan, and there are several extremely sweet drinks, including honey water and sugar cane juice, both of which are served ice cold.

YOGURT AND MILK DRINKS

Yogurt, diluted with water, is a favourite thirst-quencher for the desert Bedouin. In Syria and Turkey, this drink is called *aryan.* It is often served with mint. *Salep* is a hot milk drink flavoured with cinnamon and thickened with sahlab, ground orchid root. *Boza* is a fermented wheat drink that has a reputation for being especially nourishing and healthy.

Wines of the Middle East

The main wine-producing countries of the Middle East are Israel, Lebanon and Turkey. Historically, Israel has been best known for kosher wine, but now produces Cabernet, Sauvignon Blanc, Grenache and Semillon. Lebanon's wine industry is centred on the Bekkah Valley and produces some fine red wines, largely derived from Cabernet Sauvignon grapes. Turkey produces a considerable amount of wine, and quality reds from Thrace, Anatolia and the Aegean region are highly regarded.

ALCOHOLIC DRINKS

The Koran forbids the drinking of alcohol. In some countries this taboo is strictly enforced. In Saudi Arabia, for example, the sale and/or consumption of any type of alcohol is strictly prohibited, and strict penalties are imposed on anyone caught flouting the law. Elsewhere in the Middle East, the situation is somewhat more relaxed. In Jordan, for example, alcohol is available in many hotels and restaurants, but drinking alcohol in public can cause deep offence. Turkey is more liberal, and has Western-style bars and pubs, though these remain largely male preserves. Beer, brewed under licence, is available, as is wine.

The most popular spirit is raki, a potent aniseed-flavoured drink distilled from grain, which clouds when mixed with water, a phenomenon that has earned it the nickname *aslan sutu* (lion's milk).

Right: The favourite spirit in the Middle East is aniseed-flavoured raki.

SOUPS, MEZZES AND APPETIZERS

In the Middle East, and some African countries, the first course is seen as a main component of the meal, rather than simply a morsel to tempt the appetite. In Iran, soup is held in such high regard that the kitchen is known as "the house of the soup maker". The art of the appetizer reaches its apogee in Lebanon, where a mezze consists of dozens of different dishes, balanced to offer a feast of colours and flavours. This chapter explores some of the options, from simple marinated olives to stuffed vegetables and exquisite salads.

CHILLED ALMOND AND GARLIC SOUP WITH ROASTED CHILLI AND GRAPES

THE COLD AND CHILLED SOUPS OF NORTH AFRICA ARE ANCIENT IN ORIGIN AND WERE ORIGINALLY INTRODUCED TO MOROCCO BY THE ARABS. THIS PARTICULAR MILKY WHITE SOUP HAS TRAVELLED FURTHER WITH THE MOORS INTO SPAIN. HEAVILY LACED WITH GARLIC, IT IS UNUSUAL BUT DELICIOUSLY REFRESHING IN HOT WEATHER, AND MAKES A DELIGHTFUL, TANGY FIRST COURSE FOR A SUMMER LUNCH PARTY.

SERVES FOUR

INGREDIENTS
  130g/4½oz/¾ cup blanched almonds
  3–4 slices day-old white bread,
    crusts removed
  4 garlic cloves
  60ml/4 tbsp olive oil
  about 1 litre/1¾ pints/4 cups
    iced water
  30ml/2 tbsp white wine vinegar
  salt
To garnish
  1 dried red chilli, roasted and
    thinly sliced
  a small bunch of sweet green grapes,
    halved and seeded
  a handful of slivered almonds

COOK'S TIP
Almonds can be bought ready-blanched, but you can also blanch them yourself in boiling water. To blanch almonds using a microwave oven, place them in a bowl, cover with boiling water and microwave on High for 2 minutes. Drain, and peel off the skins.

1 Place the blanched almonds in a blender or food processor and process to form a smooth paste. Add the bread, garlic, olive oil and half the water and process again until smooth.

2 With the motor running, continue to add the remaining water in a slow, steady stream until the mixture is smooth with the consistency of single (light) cream. Add the vinegar and salt.

3 Transfer the soup to a serving bowl and then chill for at least 1 hour.

4 When the soup is chilled, stir gently before serving into individual bowls. Garnish each bowl with the sliced roasted chilli, halved grapes and a few slivered almonds.

Energy 352Kcal/1459kJ; Protein 8.6g; Carbohydrate 13.8g, of which sugars 3.4g; Fat 29.5g, of which saturates 3.1g; Cholesterol 0mg; Calcium 102mg; Fibre 2.8g; Sodium 110mg.

CINNAMON-SCENTED CHICKPEA AND LENTIL SOUP WITH FENNEL AND HONEY BUNS

THIS THICK LENTIL AND VEGETABLE SOUP, FLAVOURED WITH GINGER AND CINNAMON, VARIES FROM VILLAGE TO VILLAGE AND TOWN TO TOWN. IT IS BELIEVED TO HAVE ORIGINATED FROM A SEMOLINA GRUEL THAT THE BERBERS PREPARED TO WARM THEMSELVES DURING THE COLD WINTERS IN THE ATLAS MOUNTAINS. OVER THE CENTURIES, IT HAS BEEN ADAPTED AND REFINED WITH SPICES AND TOMATOES FROM THE NEW WORLD.

SERVES EIGHT

INGREDIENTS
    30–45ml/2–3 tbsp smen or olive oil
    2 onions, halved and sliced
    2.5ml/½ tsp ground ginger
    2.5ml/½ tsp ground turmeric
    5ml/1 tsp ground cinnamon
    pinch of saffron threads
    2 x 400g/14oz cans chopped tomatoes
    5–10ml/1–2 tsp caster
      (superfine) sugar
    175g/6oz/¾ cup brown or green
      lentils, picked over and rinsed
    about 1.75 litres/3 pints/7½ cups
      meat or vegetable stock, or water
    200g/7oz/1 generous cup dried
      chickpeas, soaked overnight,
      drained and boiled until tender
    200g/7oz/1 generous cup dried broad
      (fava) beans, soaked overnight,
      drained and boiled until tender
    small bunch of fresh coriander
      (cilantro), chopped
    small bunch of flat leaf parsley, chopped
    salt and ground black pepper
For the buns
    2.5ml/½ tsp dried yeast
    300g/11oz/2¾ cups unbleached
      strong white bread flour
    a pinch of salt
    15–30ml/1–2 tbsp clear honey
    5ml/1 tsp fennel seeds
    250ml/8fl oz/1 cup milk
    1 egg yolk, stirred with a little milk

1 Make the fennel and honey buns. Dissolve the yeast in about 15ml/1 tbsp lukewarm water. Sift the flour and salt into a bowl. Make a well in the centre and add the dissolved yeast, honey and fennel seeds. Gradually pour in the milk, using your hands to work it into the flour along with the honey and yeast, until the mixture forms a dough – if the dough becomes too sticky to handle, add more flour.

2 Turn the dough out on to a floured surface and knead well for about 10 minutes, until it is smooth and elastic. Flour the surface under the dough and cover it with a damp cloth, then leave the dough to rise until it has doubled in size.

3 Preheat the oven to 230ºC/450ºF/ Gas 8. Grease two baking sheets. Divide the dough into 8 balls. On a floured surface, flatten the balls of dough with the palm of your hand, then place them on a baking sheet. Brush the tops of the buns with egg yolk, then bake for about 15 minutes, until they are risen slightly and sound hollow when tapped underneath. Transfer to a wire rack to cool.

4 To make the soup, heat the smen or olive oil in a stockpot or large pan. Add the onions and stir over a low heat for about 15 minutes, or until they are soft.

5 Add the ginger, turmeric, cinnamon and saffron, then the tomatoes and a little sugar. Stir in the lentils and pour in the stock or water. Bring the liquid to the boil, then reduce the heat, cover and simmer for about 25 minutes, or until the lentils are tender.

6 Stir in the cooked chickpeas and beans, bring back to the boil, then cover and simmer for a further 10–15 minutes. Stir in the fresh herbs and season the soup to taste. Serve piping hot, with the fennel and honey buns.

Energy 376Kcal/1594kJ; Protein 18.7g; Carbohydrate 66.4g, of which sugars 12g; Fat 5.9g, of which saturates 1g; Cholesterol 2mg; Calcium 181mg; Fibre 8.6g; Sodium 70mg.

MOROCCAN PUMPKIN SOUP

MODERN MOROCCAN STREET STALLS AND MARKETS ARE PILED HIGH WITH COLOURFUL SEASONAL PRODUCE. THE PUMPKIN SEASON IS PARTICULARLY DELIGHTFUL, WITH THE HUGE ORANGE VEGETABLES DISPLAYED ON TABLES AND WOODEN CARTS. THE SELLERS PATIENTLY PEEL AND SLICE THE PUMPKINS READY FOR MAKING THIS SIMPLE AND TASTY WINTER SOUP, WITH ITS HINT OF SUGAR AND SPICE.

SERVES FOUR

INGREDIENTS
about 1.1kg/2lb 7oz pumpkin
750ml/1¼ pints/3 cups
  chicken stock
750ml/1¼ pints/3 cups milk
10–15ml/2–3 tsp sugar
75g/3oz/½ cup cooked white rice
salt and ground black pepper
5ml/1 tsp ground cinnamon,
  to garnish

COOK'S TIPS
Use butternut squash in place of pumpkin. Use cooked brown rice in place of white rice, if preferred.

1 Remove any seeds or strands of fibre from the pumpkin, cut off the peel and chop the flesh. Put the prepared pumpkin in a pan and add the stock, milk, sugar and seasoning.

2 Bring to the boil, then reduce the heat and simmer for about 20 minutes, until the pumpkin is tender. Drain the pumpkin, reserving the liquid, and purée it in a blender or food processor, then return it to the pan.

3 Bring the soup back to the boil again, throw in the rice and simmer for a few minutes, until the grains are reheated. Check the seasoning, pour into bowls and dust with cinnamon. Serve piping hot, with chunks of fresh, crusty bread.

Energy 148Kcal/627kJ; Protein 8.8g; Carbohydrate 20.7g, of which sugars 13.5g; Fat 4g, of which saturates 2.3g; Cholesterol 11mg; Calcium 308mg; Fibre 2.8g; Sodium 81mg.

CHORBA WITH RAS EL HANOUT AND NOODLES

THIS FULL-FLAVOURED CHORBA IS THE DAILY SOUP IN MANY MOROCCAN HOUSEHOLDS. THE RAS EL HANOUT GIVES IT A LOVELY, WARMING KICK. YOU CAN PURÉE THE SOUP, IF YOU PREFER, BUT HERE IT IS LEFT AS IT IS, FINISHED OFF WITH A SWIRL OF YOGURT AND FINELY CHOPPED CORIANDER. GARLIC LOVERS MAY LIKE TO ADD A CRUSHED GARLIC CLOVE AND A LITTLE SALT TO THE YOGURT.

SERVES FOUR

INGREDIENTS
    45–60ml/3–4 tbsp olive oil
    3–4 whole cloves
    2 onions, chopped
    1 butternut squash
    4 celery sticks, chopped
    2 carrots, chopped
    8 large, ripe tomatoes
    5–10ml/1–2 tsp sugar
    15ml/1 tbsp tomato purée (paste)
    5–10ml/1–2 tsp ras el hanout
    2.5ml/½ tsp ground turmeric
    a big bunch of fresh coriander
      (cilantro), chopped
    1.75 litres/3 pints/7½ cups
      vegetable stock
    a handful of dried egg noodles or
      capellini, broken into pieces
    salt and ground black pepper
    natural (plain) yogurt, to garnish

1 Peel, seed and cut the squash into small chunks. Skin, and roughly chop the tomatoes. In a deep, heavy pan, heat the oil and add the cloves, onions, squash, celery and carrots. Fry until they begin to colour, then stir in the chopped tomatoes and sugar. Cook until the liquid reduces and the tomatoes begin to pulp.

2 Stir in the tomato purée, ras el hanout, turmeric and chopped coriander. Pour in the stock and bring the liquid to the boil. Reduce the heat and simmer, uncovered, for 30–40 minutes until the vegetables are very tender and the liquid has reduced a little.

3 To make a puréed soup, let the liquid cool slightly before processing in a blender or food processor, then pour back into the pan and add the pasta.

4 Alternatively, to make a chunky soup, simply add the pasta to the unblended soup and cook for a further 8–10 minutes, or until the pasta is soft.

5 Season the soup to taste and ladle it into bowls. Spoon a swirl of yogurt into each one, garnish with coriander sprigs and serve with a freshly baked Moroccan loaf.

Energy 265Kcal/1108kJ; Protein 6.9g; Carbohydrate 37.8g, of which sugars 20.2g; Fat 10.2g, of which saturates 1.7g; Cholesterol 0mg; Calcium 158mg; Fibre 8.1g; Sodium 64mg.

LAMB, BEAN AND PUMPKIN SOUP

ASIDE FROM THE GREEN BANANAS, WHICH ARE VERY MUCH AN AFRICAN TOUCH, THIS SOUP COULD HAVE COME FROM ANY OF THE LANDS OF THE MIDDLE EAST. PUMPKIN, CARROT AND TURMERIC GIVE IT A RICH COLOUR AND THE SPICES PROVIDE A WARMTH DESIGNED TO BANISH WINTER CHILLS.

SERVES FOUR

INGREDIENTS

115g/4oz black-eyed beans (peas),
  soaked for 1–2 hours, or overnight
675g/1½lb neck of lamb, cut into
  medium-size chunks
5ml/1 tsp chopped fresh thyme, or
  2.5ml/½ tsp dried
2 bay leaves
1.2 litres/2 pints/5 cups stock
  or water
1 onion, sliced
225g/8oz pumpkin, diced
2 black cardamom pods
7.5ml/1½ tsp ground turmeric
15ml/1 tbsp chopped fresh coriander
  (cilantro)
2.5ml/½ tsp caraway seeds
1 fresh green chilli, seeded
  and chopped
2 green bananas
1 carrot
salt and ground black pepper

1 Drain the beans, place in a pan and cover with cold water. Bring to the boil and boil rapidly for 10 minutes, then reduce the heat and simmer, covered, for 40–50 minutes until tender, adding more water if necessary. Remove from the heat and set aside to cool.

2 Meanwhile, put the lamb in a large pan, add the thyme, bay leaves and stock or water and bring to the boil. Cover and simmer over a medium heat for 1 hour, until tender.

3 Add the onion, pumpkin, cardamoms, turmeric, coriander, caraway seeds, chilli and seasoning and stir. Bring back to a simmer and then cook, uncovered, for 15 minutes, until the pumpkin is tender, stirring occasionally.

4 When the beans are cool, spoon into a blender or food processor with their liquid and process to a smooth purée.

5 Cut the bananas into medium slices and the carrot into thin slices. Stir into the soup with the bean purée. Cook for 10–12 minutes, until the vegetables are tender. Adjust the seasoning and serve.

Energy 442Kcal/1855kJ; Protein 40.8g; Carbohydrate 27.2g, of which sugars 13.1g; Fat 19.7g, of which saturates 9g; Cholesterol 128mg; Calcium 74mg; Fibre 6.4g; Sodium 155mg.

GHANIAN FISH AND OKRA SOUP

OKRA GROWS WELL IN MANY PARTS OF WEST AFRICA AND THE SUDAN, AND SOUPS LIKE THIS ONE WERE THE INSPIRATION FOR GUMBO, WHICH SLAVES INTRODUCED TO THE CARIBBEAN AND NORTH AMERICA. OKRA THICKENS THE SOUP AND GIVES IT A UNIQUE TEXTURE AND FLAVOUR.

SERVES FOUR

INGREDIENTS
    2 green bananas
    50g/2oz/¼ cup butter or margarine
    1 onion, finely chopped
    2 tomatoes, skinned and
      finely chopped
    115g/4oz okra, trimmed
    225g/8oz smoked haddock
      or cod fillet, cut into
      bitesize pieces
    900ml/1½ pints/3¾ cups
      fish stock
    1 fresh red or green chilli, seeded
      and chopped
    salt and ground black pepper
    chopped fresh parsley,
      to garnish

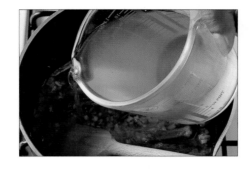

3 Add the fish, fish stock, chilli and seasoning. Bring to the boil, then reduce the heat and simmer for about 20 minutes, until the fish is cooked through and flakes easily.

4 Peel the cooked bananas and cut into slices. Stir into the soup, heat through for a few minutes and then ladle into soup bowls. Sprinkle with chopped parsley and serve.

1 Slit the skins of the bananas and place in a large pan. Cover with water, bring to the boil and cook over a medium heat for 25 minutes. Drain.

2 Melt the butter or margarine in a large pan and sauté the onion for about 5 minutes. Stir in the tomatoes and okra and sauté for a further 10 minutes.

Energy 295Kcal/1233kJ; Protein 20g; Carbohydrate 24.6g, of which sugars 21.2g; Fat 13.8g, of which saturates 7.5g; Cholesterol 47mg; Calcium 477mg; Fibre 12.7g; Sodium 532mg.

PLANTAIN AND CORN SOUP

CAMEROON IS THE HOME OF THIS COLOURFUL AND UNUSUAL SOUP. IT IS IMPORTANT TO USE RIPE PLANTAINS, WHICH COOK DOWN AND BECOME BEAUTIFULLY TENDER. NUTMEG ADDS THE FINAL TOUCH.

SERVES FOUR

INGREDIENTS

25g/1oz/2 tbsp butter or margarine
1 onion, finely chopped
1 garlic clove, crushed
275g/10oz yellow plantains, peeled
  and sliced
1 large tomato, peeled and chopped
175g/6oz/1 cup corn
5ml/1 tsp dried tarragon, crushed
900ml/1½ pints/3¾ cups vegetable
  or chicken stock
1 fresh green chilli, seeded
  and chopped
pinch of freshly grated nutmeg
salt and ground black pepper

1 Melt the butter or margarine in a pan over a medium heat, add the onion and garlic and sauté for a few minutes until the onion is soft.

2 Add the plantains, tomato and corn and cook for 5 minutes.

3 Add the tarragon, vegetable or chicken stock, chilli and salt and pepper and simmer for 10 minutes or until the plantain is tender. Stir in the nutmeg and serve immediately.

GROUNDNUT SOUP

GROUNDNUTS – OR PEANUTS – ARE VERY WIDELY USED IN SAUCES IN AFRICAN COOKING. GROUNDNUT PASTE IS AVAILABLE FROM MANY HEALTH FOOD SHOPS AND IS WORTH SEEKING OUT AS IT MAKES A WONDERFULLY RICH AND CREAMY SOUP.

SERVES FOUR

INGREDIENTS

45ml/3 tbsp pure groundnut paste
  or peanut butter
1.5 litres/2½ pints/6¼ cups stock
30ml/2 tbsp tomato purée (paste)
1 onion, chopped
2 slices fresh root ginger, peeled and
  finely chopped
1.5ml/¼ tsp dried thyme
1 bay leaf
salt and chilli powder
225g/8oz white yam, diced
10 small okras, trimmed (optional)

1 Place the groundnut paste or peanut butter in a bowl, add 300ml/½ pint/ 1¼ cups of the stock and the tomato purée and blend together to make a smooth paste.

2 Spoon the nut mixture into a pan and add the onion, chopped ginger, thyme, bay leaf, salt, chilli powder and the remaining stock. Heat gently until the liquid is simmering.

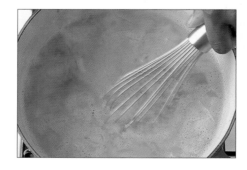

3 Cook for 1 hour, stirring from time to time to prevent the nut mixture sticking.

4 Add the white yam and cook for a further 10 minutes. Add the okra, if using, and simmer until tender. Serve.

COOK'S TIP
Use peanut butter in place of groundnut paste, but only use the smooth variety for this recipe.

TOP Energy 185Kcal/775kJ; Protein 5.8g; Carbohydrate 22.6g, of which sugars 5.2g; Fat 8.3g, of which saturates 1.9g; Cholesterol 0mg; Calcium 66mg; Fibre 3.3g; Sodium 75mg.
BOTTOM Energy 198Kcal/837kJ; Protein 2.7g; Carbohydrate 35.6g, of which sugars 11g; Fat 6g, of which saturates 3.4g; Cholesterol 13mg; Calcium 20mg; Fibre 2.3g; Sodium 162mg.

CHICKEN, TOMATO AND CHRISTOPHENE SOUP

CHRISTOPHENE IS A PALE GREEN GOURD. IN SOUTHERN AFRICA IS IS CALLED CHO-CHO, WHILE ELSEWHERE IT IS CALLED CHOKO, CHAYOTE OR VEGETABLE PEAR. THE FLESH HAS A DELICATE FLAVOUR.

SERVES FOUR

INGREDIENTS
225g/8oz skinless, boneless
  chicken breasts
1 garlic clove, crushed
pinch of freshly grated nutmeg
25g/1oz/2 tbsp butter or margarine
½ onion, finely chopped
15ml/1 tbsp tomato purée (paste)
400g/14oz can tomatoes, puréed
1.2 litres/2 pints/5 cups
  chicken stock
1 fresh red or green chilli, seeded
  and chopped
5ml/1 tsp dried oregano
2.5ml/½ tsp dried thyme
1 christophene, about 350g/12oz
  total weight, peeled and diced
50g/2oz smoked haddock fillet,
  skinned and diced
salt and ground black pepper
chopped fresh chives, to garnish

1 Dice the chicken, place in a bowl and season with salt, pepper, garlic and nutmeg. Mix well to flavour the chicken and then set aside for about 30 minutes.

COOK'S TIP
Christophene is a vegetable of the squash family native to central America. The flesh is crisp and light green in colour, and the flavour is delicate and very mild. It may be used in a similar way to courgettes (zucchini) in cooking.

2 Melt the butter or margarine in a large pan, add the chicken and sauté over a medium heat for 5–6 minutes. Stir in the onion and sauté gently for a further 5 minutes, until the onion is slightly softened.

3 Add the tomato purée, puréed tomatoes, stock, chilli, dried herbs and christophene. Bring to the boil, cover and simmer gently for 35 minutes, until the christophene is tender.

4 Add the smoked fish, simmer for a further 5 minutes, until the fish is cooked through, adjust the seasoning and pour into warmed soup bowls. Garnish with a sprinkling of chopped chives and serve.

Energy 133Kcal/558kJ; Protein 16.7g; Carbohydrate 3.2g, of which sugars 2.4g; Fat 6g, of which saturates 3.5g; Cholesterol 57mg; Calcium 36mg; Fibre 1.1g; Sodium 167mg.

CAMEROON VEGETABLE SOUP

COCONUT CROPS UP IN MANY POPULAR CAMEROONIAN DISHES, INCLUDING THEIR FAMOUS BEEF AND PINEAPPLE CURRY. HERE IT IS TEAMED WITH SWEET POTATO AND SPICES TO MAKE A TASTY SOUP.

SERVES FOUR

INGREDIENTS
30ml/2 tbsp butter or margarine
½ red onion, finely chopped
175g/6oz each turnip, sweet potato
 and pumpkin, peeled and
 roughly chopped
5ml/1 tsp dried marjoram
2.5ml/½ tsp ground ginger
1.5ml/¼ tsp ground cinnamon
15ml/1 tbsp chopped spring onion
 (scallion)
1 litre/1¾ pints/4 cups
 well-flavoured vegetable stock
30ml/2 tbsp flaked (sliced) almonds
1 fresh red or green chilli, seeded
 and chopped
5ml/1 tsp sugar
25g/1oz creamed coconut or
 60ml/4 tbsp coconut cream
salt and ground black pepper
chopped fresh coriander (cilantro),
 to garnish

COOK'S TIP
Take care when preparing fresh chillies. Avoid touching your eyes and wash your hands thoroughly afterwards (or wear disposable gloves).

1 Melt the butter or margarine in a large non-stick pan. Fry the onion for 4–5 minutes. Add the chopped vegetables and fry for 3–4 minutes.

2 Add the marjoram, ginger, cinnamon, spring onion, salt and pepper. Sauté over a low heat for about 10 minutes, stirring frequently.

3 Add the vegetable stock, flaked almonds, chilli and sugar and stir well to mix, then cover and simmer gently for 10–15 minutes, until the vegetables are just tender.

4 Grate the creamed coconut into the soup, or add the coconut cream, and stir to mix. Spoon the soup into warmed bowls and serve, sprinkled with chopped coriander.

Energy 168Kcal/701kJ; Protein 2.3g; Carbohydrate 13.2g, of which sugars 5.5g; Fat 12.2g, of which saturates 7.9g; Cholesterol 16mg; Calcium 50mg; Fibre 2.4g; Sodium 66mg.

IRANIAN BEEF AND HERB SOUP WITH YOGURT

THIS RECIPE IS CALLED AASHE MASTE IN IRAN. IT DATES FROM ANCIENT PERSIAN TIMES, WHEN SOUP WAS SO IMPORTANT THAT THE WORD FOR COOK WAS ASH-PAZ, LITERALLY "MAKER OF THE SOUP".

SERVES SIX

INGREDIENTS
2 large onions
30ml/2 tbsp oil
15ml/1 tbsp ground turmeric
90g/3½oz/½ cup yellow split peas
1.2 litres/2 pints/5 cups water
225g/8oz minced (ground) beef
200g/7oz/1 cup long-grain rice
45ml/3 tbsp each chopped fresh
  parsley, coriander (cilantro),
  and chives
15g/½oz/1 tbsp butter
1 large garlic clove, finely chopped
60ml/4 tbsp chopped fresh mint
2–3 saffron threads dissolved in
  15ml/1 tbsp boiling water (optional)
salt and ground black pepper
natural (plain) yogurt and naan
  bread, to serve

1 Chop one of the onions, then heat the oil in a large pan and fry the onion until golden brown. Add the turmeric, split peas and water, bring to the boil, then reduce the heat and simmer for 20 minutes.

COOK'S TIP
Fresh spinach is also delicious in this soup. Add 50g/2oz finely chopped spinach leaves to the soup with the parsley, coriander and chives.

2 Meanwhile, grate the other onion into a bowl, add the minced beef and seasoning and mix. Using your hands, form the mixture into small balls, about the size of walnuts. Carefully add to the pan and simmer for 10 minutes.

3 Add the rice, then stir in the chopped parsley, coriander and chives and simmer for about 30 minutes, until the rice is tender, stirring frequently.

4 Melt the butter in a small pan and gently fry the garlic. Add the chopped mint, stir briefly, and then sprinkle the mixture over the soup with the saffron liquid, if using. Serve the soup with yoghurt and naan bread.

Energy 338Kcal/1409kJ; Protein 14.8g; Carbohydrate 42g, of which sugars 5.3g; Fat 12.5g, of which saturates 4.5g; Cholesterol 28mg; Calcium 64mg; Fibre 2.5g; Sodium 57mg.

SPINACH AND LEMON SOUP WITH MEATBALLS

THIS SOUP — OR A VARIATION OF IT — IS STANDARD FARE THROUGHOUT THE MIDDLE EAST. IN TURKEY, WITHOUT MEATBALLS, IT IS POPULARLY REFERRED TO AS WEDDING SOUP.

SERVES SIX

INGREDIENTS
2 large onions
45ml/3 tbsp oil
15ml/1 tbsp ground turmeric
90g/3½oz/½ cup yellow split peas
1.2 litres/2 pints/5 cups water
225g/8oz minced (ground) lamb
450g/1lb spinach, chopped
50g/2oz/½ cup rice flour
juice of 2 lemons
1–2 garlic cloves, very finely chopped
30ml/2 tbsp chopped fresh mint
4 eggs, beaten
salt and ground black pepper

1 Chop one of the onions, heat 30ml/2 tbsp of the oil in a large frying pan and fry the onion until golden. Add the turmeric, split peas and water, bring to the boil then simmer for 20 minutes.

2 Grate the remaining onion into a bowl, add the minced lamb and seasoning and mix. With your hands, form into small balls, about the size of walnuts. Carefully add to the pan and simmer for 10 minutes, then add the spinach, cover and simmer for 20 minutes.

3 Mix the rice flour with about 250ml/8fl oz/1 cup cold water to make a smooth paste, then slowly add to the pan, stirring all the time to prevent lumps. Stir in the lemon juice, season with salt and pepper and cook over a gentle heat for 20 minutes.

4 Meanwhile, heat the remaining oil in a small pan and fry the garlic briefly until golden. Stir in the chopped mint and remove the pan from the heat.

COOK'S TIP
If preferred, use less lemon juice to begin with and then add more to taste once the soup is cooked. Use minced beef or pork in place of minced lamb.

5 Remove the soup from the heat and stir in the beaten eggs. Ladle the soup into warmed soup bowls. Sprinkle the garlic and mint garnish over the soup and serve.

Energy 293Kcal/1222kJ; Protein 18.3g; Carbohydrate 21.6g, of which sugars 5.2g; Fat 15.2g, of which saturates 4.3g; Cholesterol 156mg; Calcium 179mg; Fibre 3.4g; Sodium 185mg.

OLIVES WITH MOROCCAN MARINADES

VISIT A MOROCCAN SUQ AND YOU'LL SEE BOWLS BRIMMING WITH FAT PURPLE, GREEN AND BLACK OLIVES. MARINATED, THEY MAKE A DELICIOUS APPETIZER AND KEEP WELL IN THE REFRIGERATOR.

SERVES SIX TO EIGHT

INGREDIENTS
    225g/8oz/1⅓ cups green or tan
      olives (unpitted) for each marinade
For the Moroccan marinade
    45ml/3 tbsp chopped fresh
      coriander (cilantro)
    45ml/3 tbsp chopped fresh flat
      leaf parsley
    1 garlic clove, finely chopped
    good pinch of cayenne pepper
    good pinch of ground cumin
    30–45ml/2–3 tbsp olive oil
    30–45ml/2–3 tbsp lemon juice
For the spicy herb marinade
    60ml/4 tbsp chopped fresh
      coriander (cilantro)
    60ml/4 tbsp chopped fresh flat
      leaf parsley
    1 garlic clove, finely chopped
    5ml/1 tsp grated fresh root ginger
    1 fresh red chilli, seeded and
      thinly sliced
    ¼ preserved lemon, cut into thin strips

1 Crack the olives, hard enough to break the flesh, but taking care not to crack the pits. Place in a bowl of cold water and leave overnight to remove the excess brine. Drain thoroughly and divide the olives equally between two jars.

COOK'S TIP
Use a sieve (strainer) or fine colander to drain the olives thoroughly.

2 Blend all the ingredients for the Moroccan marinade together, then pour it over the olives in one jar, adding more olive oil and lemon juice to cover, if necessary.

3 To make the spicy herb marinade, mix together the chopped coriander, chopped parsley, garlic, ginger, chilli and preserved lemon. Add to the olives in the second jar. Store the olives in the fridge for at least 1 week, shaking the jars occasionally.

BYESAR

THE ARAB DISH BYESAR IS SIMILAR TO MIDDLE EASTERN HUMMUS, BUT USES BROAD BEANS INSTEAD OF CHICKPEAS. IN MOROCCO, BREAD IS ALWAYS SERVED WITH BYESAR. THE BREAD IS TORN INTO PIECES, DIPPED INTO GROUND SPICES AND USED TO SCOOP UP THE PURÉE.

SERVES FOUR TO SIX

INGREDIENTS
    115g/4oz dried broad (fava)
      beans, soaked overnight
    2 garlic cloves, peeled
    5ml/1 tsp cumin seeds
    about 60ml/4 tbsp olive oil
    salt
    fresh mint sprigs, to garnish
    extra cumin seeds, cayenne pepper
      and bread, to serve

VARIATION
Use dried chickpeas in place of broad beans if you prefer.

1 Put the dried broad beans in a pan with the whole garlic cloves and cumin seeds and add enough water just to cover. Bring to the boil, then reduce the heat, cover and simmer until the beans are tender. Drain, cool and then slip off the outer skin of each bean.

2 Process the beans in a blender or food processor, adding sufficient olive oil and water to give a smooth soft dip. Season to taste with plenty of salt. Garnish with sprigs of mint and serve with extra cumin seeds, cayenne pepper and bread.

TOP Energy 74Kcal/305kJ; Protein 0.6g; Carbohydrate 0.2g, of which sugars 0.2g; Fat 7.9g, of which saturates 1.2g; Cholesterol 0mg; Calcium 38mg; Fibre 1.5g; Sodium 846mg.
BOTTOM Energy 113Kcal/468kJ; Protein 1g; Carbohydrate 2.3g, of which sugars 0.2g; Fat 11.2g, of which saturates 1.6g; Cholesterol 0mg; Calcium 7mg; Fibre 0.5g; Sodium 2mg.

FALAFEL

THESE TASTY DEEP-FRIED PATTIES ARE ONE OF THE NATIONAL DISHES OF EGYPT AND ARE ALSO POPULAR IN ISRAEL AND OTHER MIDDLE EASTERN COUNTRIES. THEY MAKE AN EXCELLENT APPETIZER.

SERVES SIX

INGREDIENTS
 450g/1lb/2½ cups dried white beans
 2 red onions, chopped
 2 large garlic cloves, crushed
 45ml/3 tbsp finely chopped
  fresh parsley
 5ml/1 tsp ground coriander
 5ml/1 tsp ground cumin
 7.5ml/1½ tsp baking powder
 vegetable oil, for deep frying
 salt and ground black pepper
 tomato salad, to serve

1 Soak the white beans overnight in water. Remove the skins and process in a blender or food processor. Add the chopped onions, garlic, chopped parsley, coriander, cumin, baking powder and seasoning and blend again to make a very smooth paste. Allow the mixture to stand at room temperature for at least 30 minutes.

2 Take walnut-size pieces of the mixture and flatten into small patties. Set aside again for about 15 minutes.

3 Heat the oil in a deep, heavy pan until it is very hot and then deep-fry the patties in batches until golden brown. Drain on kitchen paper and then serve hot with a tomato salad.

HUMMUS

THIS POPULAR MIDDLE EASTERN DIP IS WIDELY AVAILABLE IN SUPERMARKETS, BUT NOTHING COMPARES TO THE FLAVOUR OF THE HOME-MADE VARIETY. IT IS VERY EASY TO PREPARE.

SERVES FOUR TO SIX

INGREDIENTS
 175g/6oz/1 cup cooked chickpeas
 120ml/4fl oz/½ cup tahini paste
 3 garlic cloves
 juice of 2 lemons
 45–60ml/3–4 tbsp water
 salt and ground black pepper
 fresh radishes, to serve
For the garnish
 15ml/1 tbsp olive oil
 15ml/1 tbsp finely chopped
  fresh parsley
 2.5ml/½ tsp paprika
 4 pitted black olives

1 Place the chickpeas, tahini paste, garlic, lemon juice, seasoning and a little of the water in a blender or food processor. Process until smooth, adding a little more water, if necessary.

2 Alternatively, if you don't have a blender or food processor, mash the ingredients together in a small bowl until smooth in consistency.

3 Spoon the mixture into a shallow dish. Make a dent in the middle and pour the olive oil garnish into it. Garnish with chopped parsley, paprika and olives and serve with the radishes.

COOK'S TIP
Canned chickpeas can be used for hummus. Drain and rinse under cold water before processing.

TOP Energy 409Kcal/1704kJ; Protein 16.9g; Carbohydrate 22.2g, of which sugars 1.5g; Fat 28.7g, of which saturates 4g; Cholesterol 0mg; Calcium 350mg; Fibre 8.1g; Sodium 26mg.
BOTTOM Energy 303Kcal/1282kJ; Protein 18.5g; Carbohydrate 44.7g, of which sugars 5.2g; Fat 6.9g, of which saturates 1.2g; Cholesterol 0mg; Calcium 88mg; Fibre 7.2g; Sodium 16mg.

TABBOULEH

THE BULGUR WHEAT THAT GIVES THIS CLASSIC ARAB SALAD ITS DELICIOUS NUTTINESS IS NOT COOKED, JUST SOAKED IN COLD WATER. TOMATOES, FRESH HERBS AND LEMON JUICE ADD TO THE FLAVOUR.

SERVES FOUR

INGREDIENTS
  175g/6oz/1 cup fine bulgur wheat
  juice of 1 lemon
  45ml/3 tbsp olive oil
  40g/1½oz fresh parsley,
    finely chopped
  45ml/3 tbsp fresh mint, chopped
  4–5 spring onions (scallions),
    chopped
  1 green (bell) pepper, seeded
    and sliced
  salt and ground black pepper
  2 large tomatoes, diced, and pitted
    black olives, to garnish

1 Put the bulgur wheat in a bowl. Add enough cold water to cover the wheat and let it stand for at least 30 minutes and up to 2 hours.

2 Drain and squeeze with your hands to remove excess water. The bulgur wheat will swell to double the size. Spread on kitchen paper to dry the bulgur wheat completely.

3 Place the bulgur wheat in a large bowl, add the lemon juice, the oil and a little salt and pepper. Allow to stand for 1–2 hours if possible, in order for the flavours to develop.

4 Add the chopped parsley, chopped mint, spring onions and pepper and mix well. Garnish with diced tomatoes and olives and serve.

CAÇIK

TRAVELLERS THROUGHOUT THE MIDDLE EAST KNOW THIS SIMPLE DISH. IT CAN BE SERVED WITH FLAT BREAD, AS AN APPETIZER, OR AS AN ACCOMPANIMENT TO A SPICY STEW OR CURRY.

SERVES FOUR

INGREDIENTS
  ½ cucumber
  1 small onion
  2 garlic cloves
  10g/¼oz fresh parsley
  475ml/16fl oz/2 cups natural
    (plain) yogurt
  1.5ml/¼ tsp paprika
  salt and white pepper
  fresh mint leaves, to garnish

1 Finely chop the cucumber and onion, crush the garlic and finely chop the parsley.

COOK'S TIP
It's not traditional, but other herbs, such as mint or chives used in place of parsley, would be equally good in this dish.

2 Lightly beat the yogurt in a bowl and then add the cucumber, onion, garlic and parsley and season with salt and pepper to taste.

3 Sprinkle with a little paprika and chill for at least 1 hour. Garnish with mint leaves and serve with warm pitta bread or as an accompaniment to meat, poultry and rice dishes.

TOP Energy 199Kcal/828kJ; Protein 3.9g; Carbohydrate 26.5g, of which sugars 3.9g; Fat 9.2g, of which saturates 1.3g; Cholesterol 0mg; Calcium 41mg; Fibre 2.1g; Sodium 13mg.
BOTTOM Energy 77Kcal/321kJ; Protein 6.6g; Carbohydrate 10.7g, of which sugars 10.3g; Fat 1.3g, of which saturates 0.6g; Cholesterol 2mg; Calcium 241mg; Fibre 0.6g; Sodium 101mg.

ROASTED RED PEPPERS WITH FETA, CAPERS AND PRESERVED LEMONS

Red peppers, particularly the long, slim, horn-shaped variety, feature widely in the cooking of North Africa and the Middle East. Roasting them really brings out their smoky flavour and they taste wonderful with crumbled white cheese. Feta is suggested here, but villagers would just use whatever was available locally, whether from goat's, ewe's or cow's milk. This dish makes a great mezze and also tastes good with kebabs.

SERVES FOUR

INGREDIENTS
4 fleshy red (bell) peppers
200g/7oz feta cheese, crumbled
30–45ml/2–3 tbsp olive oil or
  argan oil
30ml/2 tbsp capers, drained
peel of 1 preserved lemon, cut into
  small pieces
salt

1 Preheat the grill (broiler) on the hottest setting. Roast the red peppers under the grill, turning frequently, until they soften and their skins begin to blacken. (Alternatively, spear the peppers, one at a time, on long metal skewers and turn them over a gas flame, or roast them in a very hot oven.)

2 Place the peppers in a plastic bag, seal and leave them to stand for 15 minutes. Peel the peppers, remove and discard the stalks and seeds and then slice the flesh and arrange on a plate.

3 Add the crumbled feta and pour over the olive or argan oil. Scatter the capers and preserved lemon over the top and sprinkle with a little salt, if required (this depends on whether the feta is salty or not). Serve with chunks of bread to mop up the delicious, oil-rich juices.

Energy 255Kcal/1058kJ; Protein 9.6g; Carbohydrate 12g, of which sugars 11.4g; Fat 19.1g, of which saturates 8.2g; Cholesterol 35mg; Calcium 194mg; Fibre 2.8g; Sodium 727mg.

ARTICHOKE HEARTS WITH GINGER, HONEY AND LEMONS

WHEN GLOBE ARTICHOKES ARE IN SEASON, THEY GRACE EVERY MOROCCAN TABLE AS A FIRST COURSE OR SALAD. THE HEARTS ARE OFTEN POACHED IN SALTED WATER UNTIL TENDER, THEN CHOPPED AND TOSSED IN OLIVE OIL WITH GARLIC, HERBS AND PRESERVED LEMON. FOR A MORE EXCITING APPETIZER, THE ARTICHOKES ARE COOKED IN A GLORIOUS SPICED HONEY DRESSING. PRESERVED LEMONS, WHICH ARE AVAILABLE IN LARGE JARS AT EVERY NORTH AFRICAN MARKET, ADD A PIQUANT NOTE.

SERVES FOUR

INGREDIENTS
    30–45ml/2–3 tbsp olive oil
    2 garlic cloves, crushed
    scant 5ml/1 tsp ground ginger
    pinch of saffron threads
    juice of ½ lemon
    15–30ml/1–2 tbsp clear honey
    peel of 1 preserved lemon,
        thinly sliced
    8 fresh globe artichoke hearts,
        quartered
    150ml/¼ pint/⅔ cup water
    salt

1 Heat the olive oil in a small, heavy pan and stir in the garlic. Before the garlic begins to colour, stir in the ginger, saffron, lemon juice, honey and preserved lemon.

2 Add the artichokes to the pan and toss them in the spices and honey. Pour in the water, add a little salt and heat until simmering.

3 Cover the pan and simmer for 10–15 minutes, until the artichokes are tender, turning them occasionally.

4 If the liquid has not reduced, take the lid off the pan and boil for about 2 minutes until reduced to a coating consistency. Serve at room temperature.

COOK'S TIP
To prepare globe artichokes, remove the outer leaves and cut off the stems. Carefully separate the remaining leaves and use a teaspoon to scoop out the choke with all the hairy bits. Trim the hearts and immerse them in water mixed with a squeeze of lemon juice to prevent them from turning black. You can use frozen hearts for this recipe.

Energy 115Kcal/478kJ; Protein 0.8g; Carbohydrate 15.6g, of which sugars 15g; Fat 5.9g, of which saturates 0.9g; Cholesterol 0mg; Calcium 32mg; Fibre 3g; Sodium 32mg.

DOLMEH

THE WORD DOLMEH MEANS "STUFFED" IN PERSIAN, AND GENERALLY REFERS TO ANY VEGETABLE FILLED WITH RICE, HERBS, AND SOMETIMES MEAT.

SERVES FOUR TO SIX

INGREDIENTS

250g/9oz vine leaves
30ml/2 tbsp olive oil
1 large onion, finely chopped
250g/9oz minced (ground) lamb
50g/2oz/¼ cup yellow split peas
75g/3oz/½ cup cooked rice
30ml/2 tbsp chopped fresh parsley
30ml/2 tbsp chopped fresh mint
30ml/2 tbsp chopped fresh chives
3–4 spring onions (scallions),
  finely chopped
juice of 2 lemons
30ml/2 tbsp tomato purée (paste)
30ml/2 tbsp sugar
salt and ground black pepper
yogurt and pitta bread, to serve

1 Blanch fresh vine leaves if using, in boiling water for 1–2 minutes to soften them, or rinse preserved, bottled or canned vine leaves under cold water.

2 Heat the olive oil in a large frying pan and fry the onion for a few minutes until slightly softened. Add the minced lamb and fry over a medium heat until well browned, stirring frequently. Season with salt and pepper.

3 Place the split peas in a small pan with enough water to cover and bring to the boil. Cover the pan and simmer gently over a low heat for 12–15 minutes, until soft. Drain the split peas if necessary.

4 Stir the split peas, cooked rice, chopped herbs, spring onions, and the juice of one of the lemons into the meat. Add the tomato purée and then knead until thoroughly blended.

5 Place each vine leaf on a chopping board with the vein side up. Place 15ml/1 tbsp of the meat mixture on the leaf and fold the stem end over the meat. Fold the sides in towards the centre and then fold into a neat parcel.

6 Line the base of a large pan with unstuffed leaves and arrange the rolled leaves in layers on top. Stir the remaining lemon juice and sugar into 150ml/¼ pint/⅔ cup water and pour over the leaves. Place a heatproof plate over the dolmeh to keep them in shape.

7 Cover the pan and cook over a very low heat for 2 hours, checking occasionally and adding extra water if necessary. Serve with yogurt and bread.

COOK'S TIP
If using preserved vine leaves, soak them overnight in cold water and then rinse several times before use.

Energy 319Kcal/1336kJ; Protein 18.4g; Carbohydrate 29.8g, of which sugars 16.2g; Fat 14.8g, of which saturates 4.8g; Cholesterol 48mg; Calcium 117mg; Fibre 4.2g; Sodium 98mg.

BABA GANOUSH

LEGEND HAS IT THAT THIS FAMOUS MIDDLE EASTERN APPETIZER WAS INVENTED BY THE LADIES OF THE SULTAN'S HAREM WHO VIED WITH ONE ANOTHER TO WIN HIS FAVOUR.

SERVES FOUR TO SIX

INGREDIENTS
  3 aubergines (eggplants)
  2 garlic cloves, crushed
  60ml/4 tbsp tahini paste
  juice of 2 lemons
  15ml/1 tbsp paprika, plus extra
    for garnishing
  salt and ground black pepper
  chopped fresh parsley, olive oil,
    plus a few green or black olives,
    to garnish
  pitta bread or vegetable crudités,
    to serve

1 Preheat the oven to 190°C/375°F/ Gas 5. Slit the skins of the aubergines, place on a baking sheet and bake in the oven for 30–40 minutes, until the skins begin to split.

2 Place the aubergines on a chopping board and cool slightly. Carefully peel away the skins from the aubergines.

COOK'S TIP
Tahini paste can be obtained from health food shops, delicatessens and many supermarkets.

3 Place the aubergine flesh in a blender or food processor. Add the garlic, tahini paste, lemon juice, paprika and salt and pepper. Process to a smooth paste, adding about 15–30ml/1–2 tbsp water if the paste is too thick.

4 Spoon into a dish and make a dip in the centre. Garnish with extra paprika, chopped parsley, a drizzle of olive oil and olives. Serve with hot pitta bread or a selection of vegetable crudités.

Energy 159Kcal/662kJ; Protein 5.5g; Carbohydrate 3.6g, of which sugars 3.2g; Fat 13.9g, of which saturates 2.1g; Cholesterol 0mg; Calcium 168mg; Fibre 4.8g; Sodium 8mg.

STUFFED PEPPERS

OF ALL THE DOLMEH, OR STUFFED VEGETABLES, THIS IS PERHAPS THE MOST COLOURFUL, ESPECIALLY WHEN MIXED COLOURS ARE USED. TRY TO FIND PEPPERS THAT ARE MORE OR LESS THE SAME SIZE.

SERVES SIX

INGREDIENTS
    6 mixed (bell) peppers red, yellow
      and green
    30ml/2 tbsp olive oil
    1 large onion, finely chopped
    3–4 spring onions (scallions),
      finely chopped
    250g/9oz minced (ground) lamb
    2 garlic cloves, crushed (optional)
    50g/2oz/¼ cup yellow split peas
    75g/3oz/½ cup cooked rice
    30ml/2 tbsp finely chopped
      fresh parsley
    30ml/2 tbsp finely chopped
      fresh mint
    30ml/2 tbsp finely chopped
      fresh chives
    5ml/1 tsp ground cinnamon
    juice of 2 lemons
    30ml/2 tbsp tomato purée
      (paste)
    400g/14oz can chopped tomatoes
    knob of butter
    salt and ground black pepper
    natural (plain) yogurt and pitta bread
      or naan bread, to serve

1 Cut off the mixed pepper tops and set aside. Remove the seeds and cores and trim the bases so they stand squarely. Cook in salted boiling water for 5 minutes, then drain, rinse under cold water and set aside.

2 Heat the oil in a large pan or flameproof casserole and fry the onion and spring onions for about 4–5 minutes until golden brown. Add the minced lamb and fry over a medium heat until well browned, stirring frequently. Stir in the garlic if using.

3 Meanwhile, place the split peas in a small pan with enough water to cover, bring to the boil and then simmer gently for 12–15 minutes until soft. Drain.

4 Stir the split peas, cooked rice, chopped herbs, cinnamon, juice of one of the lemons, and tomato purée into the meat. Season and stir until combined.

5 Spoon the rice and split pea mixture into the peppers and place the reserved lids on top.

6 Pour the chopped tomatoes into a large pan or flameproof casserole and add the remaining lemon juice and butter. Arrange the peppers neatly in the pan with the stems upwards. Bring to the boil and then cover tightly and cook over a low heat for 40–45 minutes, until the peppers are tender.

7 Serve the peppers with the tomato sauce accompanied by yogurt and warm pitta bread or naan bread.

COOK'S TIP
Make sure that the pan or casserole that you choose is just large enough so that the peppers fit quite snugly.

Energy 267Kcal/1115kJ; Protein 13.9g; Carbohydrate 26.1g, of which sugars 15.3g; Fat 12.5g, of which saturates 4.7g; Cholesterol 37mg; Calcium 81mg; Fibre 4.4g; Sodium 84mg.

IMAM BAYILDI

THE NAME OF THIS MUCH LOVED TURKISH DISH TRANSLATES AS "THE IMAM FAINTED", AND IS SAID TO REPRESENT HIS REACTION ON TASTING THE SUPERB STUFFED AUBERGINES.

SERVES SIX

INGREDIENTS
3 aubergines (eggplants)
60ml/4 tbsp olive oil
1 large onion, chopped
1 small red (bell) pepper, seeded
  and diced
1 small green (bell) pepper, seeded
  and diced
3 garlic cloves, crushed
5–6 tomatoes, skinned and chopped
30ml/2 tbsp chopped fresh parsley
about 250ml/8fl oz/1 cup
  boiling water
15ml/1 tbsp lemon juice
salt and ground black pepper
chopped fresh parsley, to garnish
bread, salad and yogurt dip, to serve

1 Preheat the oven to 190°C/375°F/ Gas 5. Cut the aubergines in half lengthways and scoop out the flesh, reserving the shells. Set aside.

2 Heat 30ml/2 tbsp of the olive oil and fry the onion and peppers for 5–6 minutes, until both are slightly softened but not too tender.

3 Add the garlic and continue to cook for a further 2 minutes, then stir in the tomatoes, chopped parsley and aubergine flesh. Season and then stir well and fry over a medium heat for 2–3 minutes.

4 Heat the remaining oil in a separate pan and fry the aubergine shells, two at a time, on both sides.

COOK'S TIP
This flavourful dish can be made in advance and is ideal for a buffet table.

5 Stuff the shells with the sautéed vegetables. Arrange the aubergines closely together in an ovenproof dish and pour enough boiling water around the aubergines to come halfway up their sides.

6 Cover with foil and bake in the oven for 45–60 minutes, until the aubergines are tender and most of the liquid has been absorbed.

7 Place a half aubergine on each plate and sprinkle with a little lemon juice. Serve hot or cold, garnished with parsley and accompanied by bread, salad and a yogurt dip.

Energy 128Kcal/532kJ; Protein 2.6g; Carbohydrate 11.4g, of which sugars 10.1g; Fat 8.3g, of which saturates 1.3g; Cholesterol 0mg; Calcium 40mg; Fibre 4.5g; Sodium 14mg.

SPINACH AND CHICKPEA PANCAKES

PANCAKES ARE POPULAR IN THOSE AFRICAN STATES THAT HAVE AT SOME TIME BEEN OCCUPIED BY THE FRENCH. THESE HAVE A SPINACH AND CHICKPEA FILLING; HIGH ON FLAVOUR, LOW ON SPICE.

SERVES FOUR TO SIX

INGREDIENTS
    15ml/1 tbsp olive oil
    1 large onion, chopped
    250g/9oz fresh spinach
    400g/14oz can chickpeas, drained
    2 courgettes (zucchini), grated
    30ml/2 tbsp chopped fresh
        coriander (cilantro)
    2 eggs, beaten
    salt and ground black pepper
    fresh coriander (cilantro) leaves,
        to garnish
For the pancake batter
    150g/5oz/1¼ cups plain
        (all-purpose) flour
    1 egg
    about 350ml/12fl oz/1½ cups milk
    15ml/1 tbsp sunflower or olive oil
    butter or oil, for greasing
For the sauce
    25g/1oz/2 tbsp butter
    30ml/2 tbsp plain (all-purpose) flour
    about 300ml/½ pint/1¼ cups milk

1 First make the pancakes. Whisk together the flour, a little salt, the egg, milk and 75ml/5 tbsp water to make a fairly thin batter. Stir in the oil.

2 Heat a large griddle, grease lightly and fry the pancakes on one side only, to make eight large pancakes. Set aside while preparing the filling.

3 Heat the oil in a frying pan and fry the onion for 4–5 minutes until soft. Wash the spinach, place in a pan and cook until wilted, shaking the pan occasionally. Chop the spinach roughly.

4 Skin the chickpeas: place them in a bowl of cold water and rub them until the skins float to the surface. Mash the skinned chickpeas roughly with a fork. Add the fried onion, grated courgettes, spinach and chopped coriander. Stir in the beaten eggs, season and mix well.

5 Place the pancakes, cooked side up, on a work surface and place spoonfuls of filling down the centre. Fold one half of the pancake over the filling and roll it up. Place in a large, buttered ovenproof dish and preheat the oven to 180°C/350°F/Gas 4.

6 Melt the butter for the sauce in a small pan, stir in the flour, and then gradually add the milk. Heat gently, stirring continuously, until the sauce is thickened and smooth. Simmer gently for 2–3 minutes, stirring. Season with salt and pepper and pour over the pancakes.

7 Bake in the oven for about 15 minutes, until golden and then serve garnished with coriander leaves.

Energy 560Kcal/2351kJ; Protein 26.2g; Carbohydrate 68.2g, of which sugars 14.8g; Fat 22.1g, of which saturates 7.5g; Cholesterol 166mg; Calcium 473mg; Fibre 8.6g; Sodium 472mg.

SCHLADA

THIS DISH FROM MOROCCO IS A GOOD EXAMPLE OF HOW RECIPES MIGRATE. IT BEGAN AS AN ANCIENT ARAB DISH CALLED GAZPACHO, WHICH MEANS "SOAKED BREAD". THE MOORS TOOK THE RECIPE TO SPAIN. AT THAT STAGE, THE INGREDIENTS WERE SIMPLY GARLIC, BREAD, OLIVE OIL AND LEMON JUICE. THE SPANISH LATER ADDED TOMATOES AND PEPPERS, AND THE DISH RETURNED TO NORTH AFRICA, WHERE IT BECAME KNOWN AS SCHLADA, AND ACQUIRED SPICES AND PICKLED LEMON.

SERVES FOUR

INGREDIENTS
  3 green (bell) peppers, quartered
  4 large tomatoes
  2 garlic cloves, finely chopped
  30ml/2 tbsp olive oil
  30ml/2 tbsp lemon juice
  good pinch of paprika
  pinch of ground cumin
  ¼ preserved lemon
  salt and ground black pepper
  fresh coriander (cilantro) and flat leaf
    parsley, to garnish

3 Peel the tomatoes by placing in boiling water for 1 minute, then plunging into cold water. Peel off the skins, then quarter them, discarding the core and seeds.

4 Chop the tomatoes roughly and add to the peppers. Scatter the chopped garlic on top and chill for 1 hour.

5 Whisk together the olive oil, lemon juice, paprika and cumin and pour over the salad. Season with salt and pepper.

6 Rinse the preserved lemon in cold water and remove the flesh and pith. Cut the peel into slivers and sprinkle over the salad. Garnish with coriander and flat leaf parsley.

1 Preheat the grill (broiler) to its hottest setting. Grill (broil) the peppers skin side up until the skins are blackened, place in a plastic bag and tie the ends. Leave for about 10 minutes, until the peppers are cool enough to handle and then peel away and discard the skins.

2 Cut the peppers into small pieces, discarding the seeds and core, and place in a serving dish.

Energy 100Kcal/423kJ; Protein 2.4g; Carbohydrate 9.1g, of which sugars 8.7g; Fat 6.5g, of which saturates 1.1g; Cholesterol 0mg; Calcium 24mg; Fibre 4.2g; Sodium 20mg.

PAN-FRIED BABY SQUID <u>WITH</u> SPICES

WHETHER SERVED AS AN APPETIZER IN AFRICA OR A MEZZE IN THE MIDDLE EAST, BABY SQUID IS HIGHLY PRIZED. IT NEEDS VERY LITTLE COOKING AND TASTES WONDERFUL WITH THIS SPICY SWEET AND SOUR SAUCE, WHICH TEAMS TURMERIC AND GINGER WITH HONEY AND LEMON JUICE.

SERVES FOUR

INGREDIENTS
  8 baby squid, prepared,
    with tentacles
  5ml/1 tsp ground turmeric
  15ml/1 tbsp smen or olive oil
  2 garlic cloves, finely chopped
  15g/½oz fresh root ginger, peeled
    and finely chopped
  5–10ml/1–2 tsp clear honey
  juice of 1 lemon
  10ml/2 tsp harissa
  salt
  small bunch of fresh coriander
    (cilantro), chopped, to garnish

1 Pat dry the squid bodies, inside and out, and dry the tentacles. Sprinkle the squid with the ground turmeric.

2 Heat the smen or olive oil in a large, heavy frying pan and stir in the garlic and ginger.

3 Just as the ginger and garlic begin to colour, add the squid and tentacles and fry quickly on both sides over a high heat. (Don't overcook the squid, otherwise it will become rubbery.)

4 Add the honey, lemon juice and harissa and stir to form a thick, spicy, caramelized sauce.

5 Season with salt, sprinkle with the chopped coriander and serve immediately.

COOK'S TIP
Smen is a pungent, aged butter used in Moroccan cooking. It is also savoured with chunks of warm, fresh bread and is used to enhance other dishes including couscous and some tagines.

Energy 154Kcal/647kJ; Protein 19.8g; Carbohydrate 5.8g, of which sugars 4.3g; Fat 5.9g, of which saturates 1g; Cholesterol 281mg; Calcium 54mg; Fibre 1g; Sodium 144mg.

HOT SPICY PRAWNS WITH CORIANDER

CORIANDER HAS A LONG HISTORY. NATIVE TO THE MEDITERRANEAN AND THE MIDDLE EAST, IT WAS KNOWN TO THE ANCIENT EGYPTIANS, AND SEEDS HAVE BEEN FOUND IN THE TOMBS OF THE PHARAOHS. TODAY, CORIANDER IS WIDELY GROWN AS A CASH CROP IN NORTH AFRICA, AND IT IS OFTEN USED TO FLAVOUR TAGINES AND SIMILAR DISHES. THE HERB'S AFFINITY FOR CUMIN IS WELL KNOWN, SO IT IS NOT SURPRISING TO FIND THE TWIN FLAVOURINGS USED IN THIS SPICY APPETIZER.

SERVES TWO TO FOUR

INGREDIENTS

60ml/4 tbsp olive oil
2–3 garlic cloves, chopped
25g/1oz fresh root ginger, peeled and grated
1 fresh red or green chilli, seeded and chopped
5ml/1 tsp cumin seeds
5ml/1 tsp paprika
450g/1lb uncooked king prawns (jumbo shrimp), shelled
bunch of fresh coriander (cilantro), chopped
salt
1 lemon, cut into wedges, to serve

1 In a large, frying pan, heat the oil with the garlic. Stir in the ginger, chilli and cumin seeds. Cook briefly, until the ingredients give off a lovely aroma, then add the paprika and toss in the prawns.

2 Fry the prawns over a fairly high heat, turning them frequently, for 3–5 minutes, until just cooked. Season to taste with salt and add the coriander. Serve immediately, with lemon wedges for squeezing over the prawns.

COOK'S TIP
When buying garlic, choose plump garlic with tightly packed cloves and dry skin. Avoid any bulbs with soft, shrivelled cloves or green shoots.

Energy 382Kcal/1591kJ; Protein 40.8g; Carbohydrate 1.1g, of which sugars 0.9g; Fat 23.9g, of which saturates 3.4g; Cholesterol 439mg; Calcium 254mg; Fibre 1.9g; Sodium 440mg.

SNACKS AND STREET FOOD

Stroll around any city in Africa or the Middle East and sooner or later you are bound to encounter a street vendor cooking the regional speciality. What is on the brazier or burner may be roasted corn, kebabs, prawns, plantain snacks or even fried yam balls. Linger and you'll learn about local ingredients and cooking methods; taste and you'll capture the flavour of the place. This chapter introduces some of the dishes you may encounter, and whether you sample them on your travels or recreate them in your own home, you'll discover a world of new and fascinating flavours.

MEAT BRIOUATES

THE MOROCCANS, WHO ENJOY THE TASTE OF SWEET AND SAVOURY TOGETHER, TRADITIONALLY SPRINKLE THESE LITTLE PASTRY SNACKS WITH GROUND CINNAMON AND ICING SUGAR. IT IS AN UNUSUAL BUT DELICIOUS COMBINATION.

MAKES ABOUT TWENTY-FOUR

INGREDIENTS
175g/6oz filo pastry sheets
40g/1½oz/3 tbsp butter, melted
sunflower oil, for frying
fresh flat leaf parsley, to garnish
ground cinnamon and icing
  (confectioners') sugar,
  to serve (optional)
For the meat filling
30ml/2 tbsp sunflower oil
1 onion, finely chopped
1 small bunch of fresh coriander
  (cilantro), chopped
1 small bunch of fresh
  parsley, chopped
375g/13oz lean minced (ground) beef
  or lamb
2.5ml/½ tsp paprika
5ml/1 tsp ground coriander
good pinch of ground ginger
2 eggs, beaten

1 First make the filling. Heat the oil in a frying pan and fry the onion and the chopped herbs over a low heat for about 4 minutes, until the onion is softened and translucent.

2 Add the meat to the frying pan and cook for about 5 minutes, stirring frequently, until the meat is evenly browned and most of the moisture has evaporated. Drain away any excess fat and stir in the spices.

3 Cook the spiced meat and onion for 1 minute, and then remove the pan from the heat and stir in the beaten eggs. Stir until they begin to set and resemble lightly scrambled eggs. Set aside.

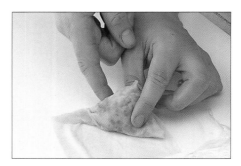

4 Take a sheet of filo pastry and cut into 8.5cm/3½in strips. Cover the remaining pastry with clear film (plastic wrap) to prevent it drying out. Brush the pastry strip with melted butter, then place a heaped teaspoon of the meat filling about 1cm/½in from one end. Fold the corner over to make a triangle shape.

5 Fold the "triangle" over itself and then continue to fold, keeping the triangle shape, until you reach the end of the strip. Continue in this way until all the pastry and filling have been used up. You should make about 24 pastries.

6 Heat about 1cm/½in oil in a heavy pan and fry the briouates in batches for 2–3 minutes until golden, turning once. Drain on kitchen paper and arrange on a serving plate. Serve garnished with fresh parsley and sprinkled with ground cinnamon and icing sugar, if liked.

Energy 95Kcal/396kJ; Protein 4.2g; Carbohydrate 4.8g, of which sugars 0.5g; Fat 6.7g, of which saturates 2.3g; Cholesterol 29mg; Calcium 19mg; Fibre 0.4g; Sodium 30mg.

PRAWN BRIOUATES

IN MOROCCO, BRIOUATES ARE MADE WITH A SPECIAL PASTRY CALLED OUARKA. LIKE FILO, IT IS VERY THIN AND APT TO DRY OUT IF NOT KEPT COVERED. MAKING THE GENUINE ARTICLE IS TRICKY AND TAKES YEARS OF PRACTICE. FORTUNATELY FILO PASTRY MAKES A PERFECT SUBSTITUTE.

MAKES ABOUT TWENTY-FOUR

INGREDIENTS
   175g/6oz filo pastry sheets
   40g/1½oz/3 tbsp butter, melted
   sunflower oil, for frying
   1 spring onion (scallion) and fresh
      coriander (cilantro) leaves, to garnish
   ground cinnamon and icing
      (confectioners') sugar, to serve
For the prawn (shrimp) filling
   15ml/1 tbsp olive oil
   15g/½oz/1 tbsp butter
   2–3 spring onions (scallions),
      finely chopped
   15g/½oz/2 tbsp plain (all-purpose) flour
   300ml/½ pint/1¼ cups milk
   2.5ml/½ tsp paprika
   350g/12oz cooked peeled prawns
      (shrimp), chopped
   salt and white pepper

1 First make the filling. Heat the olive oil and butter in a pan and fry the spring onions over a very gentle heat for 2–3 minutes until soft.

2 Stir in the flour, and then gradually add the milk. Heat gently, stirring continuously, until the sauce is thickened and smooth. Simmer gently for 2–3 minutes, stirring.

3 Season the sauce with paprika, salt and pepper and stir in the prawns.

COOK'S TIP
Chilled fresh or frozen filo pastry sheets are widely available from many supermarkets.

4 Take a sheet of filo pastry and cut it in half widthways, to make a rectangle about 18 x 14cm/7 x 5½in. Cover the remaining pastry with clear film (plastic wrap) to prevent it drying out.

5 Brush the pastry with melted butter and then place a heaped teaspoon of filling at one end of the pastry. Roll up like a cigar, tucking in the sides as you go. Continue in this way until you have used all the pastry and filling.

6 Heat about 1cm/½in oil in a heavy pan and fry the briouates, in batches if necessary, for 2–3 minutes until golden, turning occasionally. Drain on kitchen paper, arrange on a serving plate and then serve garnished with a spring onion and coriander leaves, and sprinkled with cinnamon and icing sugar, if liked.

Energy 77Kcal/320kJ; Protein 4.3g; Carbohydrate 5.5g, of which sugars 0.7g; Fat 4.3g, of which saturates 1.6g; Cholesterol 17mg; Calcium 47mg; Fibre 0.2g; Sodium 251mg.

BÖREKS

PROOF POSITIVE THAT COOKING CROSSES CONTINENTS, THESE TURKISH PASTRIES HAVE MUCH IN COMMON WITH THE BRIOUATES OF MOROCCO, BUT LACK THE SWEET CINNAMON COATING. THE TWO CHEESE FILLING IS A FAVOURITE COMBINATION, INEVITABLY ENLIVENED WITH FRESH HERBS AND JUST A PINCH OF NUTMEG. BÖREKS ARE MORE OFTEN BAKED THAN FRIED.

MAKES THIRTY-FIVE TO FORTY

INGREDIENTS
    225g/8oz feta cheese, grated
    225g/8oz mozzarella, grated
    2 eggs, beaten
    45ml/3 tbsp chopped fresh parsley
    45ml/3 tbsp chopped fresh chives
    45ml/3 tbsp chopped fresh mint
    pinch of freshly grated nutmeg
    225g/8oz filo pastry sheets
    45–60ml/3–4 tbsp melted butter
    ground black pepper

1 Preheat the oven to 180°C/350°F/ Gas 4. In a bowl, blend the feta and mozzarella cheeses with the beaten eggs. Add the chopped herbs, black pepper and nutmeg, and mix well.

2 Cut the sheets of pastry into four rectangular strips approximately 7.5cm/ 3in wide. Cover all but one or two strips of the pastry with a damp cloth to prevent them from drying out.

3 Brush one strip of pastry at a time with a little melted butter.

4 Place 5ml/1 tsp of filling at the bottom edge. Fold one corner over the filling to make a triangle shape. Continue folding the pastry over itself until you get to the end of the strip. Keep making triangles until all the filling is used up.

5 Place the böreks on a greased baking sheet and bake in the oven for about 30 minutes, until golden brown and crisp. Serve warm or cold.

COOK'S TIPS
A mixture of almost any cheeses can be used but avoid cream cheeses. Use chopped fresh basil in place of mint.

Energy 64Kcal/269kJ; Protein 3.1g; Carbohydrate 4.1g, of which sugars 0.2g; Fat 4.1g, of which saturates 2.5g; Cholesterol 22mg; Calcium 61mg; Fibre 0.3g; Sodium 131mg.

ASSIETTE OF PLANTAINS

MORE THAN HALF THE WORLD'S PLANTAINS GROW BETWEEN COASTAL WEST AFRICA AND THE CENTRAL BASIN OF ZAÏRE, SO IT IS NOT SURPRISING THAT THESE STARCHY FRUIT VEGETABLES HAVE BECOME AN IMPORTANT STAPLE. THIS SUCCULENT SNACK COMES FROM CÔTE D'IVOIRE.

SERVES FOUR

INGREDIENTS
  2 green plantains
  vegetable oil, for shallow frying
  1 yellow plantain
  ½ onion
  pinch of garlic powder
  salt and cayenne pepper

1 Peel one of the green plantains and cut into very thin rounds using a vegetable peeler. Heat the oil in a large frying pan over a moderate heat.

2 Fry the plantain rounds in the oil for about 3 minutes, turning until golden brown. Drain on kitchen paper and keep warm.

3 Coarsely grate the other green plantain and put on a plate. Slice the onion into wafer-thin shreds and mix with the grated plantain.

4 Heat a little more oil in the frying pan and fry handfuls of the mixture, in batches if necessary, for 2–3 minutes, until golden, turning once. Drain on kitchen paper and keep warm with the green plantain rounds.

5 Heat a little more oil in the frying pan and, while it is heating, peel the yellow plantain, cut in half lengthways and dice. Sprinkle with garlic powder and cayenne pepper and then fry until golden brown. Drain on kitchen paper and arrange each variety in shallow dishes. Sprinkle with salt and serve.

Energy 261Kcal/1093kJ; Protein 1.4g; Carbohydrate 34.3g, of which sugars 7.3g; Fat 14.1g, of which saturates 1.7g; Cholesterol 0mg; Calcium 14mg; Fibre 1.7g; Sodium 5mg.

SESAME-COATED MAJOUN

THE NOT-SO-SECRET INGREDIENT THAT TRADITIONALLY GIVES THESE SWEET AND SPICY SNACKS EXTRA FLAVOUR IS HASHISH. IT HAS BEEN OMITTED HERE, FOR OBVIOUS REASONS, BUT IS AS INTEGRAL TO THE GENUINE MOROCCAN RECIPE AS THE SPICES THAT FLAVOUR THE FRUIT, NUT AND HONEY MIX. MAJOUN, OFTEN CALLED HASHISH BALLS, ARE FAMED FOR THEIR NARCOTIC OR APHRODISIAC QUALITIES. THESE MAY NOT HAVE THE SAME EFFECT BUT ARE STILL DELICIOUS.

MAKES ABOUT TWENTY

INGREDIENTS
   500g/1¼lb/scant 3 cups
     blanched almonds
   250g/9oz/1½ cups walnuts
   500g/1¼lb/3⅓ cups raisins
   130g/4½oz/generous ½ cup butter
   250g/9oz/generous 1 cup clear honey
   7.5ml/1½ tsp ras el hanout
   7.5ml/1½ tsp ground ginger
   65–75g/2½–3oz sesame seeds

1 Finely chop the almonds, walnuts and raisins in a food processor or blender until they form a coarse, slightly sticky mixture. Alternatively, pound these ingredients together in batches in a large mortar using a pestle until the correct consistency is reached.

VARIATIONS
Use mixed spice (apple pie spice) or cinnamon in place of ginger. Use dried apricots in place of raisins.

2 Melt the butter in a large, heavy pan and stir in the honey, ras el hanout and ginger. Add the nuts and raisins and stir over a gentle heat for a few seconds until the mixture is thoroughly combined, firm and sticky.

3 Let the mixture cool a little, then shape into about 20 balls. Roll the balls in sesame seeds to coat completely. Serve warm or cold.

Energy 411Kcal/1711kJ; Protein 8.3g; Carbohydrate 29.1g, of which sugars 28.3g; Fat 29.8g, of which saturates 5.5g; Cholesterol 14mg; Calcium 107mg; Fibre 3g; Sodium 61mg.

TUNISIAN PLANTAIN SNACKS

SWEET AND CRISP, DEEP-FRIED SLICES OF PLAINTAIN ARE NOT ONLY A GREAT STREET SNACK, BUT ALSO MAKE EXCELLENT NIBBLES WITH DRINKS. THE SPICE MIXTURE USED HERE — ZAHTAR — IS POPULAR THROUGHOUT NORTH AFRICA AND IS ALSO WIDELY USED IN TURKEY AND JORDAN. ITS BLEND OF SESAME SEEDS, SUMAC AND THYME IS PERFECT WITH PLANTAINS, AND THE CHILLI ADDS A WARM NOTE.

SERVES TWO TO FOUR AS A SNACK

INGREDIENTS
  2 large ripe plantains
  sunflower oil, for deep-frying
  1 dried red chilli, roasted, seeded
    and chopped
  15–30ml/1–2 tbsp zhatar
  coarse salt

1 To peel the plantains, cut off their ends with a sharp knife and make two or three incisions in the skin from end to end, then peel off the skin. Cut the plantains into thick slices.

2 Heat the oil for deep-frying in a heavy pan to 180°C/350°F, or until a cube of bread browns in 30–45 seconds. Fry the plantain slices in batches until golden brown. Drain each batch on a double layer of kitchen paper.

3 While still warm, place them in a shallow bowl and sprinkle liberally with the dried chilli, zahtar and salt. Toss them thoroughly and eat immediately.

COOK'S TIP
To roast the chilli, place the chilli in a small, heavy frying pan and cook over a medium heat, stirring constantly, until the chilli darkens and gives off a peppery aroma.

Energy 334Kcal/1408kJ; Protein 1.9g; Carbohydrate 59.4g, of which sugars 14.4g; Fat 11.5g, of which saturates 1.3g; Cholesterol 0mg; Calcium 8mg; Fibre 2.9g; Sodium 4mg.

YAM BALLS

MOST AFRICAN COUNTRIES HAVE A VERSION OF THIS POPULAR SNACK, MADE BY ROLLING A SPICY MIXTURE OF MASHED YAM AND VEGETABLES INTO BALLS, WHICH ARE THEN DEEP FRIED. THE SMOOTH TEXTURE OF THE MASHED YAM CONTRASTS BEAUTIFULLY WITH THE CHOPPED VEGETABLES.

MAKES ABOUT TWENTY-FOUR

INGREDIENTS
450g/1lb white yam
30ml/2 tbsp finely chopped onion
45ml/3 tbsp chopped tomatoes
2.5ml/½ tsp chopped fresh thyme
1 fresh green chilli, finely chopped
15ml/1 tbsp finely chopped
  spring onion (scallion)
1 garlic clove, crushed
1 egg, beaten
salt and ground black pepper
vegetable oil, for shallow frying
seasoned flour, for dusting

COOK'S TIP
Add a selection of chopped fresh herbs to the yam mixture; parsley, chives and coriander (cilantro) make a good combination. Mix in 30ml/2 tbsp with the egg and seasoning.

1 Peel the yam, cut into pieces and boil in salted water for about 30 minutes until tender. Drain and mash.

2 Add the onion, tomatoes, thyme, chilli, spring onion, garlic, then stir in the egg and seasoning and mix well.

3 Using a dessertspoon, scoop a little of the mixture at a time and with your hands mould them into balls. Roll the yam balls in the seasoned flour and set aside until you have formed all the mixture into balls.

4 Heat a little oil in a large frying pan, and then fry the balls in batches for a few minutes, until golden brown. Drain the yam balls on kitchen paper and keep them warm while cooking the rest of the mixture. Serve hot.

TATALE

GHANAIANS WOULDN'T DREAM OF THROWING OVER-RIPE PLAINTAINS AWAY. INSTEAD, THEY MASH THEM WITH ONION, CHILLI AND FLOUR AND TRANSFORM THEM INTO THESE TASTY SNACKS.

SERVES FOUR

INGREDIENTS
2 over-ripe plantains
25–50g/1–2oz/¼–½ cup self-raising
  (self-rising) flour
1 small onion, finely chopped
1 egg, beaten
5ml/1 tsp palm oil (optional)
1 fresh green chilli, seeded
  and chopped
salt
vegetable oil, for shallow frying

1 Peel and mash the plantains. Place in a bowl and add enough flour to bind, stirring thoroughly.

2 Add the onion, egg, palm oil, if using, chilli and salt. Mix well and then leave to stand for 20 minutes.

3 Heat a little oil in a large frying pan. Spoon dessertspoons of mixture into the pan and fry in batches for 3–4 minutes until golden, turning once. Drain the fritters on kitchen paper and serve hot or cold.

TOP Energy 179Kcal/754kJ; Protein 1.7g; Carbohydrate 31.8g, of which sugars 5.9g; Fat 5.9g, of which saturates 0.8g; Cholesterol 0mg; Calcium 21mg; Fibre 1.6g; Sodium 4mg.
BOTTOM Energy 47Kcal/195kJ; Protein 0.6g; Carbohydrate 5.6g, of which sugars 0.4g; Fat 2.6g, of which saturates 0.4g; Cholesterol 8mg; Calcium 5mg; Fibre 0.3g; Sodium 4mg.

BASTELA WITH GINGER AND CASHEW NUTS

CRISP PASTRY AND A MELT-IN-THE-MOUTH NUT AND EGG FILLING ARE WHAT MAKE THIS DELICIOUS PIE SO SPECIAL. VERSIONS ARE MADE THROUGHOUT NORTH AFRICA, AND THE DISH HAS MIGRATED ACROSS THE STRAIT OF GIBRALTAR TO SOUTHERN SPAIN. IN THIS SIMPLIFIED VERSION, GROUND CASHEWS ARE USED IN PLACE OF THE MORE COMMON ALMONDS, AND GINGER, CORIANDER AND CINNAMON PROVIDE THE WARM SPICE NOTES.

SERVES SIX

INGREDIENTS
- 30ml/2 tbsp olive oil
- 115g/4oz/½ cup butter
- 8 spring onions (scallions), trimmed and chopped
- 2 garlic cloves, chopped
- 25g/1oz fresh root ginger, peeled and chopped
- 225g/8oz/1⅓ cups cashew nuts, roughly chopped
- 5–10ml/1–2 tsp ground cinnamon, plus extra to garnish
- 5ml/1 tsp paprika
- 2.5ml/½ tsp ground coriander
- 6 eggs, beaten
- bunch of fresh flat leaf parsley, finely chopped
- large bunch of fresh coriander (cilantro), finely chopped
- 8 sheets of ouarka or filo pastry
- salt and ground black pepper

1 Preheat the oven to 200°C/400°F/ Gas 6. Heat the olive oil with a little of the butter in a heavy pan and stir in the spring onions, garlic and ginger. Add the cashew nuts and cook for a few minutes, then stir in the cinnamon, paprika and ground coriander.

2 Season the mixture well, then add the beaten eggs. Cook, stirring constantly, until the eggs begin to scramble but remain moist. Remove the pan from the heat, add the chopped parsley and fresh coriander, and leave to cool.

VARIATION
Instead of making a single large pie, you can make small, individual pies for a picnic or to serve with drinks at a party. Simply cut the filo into strips or triangles, add a spoonful of the filling and fold them up into tight little parcels, making sure the edges are well sealed.

3 Melt the remaining butter. Separate the sheets of ouarka or filo and keep them under a slightly damp cloth. Brush the base of an ovenproof dish with a little of the melted butter and cover with a sheet of pastry, allowing the sides to flop over the rim.

4 Brush the pastry with a little more of the melted butter and place another sheet of pastry on top of the first. Repeat with another two sheets of pastry to make four layers.

5 Spread the cashew nut mixture on the pastry and fold the pastry edges over the filling. Cover with the remaining sheets of pastry, brushing each one with melted butter and tucking the edges under the pie, as though making a bed.

6 Brush the top of the pie with the remaining melted butter and bake for 25 minutes, until the pastry is crisp and golden. Dust the top of the pie with a little extra ground cinnamon and then serve immediately.

Energy 528Kcal/2190kJ; Protein 15.9g; Carbohydrate 17.6g, of which sugars 3.1g; Fat 44.5g, of which saturates 15.9g; Cholesterol 231mg; Calcium 93mg; Fibre 2.4g; Sodium 300mg.

FISH AND CHERMOULA MINI PIES

THESE LITTLE SAVOURY PIES ARE MADE WITH THE MOROCCAN FINE PASTRY OUARKA, BUT FILO PASTRY WILL WORK JUST AS WELL. THE FILLING IS HIGHLY FLAVOURED WITH CHERMOULA, WHICH IS A MIXTURE OF SPICES AND MASSES OF FRESH CORIANDER AND FLAT LEAF PARSLEY. THE CHERMOULA MAY BE MADE IN ADVANCE AND STORED IN THE REFRIGERATOR FOR A FEW DAYS. YOU CAN VARY THE FILLING BY ADDING MUSSELS OR SCALLOPS, IF YOU LIKE.

MAKES EIGHT

INGREDIENTS
500g/1¼lb firm white fish fillets
225g/8oz uncooked king prawns
  (jumbo shrimp)
16 sheets of ouarka or filo pastry
60–75ml/4–5 tbsp sunflower oil
1 egg yolk, mixed with a few drops
  of water
salt

For the chermoula
75ml/5 tbsp olive oil
juice of 1 lemon
5ml/1 tsp ground cumin
5–10ml/1–2 tsp paprika
2–3 garlic cloves, crushed
1 red chilli, seeded and chopped
large bunch of fresh flat leaf
  parsley, chopped
large bunch of fresh coriander
  (cilantro), chopped

1 Prepare the chermoula. Combine all the ingredients in a bowl and set aside. Place the fish in a frying pan and add just enough water to cover the fillets.

2 Season the fish with a little salt and heat until just simmering, then cook gently for 3 minutes, until the fish just begins to flake. Use a slotted spoon to remove the fish from the liquid and break it up, taking care to remove all bones as you do so.

3 Poach the prawns in the fish liquor for 10 minutes, until they turn pink, then drain and shell them. Gently toss the prawns and fish in the chermoula, cover and set aside for 1 hour.

4 Preheat the oven to 180°C/350°F/ Gas 4 and grease two baking sheets. To make the pies, lay the filo pastry under a damp cloth. Take two sheets of filo: brush one with oil, lay the second one on top, then brush it with oil.

5 Place some of the fish mixture in the middle of the length of the sheet but to one side of its width. Fold the edge of the pastry over the filling, then fold the long side over to cover the filling.

VARIATION
Instead of neat parcels, the filo and filling can be shaped into open boats or slipper shapes, as shown below.

6 Wrap the ends of the pastry around the filling like a collar to make a neat package with the edges tucked in, then brush with egg yolk.

7 Continue as before with the rest of the fish and chermoula mixture. Bake the pies for about 20 minutes, until the pastry is crisp and golden brown. Serve hot or warm.

Energy 236Kcal/984kJ; Protein 18.2g; Carbohydrate 10g, of which sugars 0.4g; Fat 13.9g, of which saturates 2g; Cholesterol 109mg; Calcium 67mg; Fibre 0.9g; Sodium 96mg.

TUNISIAN CHICKEN WINGS <u>WITH</u> ORANGES

THIS IS A GREAT RECIPE FOR THE BARBECUE — IT IS QUICK AND EASY TO PREPARE AND MAKES WONDERFUL FINGER FOOD. THE RUB THAT GIVES THE CHICKEN WINGS THEIR FIERY FLAVOUR IS BASED ON A CLASSIC TUNISIAN SPICE MIX CALLED HARISSA. TO BALANCE THE HEAT, ADD SEGMENTS OF BLOOD ORANGES, EITHER SERVED SEPARATELY OR COOKED ON SKEWERS WITH THE CHICKEN PORTIONS. CHERRY TOMATOES COULD BE USED INSTEAD OF THE ORANGES.

<u>SERVES FOUR</u>

INGREDIENTS
    60ml/4 tbsp fiery harissa
    30ml/2 tbsp olive oil
    16–20 chicken wings
    4 blood oranges, quartered
    icing (confectioners') sugar
    small bunch of fresh coriander
      (cilantro), chopped, to garnish
    salt

1 Preheat the grill (broiler) to its hottest setting. Put the harissa in a small bowl with the olive oil and mix to form a loose paste. Add a little salt and stir to combine.

2 Brush harissa mixture over the chicken wings so that they are well coated. Grill (broil) the wings for 5–8 minutes on each side, until cooked and a dark golden brown.

3 Once the wings begin to cook, dip the orange quarters lightly in icing sugar and grill them for a few minutes, until they are slightly burnt but not black and charred. Serve the chicken wings immediately with the oranges, sprinkled with a little chopped fresh coriander.

VARIATION
When blood oranges are out of season, normal oranges can be used instead.

Energy 500Kcal/2077kJ; Protein 44.8g; Carbohydrate 0g, of which sugars 0g; Fat 35.6g, of which saturates 8.9g; Cholesterol 196mg; Calcium 14mg; Fibre 0g; Sodium 132mg.

BUS-STATION KEFTA WITH EGG AND TOMATO

THE TITLE SAYS IT ALL. THIS IS THE TYPE OF SNACK THAT IS ON SALE IN BUS AND TRAIN STATIONS THROUGHOUT NORTH AFRICA AND THE MIDDLE EAST. IT IS COOKED ON THE SPOT AND EATEN STRAIGHT FROM THE PAN. SPEED IS ESSENTIAL WHEN TRAVELLERS ARE ABOUT TO DEPART, SO THIS IS THE PERFECT DISH FOR A QUICK BRUNCH OR SUPPER. MAKE THE TINY MEATBALLS IN ADVANCE AND KEEP THEM CHILLED UNTIL THEY ARE NEEDED.

SERVES FOUR

INGREDIENTS
225g/8oz minced (ground) lamb
1 onion, finely chopped
50g/2oz/1 cup fresh breadcrumbs
5 eggs
5ml/1 tsp ground cinnamon
bunch of flat leaf parsley, chopped
30ml/2 tbsp olive oil
400g/14oz can chopped tomatoes
10ml/2 tsp sugar
5ml/1 tsp ras el hanout
small bunch of fresh coriander
  (cilantro), roughly chopped
salt and ground black pepper
crusty bread, to serve

1 In a bowl, knead the minced lamb with the onion, breadcrumbs, 1 egg, cinnamon, chopped parsley and salt and pepper until well mixed. Lift the mixture in your hand and slap it down into the bowl several times.

2 Take a small amount of mixture and shape it into a small ball about the size of a walnut. Repeat with the remaining mixture to make about 12 balls.

3 Heat the olive oil in a large, heavy frying pan. Fry the meatballs until nicely browned, turning them occasionally so they cook evenly.

4 Stir the tomatoes, sugar, ras el hanout and most of the chopped coriander in to the pan. Bring to the boil, cook for a few minutes to reduce the liquid, and roll the balls round in the sauce. Season to taste with salt and pepper.

5 Make room for the remaining eggs in the pan and crack them into spaces between the meatballs. Cover the pan, reduce the heat and cook for about 3 minutes or until the eggs are just set.

6 Sprinkle with the remaining chopped coriander and serve in the pan, with chunks of bread to use as scoops.

Energy 330Kcal/1381kJ; Protein 21.5g; Carbohydrate 16.7g, of which sugars 6.6g; Fat 20.4g, of which saturates 6.2g; Cholesterol 281mg; Calcium 97mg; Fibre 1.7g; Sodium 264mg

CAMEROONIAN SUYA

SUYA IS SAID TO HAVE ORIGINATED IN GHANA, BUT IS POPULAR THROUGHOUT AFRICA. A SPICY PEANUT RUB GIVES THE SUCCULENT BEEF KEBABS THEIR INIMITABLE FLAVOUR.

SERVES SIX

INGREDIENTS
450g/1lb frying (flank) steak
2.5ml/½ tsp sugar
5ml/1 tsp garlic powder
5ml/1 tsp ground ginger
5ml/1 tsp paprika
5ml/1 tsp ground cinnamon
pinch of chilli powder
10ml/2 tsp onion salt
50g/2oz/⅓ cup peanuts,
    finely crushed
vegetable oil, for brushing

COOK'S TIP
If cooking the meat on a barbecue, don't cook it too near to the burning coals, or wait until the heat is past its fiercest, to avoid scorching.

1 Cut the steak into 2.5cm/1in wide strips. Place in a bowl or a shallow dish.

2 Mix the sugar, garlic powder, spices, onion salt and crushed peanuts together in a small bowl, then mix with the steak.

3 Thread the steak on to six satay sticks, pushing the meat close together. Place in a shallow dish, cover loosely with foil and leave to marinate in a cool place for a few hours.

4 Preheat a grill (boiler) or barbecue. Brush the meat with a little oil and then cook on a moderate heat for about 15 minutes, until evenly browned. Serve hot.

AKKRAS

THESE WEST AFRICAN BEAN FRITTERS ARE MADE IN MUCH THE SAME WAY AS MIDDLE EASTERN FALAFEL. SLAVES TOOK THE RECIPE TO THE CARIBBEAN, WHERE IT REMAINS VERY POPULAR TODAY.

SERVES FOUR

INGREDIENTS
225g/8oz/1¼ cups dried
    black-eyed beans (peas)
1 onion, chopped
1 fresh red chilli, halved, with seeds
    removed (optional)
about 150ml/¼ pint/⅔ cup water
vegetable oil, for deep-frying

1 Soak the black-eyed beans in plenty of cold water for 6–8 hours or overnight. Drain the beans and then briskly rub the beans between the palms of your hands to remove the skins.

2 Return the beans to a bowl, top up with water and the skins will float to the surface. Discard the skins and soak the beans again for 2 hours.

3 Place the beans in a blender or food processor with the onion, chilli, if using, and a little water. Process to make a thick paste. Pour the mixture into a large bowl and whisk for a few minutes.

4 Heat the oil in a large, heavy pan and fry spoonfuls of the mixture for 4 minutes, until golden brown. Serve.

TOP Energy 195Kcal/810kJ; Protein 19.2g; Carbohydrate 1.1g, of which sugars 0.5g; Fat 12.6g, of which saturates 3.8g; Cholesterol 44mg; Calcium 9mg; Fibre 0.5g; Sodium 376mg.
BOTTOM Energy 238Kcal/1004kJ; Protein 13.7g; Carbohydrate 33.4g, of which sugars 3.7g; Fat 6.5g, of which saturates 0.9g; Cholesterol 0mg; Calcium 55mg; Fibre 5.2g; Sodium 10mg.

SIZZLING PRAWNS

IN COASTAL REGIONS OF AFRICA AND THE MIDDLE EAST, STREET FOOD OFTEN MEANS A MAN WITH A PAN COOKING SPICY SEAFOOD OVER A SMALL BRAZIER. PRAWNS COOKED THIS WAY TASTE GREAT.

SERVES FOUR

INGREDIENTS
    450g/1lb raw king prawns (jumbo
      shrimp) in their shells
    30ml/2 tbsp olive oil
    25–40g/1–1½oz/2–3 tbsp butter
    2 garlic cloves, crushed
    5ml/1 tsp ground cumin
    2.5ml/½ tsp ground ginger
    10ml/2 tsp paprika
    1.5ml/¼ tsp cayenne pepper
    lemon wedges and fresh coriander
      (cilantro) sprigs, to garnish

1 Pull the heads off the prawns and then peel away and discard the shells, legs and tails. Using a sharp knife, cut along the back of each prawn and pull away and discard the dark thread.

2 Heat the olive oil and butter in a frying pan. When the butter begins to sizzle, add the garlic and cook for about 30 seconds.

3 Add the cumin, ginger, paprika and cayenne pepper. Cook briefly, stirring for a few seconds, and then add the prawns. Cook for 2–3 minutes over a high heat, until they turn pink, stirring frequently.

4 Transfer the prawns to four warmed serving dishes and pour the butter and spicy mixture over. Garnish with lemon wedges and coriander and serve.

GRILLED KEFTAS

CLOSELY RELATED TO THE KOFTAS OF INDIA AND THE MIDDLE EAST, THESE SPICY LAMB SAUSAGE SKEWERS WITH A MINT AND YOGURT DRESSING ARE A MOROCCAN SPECIALITY.

MAKES TWELVE TO FOURTEEN

INGREDIENTS
    675g/1½lb lean lamb
    1 onion, quartered
    3–4 fresh parsley sprigs
    2–3 fresh coriander (cilantro) sprigs
    1–2 fresh mint sprigs
    2.5ml/½ tsp ground cumin
    2.5ml/½ tsp mixed spice (apple
      pie spice)
    5ml/1 tsp paprika
    salt and ground black pepper
    Moroccan bread, to serve
For the mint dressing
    30ml/2 tbsp finely chopped
      fresh mint
    90ml/6 tbsp natural (plain) yogurt

1 Roughly chop the lamb, place in a food processor and process until smooth. Transfer to a plate.

2 Add the onion, parsley, coriander and mint to the processor and process until finely chopped. Add the lamb together with the ground spices and seasoning and process again until very smooth. Transfer to a bowl and chill for about 1 hour.

3 Make the dressing. Blend the chopped mint with the yogurt and chill until required.

4 Mould the meat into small sausage shapes and skewer with wooden or metal kebab sticks. Preheat a grill (broiler) or barbecue to a medium heat.

5 Cook the keftas for 5–6 minutes, turning once. Serve immediately with the mint dressing. Moroccan bread makes a good accompaniment.

TOP Energy 182Kcal/756kJ; Protein 19.9g; Carbohydrate 0g, of which sugars 0g; Fat 11.3g, of which saturates 4.2g; Cholesterol 233mg; Calcium 90mg; Fibre 0g; Sodium 252mg.
BOTTOM Energy 111Kcal/463kJ; Protein 11.7g; Carbohydrate 1.7g, of which sugars 1.3g; Fat 6.4g, of which saturates 3g; Cholesterol 43mg; Calcium 29mg; Fibre 0.2g; Sodium 56mg.

MARRAKESH PIZZA

IN MOROCCO, COOKS TEND TO PLACE FLAVOURINGS INSIDE RATHER THAN ON TOP OF THE DOUGH, SO THAT THE FLAVOURS PERMEATE RIGHT THROUGH. THE RESULT IS SURPRISING — AND QUITE DELICIOUS.

MAKES FOUR

INGREDIENTS
5ml/1 tsp sugar
10ml/2 tsp dried yeast
450g/1lb/4 cups strong white
   bread flour
10ml/2 tsp salt
melted butter, for brushing
rocket (arugula) salad and olives, to
   serve
For the filling
1 small onion, very finely chopped
2 tomatoes, skinned, seeded
   and chopped
25ml/1½ tbsp chopped fresh parsley
25ml/1½ tbsp chopped fresh
   coriander (cilantro)
5ml/1 tsp paprika
5ml/1 tsp ground cumin
50g/2oz/⅓ cup shredded vegetable
   suet (chilled, grated shortening)
40g/1½oz Cheddar cheese, grated

1 First prepare the yeast. Place 150ml/ ¼ pint/⅔ cup warm water in a small bowl, stir in the sugar and then sprinkle with the yeast. Stir once or twice, then set aside in a warm place for about 10 minutes until frothy.

2 Meanwhile, make the filling. Mix together the onion, tomatoes, chopped parsley, chopped coriander, paprika, cumin, suet and cheese, then season with salt and set aside.

3 In a large bowl, mix together the flour and 10ml/2 tsp salt. Add the yeast mixture and enough warm water to make a fairly soft dough (about 250ml/ 8fl oz/1 cup). Knead the mixture into a ball and then knead on a floured work surface for 10–12 minutes until the dough is firm and elastic.

4 Divide the dough into four pieces and roll each into a rectangle, measuring 20 x 30cm/8 x 12in. Spread the filling down the centre of each rectangle, then fold into three, to make a rectangle 20 x 10cm/8 x 4in.

5 Roll out the dough again, until it is the same size as before and again fold into three to make a smaller rectangle. (The filling will be squeezed out in places, but don't worry – just push it back inside the dough.)

6 Place the pizzas on a buttered baking sheet, cover with oiled clear film (plastic wrap) and leave in a warm place for about 1 hour until slightly risen.

7 Heat a griddle and brush with butter. Prick the pizzas with a fork five or six times on both sides and then fry for about 8 minutes on each side, until crisp and golden.

8 Serve the pizzas immediately, with a little melted butter if liked, and accompanied by rocket salad and black olives.

Energy 548Kcal/2313kJ; Protein 14.2g; Carbohydrate 92.7g, of which sugars 5.3g; Fat 16g, of which saturates 8g; Cholesterol 11mg; Calcium 259mg; Fibre 4.8g; Sodium 1063mg.

ISRAELI SPICED SEED BREADS

ORANGE FLOWER WATER SCENTS THESE DELICIOUS BREADS, WHICH ARE FLAVOURED WITH SESAME SEEDS AND FENNEL SEEDS. THEY ARE BEST SERVED WARM, WITH BUTTER AND HONEY.

MAKES TWELVE

INGREDIENTS
   5ml/1 tsp sugar
   10ml/2 tsp dried yeast
   75g/3oz/6 tbsp butter, melted
   15ml/1 tbsp orange flower water or
      almond essence (extract) (optional)
   400g/14oz/3½ cups strong white
      bread flour
   75g/3oz/¾ cup icing
      (confectioners') sugar
   5ml/1 tsp salt
   30ml/2 tbsp sesame seeds
   15ml/1 tbsp fennel seeds
   beaten egg, to glaze

1 First start the yeast. Place 120ml/ 4fl oz/½ cup warm water in a jug, stir in the sugar and sprinkle the yeast on top. Stir and then set aside for about 10 minutes until frothy.

2 Place the melted butter, orange flower water or almond essence, and 175ml/ 6fl oz/¾ cup warm water in a separate jug and stir to mix. Stir the flour, icing sugar, salt, sesame seeds and fennel seeds together in the bowl of a food processor fitted with the dough blade.

3 Add the yeast and half of the butter and water mixture to the flour and process so that they slowly combine. Continue processing, adding the remaining butter and water to make a smooth and glossy dough. (You may need to add extra flour/warm water.)

4 Continue processing for 1–2 minutes, then transfer the dough to a floured board and knead by hand for a few minutes until the dough is smooth and elastic.

5 Place in a clean, lightly oiled bowl, cover with clear film (plastic wrap) and leave in a warm place for 1–1½ hours until doubled in size. Knead again for a few minutes and then divide and shape into 12 small balls and flatten slightly with oiled hands. Place on a greased baking sheet, cover with oiled clear film and leave to rise for 1 hour.

6 Preheat the oven to 190°C/375°F/ Gas 5. Brush the breads with beaten egg and then bake for 12–15 minutes, until golden brown. Serve warm or cold.

Energy 201Kcal/847kJ; Protein 3.7g; Carbohydrate 32.8g, of which sugars 7.4g; Fat 7g, of which saturates 3.5g; Cholesterol 13mg; Calcium 68mg; Fibre 1.2g; Sodium 204mg.

FISH DISHES

Harvesting the riches of rivers and the sea has always been an important activity for the peoples of Africa and the Middle East, for, as the Angolan proverb says, "The smallest fish is better than an empty dish". The daily catch is sold as soon as the boats return to shore, to be cooked the same day, or preserved by drying, salting or pickling. Africans and Arabs have a vast store of fish recipes, but often prefer the simplest methods of cooking, and grilling, especially over an open fire, is universally popular.

KING PRAWNS IN ALMOND SAUCE

A DELECTABLE SEAFOOD CURRY FROM MAURITIUS, WHERE THE PRAWNS ARE LARGE AND SUCCULENT
AND CHRISTOPHENE — OR CHO-CHO AS IT'S LOCALLY KNOWN — IS A POPULAR VEGETABLE.

SERVES FOUR

INGREDIENTS
  450g/1lb raw king prawns
    (jumbo shrimp)
  600ml/1 pint/2½ cups water
  3 thin slices fresh root ginger, peeled
  10ml/2 tsp curry powder
  2 garlic cloves, crushed
  15g/½oz/1 tbsp butter or margarine
  60ml/4 tbsp ground almonds
  1 fresh green chilli, seeded and
    finely chopped
  45ml/3 tbsp single (light) cream
  salt and ground black pepper
For the vegetables
  15ml/1 tbsp mustard oil
  15ml/1 tbsp vegetable oil
  1 onion, sliced
  ½ red (bell) pepper, seeded and
    thinly sliced
  ½ green (bell) pepper, seeded and
    thinly sliced
  1 christophene, peeled, stoned
    (pitted) and cut into strips

1 Shell the prawns and place the shells in a pan with the water and ginger. Simmer, uncovered, for 15 minutes until reduced by half. Strain into a jug (pitcher), discard the shells and ginger.

2 De-vein the prawns, place in a bowl and season with the curry powder, garlic and salt and pepper and set aside.

3 Heat the mustard and vegetable oils in a large frying pan, add the vegetables and stir-fry for 5 minutes. Season, spoon into a dish and keep warm.

4 Wipe out the frying pan, then melt the butter or margarine in the pan and sauté the prawns for about 5 minutes, until pink. Spoon over the bed of vegetables, cover and keep warm.

5 Add the ground almonds and chilli to the pan, stir-fry for a few seconds and then add the reserved stock and bring to the boil. Reduce the heat, stir in the cream and cook for a few minutes, without boiling. Pour the sauce over the vegetables and prawns before serving.

FRIED POMFRET IN COCONUT SAUCE

POMFRET ARE FOUND IN THE MEDITERRANEAN, BUT THE BEST-FLAVOURED FISH COME FROM THE
INDIAN OCEAN. THIS IS HOW IT IS COOKED IN ZANZIBAR.

SERVES FOUR

INGREDIENTS
  4 medium pomfret
  juice of 1 lemon
  5ml/1 tsp garlic powder
  salt and ground black pepper
  vegetable oil, for shallow frying
For the coconut sauce
  450ml/¾ pint/scant 2 cups water
  2 thin slices fresh root ginger, peeled
  25–40g/1–1½oz creamed coconut or
    60–90ml/4–6 tbsp coconut cream
  30ml/2 tbsp vegetable oil
  1 red onion, sliced
  2 garlic cloves, crushed
  1 green chilli, seeded and sliced
  15ml/1 tbsp chopped fresh
    coriander (cilantro)

1 Cut the fish in half and sprinkle with the lemon juice. Season with garlic powder, salt and pepper and marinate in a cool place for a few hours.

2 Heat a little oil in a large frying pan. Pat the fish dry, fry in the oil for 10 minutes, turning once. Set aside.

3 To make the sauce, place the water in a pan with the slices of ginger, bring to the boil and simmer until the liquid is reduced to just over 300ml/½ pint/1¼ cups. Remove the ginger and reserve, then add the creamed coconut or coconut cream to the pan and stir until the coconut has melted.

4 Heat the oil in a wok or large pan and fry the onion and garlic for 2–3 minutes. Add the reserved ginger and coconut stock, the chilli and chopped coriander, stir well and then gently add the fish. Simmer for 10 minutes, until the fish is cooked through. Transfer the fish to a warmed serving plate, adjust the seasoning for the sauce and pour over the fish. Serve immediately.

TOP Energy 301Kcal/1251kJ; Protein 24.3g; Carbohydrate 6.1g, of which sugars 5.1g; Fat 20.1g, of which saturates 4.8g; Cholesterol 234mg; Calcium 154mg; Fibre 2.4g; Sodium 244mg.
BOTTOM Energy 210Kcal/875kJ; Protein 23.2g; Carbohydrate 2.3g, of which sugars 2g; Fat 12g, of which saturates 1.5g; Cholesterol 58mg; Calcium 23mg; Fibre 0.2g; Sodium 101mg.

Nigerian Lobster Piri Piri

Dried shrimps intensify the flavour of this seafood dish. The sauce uses easy-to-obtain ingredients like onions, tomatoes and chilli, with chopped ginger for added piquancy.

SERVES TWO TO FOUR

INGREDIENTS
  60ml/4 tbsp vegetable oil
  2 onions, chopped
  5ml/1 tsp chopped fresh root ginger
  450g/1lb fresh or canned
    tomatoes, chopped
  15ml/1 tbsp tomato purée (paste)
  225g/8oz cooked, peeled
    prawns (shrimp)
  10ml/2 tsp ground coriander
  1 green chilli, seeded and chopped
  15ml/1 tbsp dried shrimps, ground
  600ml/1 pint/2½ cups water
  1 green (bell) pepper, seeded
    and sliced
  2 cooked lobsters, halved
  salt and ground black pepper
  fresh coriander (cilantro) sprigs,
    to garnish

1 Heat the oil in a large, flameproof casserole and fry the onions, ginger, tomatoes and tomato purée for 5 minutes, until the onions are soft. Add the prawns, ground coriander, chilli and ground shrimps and stir well to mix.

2 Stir in the water, green pepper and salt and pepper, bring to the boil and simmer, uncovered, over a medium heat for about 20–30 minutes, until the sauce is reduced.

3 Add the lobsters to the sauce and cook for a few minutes to heat through. Arrange the lobster halves on warmed serving plates and pour the sauce over each one. Garnish with coriander sprigs and serve with fluffy white rice.

VARIATION
Use ground dried crayfish in place of ground dried shrimps, if preferred.

Energy 588Kcal/2464kJ; Protein 64.9g; Carbohydrate 24.5g, of which sugars 20.4g; Fat 26.6g, of which saturates 3.3g; Cholesterol 419mg; Calcium 270mg; Fibre 5.1g; Sodium 918mg.

TILAPIA IN MANGO AND TOMATO SAUCE

THE FLESH OF TILAPIA IS WHITE AND MOIST, WITH A SWEET FLAVOUR THAT IS ACCENTUATED WHEN IT IS COOKED WITH FRUIT, AS HERE. THE FISH IS POPULAR IN AFRICA, AND IN ISRAEL AND LEBANON.

SERVES FOUR

INGREDIENTS

4 tilapia
juice of ½ lemon
2 garlic cloves, crushed
2.5ml/½ tsp dried thyme
30ml/2 tbsp chopped spring onion
  (scallion)
vegetable oil, for shallow frying
plain (all-purpose) flour, for dusting
30ml/2 tbsp groundnut (peanut) oil
15g/½oz/1 tbsp butter or margarine
1 onion, finely chopped
3 tomatoes, skinned and
  finely chopped
5ml/1 tsp ground turmeric
60ml/4 tbsp white wine
1 fresh green chilli, seeded and
  finely chopped
600ml/1 pint/2½ cups well-flavoured
  fish stock
5ml/1 tsp sugar
1 under-ripe medium mango, peeled,
  stoned (pitted) and diced
15ml/1 tbsp chopped fresh parsley
salt and ground black pepper

1 Place the fish in a shallow bowl, drizzle the lemon juice all over the fish and gently rub in the garlic, thyme and some salt and pepper.

2 Place some of the spring onion in the cavity of each fish, cover loosely with clear film (plastic wrap) and leave to marinate for a few hours or overnight in the fridge.

3 Heat a little vegetable oil in a large frying pan, coat the fish with some flour, and then fry the fish on both sides for a few minutes, until golden brown. Remove with a slotted spoon to a plate and set aside.

4 Heat the groundnut oil and butter or margarine in a pan and fry the onion for 4–5 minutes, until soft. Stir in the tomatoes and cook briskly for a few minutes.

5 Add the turmeric, white wine, chilli, fish stock and sugar and stir well. Bring to the boil, then simmer gently, covered, for 10 minutes. Add the fish and cook for about 15–20 minutes.

6 Add the mango, arranging it around the fish, and cook briefly for 1–2 minutes to heat through. Arrange the fish on a warmed serving plate with the mango and tomato sauce poured over. Garnish with chopped parsley and serve immediately.

Energy 238Kcal/998kJ; Protein 23.4g; Carbohydrate 10.1g, of which sugars 9.6g; Fat 10.8g, of which saturates 3.1g; Cholesterol 8mg; Calcium 168mg; Fibre 2g; Sodium 97mg.

TANZANIAN FRIED FISH WITH COCONUT

A SPINACH AND COCONUT MILK SAUCE, STUDDED WITH PRAWNS AND RED CHILLI, LOOKS VERY PRETTY WHEN PUDDLED AROUND GOUJONS OF FRIED FISH THAT HAVE BEEN MARINATED IN SPICES.

SERVES FOUR

INGREDIENTS
  450g/1lb white fish fillets (cod
    or haddock)
  15ml/1 tbsp lemon or lime juice
  2.5ml/½ tsp garlic powder
  5ml/1 tsp ground cinnamon
  2.5ml/½ tsp dried thyme
  2.5ml/½ tsp paprika
  2.5ml/½ tsp ground black pepper
  seasoned flour, for dusting
  vegetable oil, for shallow frying
  salt
For the sauce
  25g/1oz/2 tbsp butter or margarine
  1 onion, finely chopped
  1 garlic clove, crushed
  300ml/½ pint/1¼ cups coconut milk
  115g/4oz fresh spinach, thinly sliced
  225–275g/8–10oz cooked, peeled
    prawns (shrimp)
  1 fresh red chilli, seeded and
    finely chopped

2 Blend together the garlic powder, cinnamon, thyme, paprika, black pepper and salt and sprinkle over the fish. Cover loosely with clear film (plastic wrap) and leave to marinate in a cool place or refrigerator for a few hours.

3 Meanwhile, make the sauce. Melt the butter or margarine in a large pan and fry the onion and garlic for 5–6 minutes, until the onion is soft, stirring frequently.

4 Place the coconut milk and spinach in a separate pan and bring to the boil. Cook gently for a few minutes until the spinach has wilted and the coconut milk has reduced a little, then remove from the heat and set aside to cool slightly.

5 Process the spinach mixture in a blender or food processor for 30 seconds then add to the onion with the prawns and red chilli. Stir well and simmer gently for a few minutes then set aside while cooking the fish.

6 Cut the marinated fish into 5cm/2in pieces and dip in the seasoned flour. Heat a little oil in a large frying pan and fry the fish pieces, in batches if necessary, for 2–3 minutes each side, until golden brown. Drain on kitchen paper.

7 Arrange the fish on a warmed serving plate. Gently reheat the sauce and serve separately in a sauce boat or poured over the fish.

VARIATION
Use 1 clove crushed fresh garlic in place of garlic powder.

Energy 259Kcal/1087kJ; Protein 32.5g; Carbohydrate 5.4g, of which sugars 5g; Fat 12.1g, of which saturates 4.3g; Cholesterol 164mg; Calcium 136mg; Fibre 0.8g; Sodium 343mg.

TANZANIAN FISH CURRY

WITH LAKES ON ITS WESTERN AND NORTHERN BORDERS, AND THE SEA TO THE EAST, TANZANIA HAS A RICH INSPIRATION FOR ITS FISH DISHES. THIS SIMPLE TREATMENT OF SNAPPER OR BREAM WORKS WELL.

SERVES TWO TO THREE

INGREDIENTS

1 large snapper or red bream
1 lemon
45ml/3 tbsp vegetable oil
1 onion, finely chopped
2 garlic cloves, crushed
45ml/3 tbsp curry powder
400g/14oz can chopped tomatoes
20ml/1 heaped tbsp smooth peanut
  butter, preferably unsalted
½ green (bell) pepper, seeded
  and chopped
2 slices fresh root ginger, chopped
1 fresh green chilli, seeded and
  finely chopped
about 600ml/1 pint/2½ cups
  fish stock
15ml/1 tbsp finely chopped fresh
  coriander (cilantro)
salt and ground black pepper

3 Stir in the tomatoes and then the peanut butter, mixing well, then add the green pepper, ginger, chilli and stock. Stir well and simmer gently for 10 minutes.

COOK'S TIP
The fish can be fried before adding to the sauce, if preferred. Dip in seasoned flour and fry in oil in a pan or a wok for a few minutes before adding to the sauce.

4 Cut the fish into pieces and gently lower into the sauce. Simmer for a further 20 minutes or until the fish is cooked, then using a slotted spoon, transfer the fish pieces to a plate.

5 Stir the coriander into the sauce and adjust the seasoning. If the sauce is very thick, add a little stock or water. Return the fish to the sauce, heat through and then serve immediately.

1 Season the fish with salt and pepper and squeeze half a lemon over it. Cover, and leave in a cool place for 2 hours.

2 Heat the oil in a pan and fry the onion and garlic for 5–6 minutes. Reduce the heat, add the curry powder and stir in.

Energy 483Kcal/2020kJ; Protein 44.5g; Carbohydrate 12.8g, of which sugars 10.9g; Fat 28.7g, of which saturates 3.7g; Cholesterol 86mg; Calcium 129mg; Fibre 3.2g; Sodium 364mg.

FISH WITH CRAB MEAT AND AUBERGINE

IN MAURITIUS, HOME OF THE FAMOUS BLUE SWIMMER CRABS AND SAND CRABS, THIS SHELLFISH IS VERY POPULAR. COMBINING IT WITH SALMON AND AUBERGINE CREATES A SOPHISTICATED DISH.

SERVES FOUR

INGREDIENTS
  450–675g/1–1½lb salmon fillet,
    skinned and cut into 4 pieces
  2 garlic cloves, crushed
  juice of ½ lemon
  15ml/1 tbsp vegetable oil
  15g/½oz/1 tbsp butter or margarine
  1 onion, cut into rings
  175g/6oz fresh or canned crab meat
  salt and ground black pepper
For the aubergine (eggplant) sauce
  25g/1oz/2 tbsp butter or margarine
  30ml/2 tbsp chopped spring onion
    (scallion)
  2 tomatoes, skinned and chopped
  ½ red (bell) pepper, seeded and
    finely chopped
  1 large aubergine (eggplant), peeled
    and chopped
  450ml/¾ pint/scant 2 cups fish or
    vegetable stock
  salt and ground black pepper

1 Place the salmon fillet in a shallow, non-metallic dish, season with the garlic and a little salt and pepper. Sprinkle with the lemon juice, cover loosely with clear film (plastic wrap) and set aside to marinate in a cool place for 1 hour.

2 Meanwhile, make the aubergine sauce. Melt the butter or margarine in a pan and gently fry the spring onion and tomatoes for 5 minutes.

3 Add the red pepper and aubergine, stir together and then add 300ml/ ½ pint/1¼ cups of the stock. Simmer for 20 minutes, until the aubergines are mushy and the liquid has been absorbed and then mash the mixture together well with a fork.

4 To cook the salmon, heat the oil and butter or margarine in a large frying pan. When the butter has melted, scatter the onion rings over the bottom of the pan and lay the salmon pieces on top. Cover each piece of salmon with crab meat and then spoon the aubergine mixture on top.

5 Pour the remaining stock around the salmon, cover with a lid and cook over a low to moderate heat, until the salmon is cooked through and flakes easily when tested with a knife. The sauce should be thick and fairly dry.

6 Arrange the fish on warmed serving plates, spoon extra sauce over and serve at once.

COOK'S TIP
Use a fish slice or metal spatula to carefully transfer the salmon fillet to serving plates, to prevent breaking up the fish.

Energy 372Kcal/1548kJ; Protein 32.4g; Carbohydrate 6.5g, of which sugars 5.8g; Fat 24.3g, of which saturates 7.9g; Cholesterol 109mg; Calcium 98mg; Fibre 3.1g; Sodium 360mg.

EGYPTIAN BAKED RED SNAPPER

A RECIPE DOESN'T HAVE TO BE ELABORATE TO TASTE GOOD. THIS COULDN'T BE SIMPLER, BUT THE FISH IS DELICIOUS WHEN BAKED WHOLE WITH ITS LIGHTLY SPICED TOMATO SAUCE.

SERVES THREE TO FOUR

INGREDIENTS

　1 large red snapper, cleaned
　juice of 1 lemon
　2.5ml/½ tsp paprika
　2.5ml/½ tsp garlic powder
　2.5ml/½ tsp dried thyme
　2.5ml/½ tsp ground black pepper
For the sauce
　30ml/2 tbsp palm or vegetable oil
　1 onion, peeled and chopped
　400g/14oz can chopped tomatoes
　2 garlic cloves
　1 fresh thyme sprig or 2.5ml/½ tsp
　　dried thyme
　1 fresh green chilli, seeded and
　　finely chopped
　½ green (bell) pepper, seeded
　　and chopped
　300ml/½ pint/1¼ cups fish stock

1 Preheat the oven to 200°C/400°F/ Gas 6 and then prepare the sauce. Heat the oil in a pan, fry the onion for 5 minutes, and then add the tomatoes, garlic, thyme and chilli.

2 Add the green pepper and stock. Bring to the boil, stirring, then reduce the heat and simmer, covered, for about 10 minutes, until the vegetables are soft. Remove from the heat and cool slightly and then place in a blender or food processor and process to form a purée.

COOK'S TIP
If you prefer less sauce, remove the foil after 20 minutes and continue baking uncovered, until cooked.

3 Wash the fish well and then score the skin with a sharp knife in a criss-cross pattern. Mix together the lemon juice, paprika, garlic, thyme and black pepper, spoon over the fish and rub in well.

4 Place the fish in a greased baking dish and pour the sauce over the top. Cover with foil and bake for about 30–40 minutes, until the fish is cooked and flakes easily when tested with a knife. Serve with boiled rice.

Energy 198Kcal/837kJ; Protein 33.1g; Carbohydrate 7.4g, of which sugars 6.6g; Fat 4.3g, of which saturates 0.8g; Cholesterol 58mg; Calcium 91mg; Fibre 1.7g; Sodium 201mg.

YELLOWTAIL WITH LEMON AND RED ONION

THIS DELICIOUS GAME FISH IS FOUND IN SOUTH AFRICAN WATERS, THE FLESH CAN BE DRY, BUT SIMMERING IT IN STOCK KEEPS IT BEAUTIFULLY MOIST. HALIBUT OR COD CAN BE SUBSTITUTED.

SERVES FOUR

INGREDIENTS

4 yellowtail, halibut or cod steaks or cutlets, about 175g/6oz each
juice of 1 lemon
5ml/1 tsp garlic powder
5ml/1 tsp paprika
5ml/1 tsp ground cumin
4ml/¾ tsp dried tarragon
about 60ml/4 tbsp olive oil
plain (all-purpose) flour, for dusting
300ml/½ pint/1¼ cups fish stock
2 fresh red chillies, seeded and finely chopped
30ml/2 tbsp chopped fresh coriander (cilantro)
1 red onion, cut into rings
salt and ground black pepper

1 Place the fish in a shallow, non-metallic bowl. Mix together the lemon juice, garlic powder, paprika, cumin, tarragon, salt and pepper. Spoon over the fish, cover with clear film (plastic wrap) and leave overnight in the fridge.

2 Gently heat the oil in a large frying pan, dust the fish with flour and then fry on each side, until golden brown.

3 Pour the fish stock around the fish, and simmer, covered, for about 5 minutes, until the fish is almost cooked through.

4 Add the red chillies and 15ml/1 tbsp of the chopped coriander to the pan. Simmer for a further 5 minutes.

5 Transfer the fish and sauce to a serving plate and keep warm.

6 Wipe the pan, heat some olive oil in the pan and stir-fry the onion rings until speckled brown. Scatter over the fish with the remaining chopped coriander and serve at once.

Energy 265Kcal/1106kJ; Protein 33g; Carbohydrate 5.4g, of which sugars 1.2g; Fat 12.5g, of which saturates 1.8g; Cholesterol 81mg; Calcium 47mg; Fibre 0.9g; Sodium 109mg.

SPICY SHELLFISH COUSCOUS

THIS IS PRECISELY THE TYPE OF DISH YOU MIGHT ENJOY ON A WARM EVENING AT A BEACH BAR IN CASABLANCA OR TANGIER. THE COUSCOUS IS FLAVOURED WITH HARISSA, A SPICY CHILLI PASTE, BEFORE BEING BAKED IN THE OVEN. IT IS TOPPED WITH MUSSELS AND PRAWNS AND MOISTENED WITH A MARVELLOUSLY CREAMY SAUCE, WHICH JUST BEGS TO BE MOPPED UP WITH BREAD.

SERVES FOUR TO SIX

INGREDIENTS
  500g/1¼lb/3 cups couscous
  5ml/1 tsp salt
  600ml/1 pint/2½ cups warm water
  45ml/3 tbsp sunflower oil
  5–10ml/1–2 tsp harissa
  25g/1oz/2 tbsp butter, diced
For the shellfish broth
  500g/1¼lb mussels in their shells,
    scrubbed, with beards removed
  500g/1¼lb uncooked prawns
    (shrimp) in their shells
  juice of 1 lemon
  50g/2oz/¼ cup butter
  2 shallots, finely chopped
  5ml/1 tsp coriander seeds, roasted
    and ground
  5ml/1 tsp cumin seeds, roasted
    and ground
  2.5ml/½ tsp ground turmeric
  2.5ml/½ tsp cayenne pepper
  5–10ml/1–2 tsp plain
    (all-purpose) flour
  600ml/1 pint/2½ cups fish stock
  120ml/4fl oz/½ cup double
    (heavy) cream
  salt and ground black pepper
  small bunch of fresh coriander
    (cilantro), finely chopped

COOK'S TIP
To roast spices, toss the spices in a heavy pan over a high heat until they begin to change colour and give off a nutty aroma, then tip them into a bowl.

1 Preheat the oven to 180°C/350°F/ Gas 4. Place the couscous in a bowl. Stir the salt into the warm water, then pour over the couscous, stirring. Set aside for 10 minutes.

2 Stir the sunflower oil into the harissa to make a paste, then, using your fingers, rub it into the couscous and break up any lumps. Tip into an ovenproof dish, arrange the butter over the top, cover with foil and cook in the oven for about 20 minutes.

3 Meanwhile, put the mussels and prawns in a pan, add the lemon juice and 50ml/2fl oz/¼ cup water, cover and cook for 3–4 minutes, shaking the pan, until the mussels have opened. Drain the shellfish, reserving the liquor, and discard any closed mussels.

4 Heat the butter in a large pan. Cook the shallots for 5 minutes, or until softened. Add the spices and fry for 1 minute. Off the heat, stir in the flour, the fish stock and shellfish cooking liquor. Bring to the boil, stirring. Add the cream and simmer, stirring occasionally, for about 10 minutes. Season with salt and pepper.

5 Shell about two-thirds of the mussels and prawns, then add the shellfish and most of the fresh coriander to the pan. Heat through, then sprinkle with the remaining coriander.

6 Fluff up the couscous with a fork or your fingers, working in the melted butter. To serve, pass round the couscous and ladle the broth over the top.

Energy 734Kcal/3050kJ; Protein 24.5g; Carbohydrate 67.1g, of which sugars 1.5g; Fat 42.3g, of which saturates 21g; Cholesterol 223mg; Calcium 113mg; Fibre 0.2g; Sodium 360mg.

TAGINE OF MONKFISH

THE FISH IS MARINATED IN CHERMOULA, A LEMONY GARLIC AND CORIANDER PASTE, WHICH GIVES IT THAT UNMISTAKABLE MOROCCAN FLAVOUR. MONKFISH IS ROBUST ENOUGH TO HOLD ITS OWN AGAINST THE SPICES AND BLACK OLIVES, AND THE RESULT IS A VERY TASTY DISH. IT DOESN'T REALLY NEED BREAD, AS POTATOES ARE INCLUDED, BUT YOU MAY NOT BE ABLE TO RESIST MOPPING UP THE JUICES.

SERVES FOUR

INGREDIENTS
  900g/2lb monkfish tail, cut
    into chunks
  15–20 small new potatoes, scrubbed,
    scraped or peeled
  45–60ml/3–4 tbsp olive oil
  4–5 garlic cloves, thinly sliced
  15–20 cherry tomatoes
  2 green (bell) peppers, grilled
    (broiled) until black, skinned,
    seeded and cut into strips
  large handful of kalamata or fleshy
    black olives
  about 100ml/3½fl oz/scant ½ cup
    water
  salt and ground black pepper
For the chermoula
  2 garlic cloves
  5ml/1 tsp coarse salt
  10ml/2 tsp ground cumin
  5ml/1 tsp paprika
  juice of 1 lemon
  small bunch of fresh coriander
    (cilantro), roughly chopped
  15ml/1 tbsp olive oil

1 Use a mortar and pestle to make the chermoula: pound the garlic with the salt to a smooth paste. Add the cumin, paprika, lemon juice and chopped coriander, and gradually mix in the oil to emulsify the mixture slightly.

2 Reserve a little chermoula for cooking, then rub the rest of the paste over the monkfish. Cover and leave to marinate in a cool place for 1 hour.

3 Par-boil the potatoes for about 10 minutes. Drain, then cut them in half lengthways. Heat the olive oil in a heavy pan and stir in the garlic. When the garlic begins to colour, add the tomatoes and cook until just softened.

4 Add the peppers to the tomatoes and garlic, together with the remaining chermoula, and season to taste.

5 Spread the potatoes over the base of a tagine, shallow pan or deep, ridged frying pan. Spoon three-quarters of the tomato and pepper mixture over and place the marinated fish chunks on top, with their marinade.

6 Spoon the rest of the tomato and pepper mixture on top of the fish and add the olives. Drizzle a little extra olive oil over the dish and pour in the water.

7 Heat until simmering, cover the tagine or pan with a lid and cook over a medium heat for about 15 minutes, until the fish is cooked through. Serve with fresh, warm crusty bread to mop up the delicious juices.

Energy 406Kcal/1710kJ; Protein 39.6g; Carbohydrate 25.2g, of which sugars 6.5g; Fat 17.1g, of which saturates 2.7g; Cholesterol 32mg; Calcium 98mg; Fibre 5.4g; Sodium 915mg.

SYRIAN BAKED FISH WITH TAHINI

TAHINI IS A SESAME SEED PASTE THAT IS POPULAR THROUGHOUT THE ARAB COUNTRIES IN BOTH SWEET AND SAVOURY DISHES. MOST PEOPLE KNOW IT AS AN INGREDIENT IN AUTHENTIC HUMMUS, BUT IT IS ALSO VERY GOOD WITH FISH. THIS RECIPE COMES FROM TARTOUS, A FISHING TOWN ON SYRIA'S MEDITERRANEAN COASTLINE.

SERVES SIX

INGREDIENTS
    6 cod or haddock fillets
    juice of 2 lemons
    60ml/4 tbsp olive oil
    2 large onions, chopped
    250ml/8fl oz/1 cup tahini paste
    1 garlic clove, crushed
    45–60ml/3–4 tbsp water
    salt and ground black pepper
    boiled rice and a green salad,
      to serve

1 Preheat the oven to 180°C/350°F/ Gas 4. Arrange the fish fillets in a shallow ovenproof dish, pour over 15ml/1 tbsp each of the lemon juice and olive oil and bake for 20 minutes.

2 Meanwhile heat the remaining oil in a large frying pan and fry the onions for 6–8 minutes, until well browned and almost crisp.

3 Put the tahini paste, garlic and seasoning in a small bowl and slowly beat in the remaining lemon juice and water, a little at a time, until the sauce is light and creamy.

4 Sprinkle the onions over the fish, pour over the tahini sauce and bake for a further 15 minutes, until the fish is cooked through and the sauce is bubbling. Serve the fish at once with boiled rice and a salad.

Energy 434Kcal/1800kJ; Protein 33.8g; Carbohydrate 0.7g, of which sugars 0.2g; Fat 32.9g, of which saturates 4.7g; Cholesterol 65mg; Calcium 296mg; Fibre 3.4g; Sodium 93mg.

EGYPTIAN BAKED FISH WITH NUTS

*THE ARABIC WORD FOR RED MULLET IS SULTAN IBRAHIM. IT IS A VERY POPULAR FISH IN THE MIDDLE
EAST AND IS OFTEN SERVED WHOLE IN THE FISH RESTAURANTS OF ALEXANDRIA AND ABU QIR ON
EGYPT'S NORTH COAST. THE SAUCE FOR THIS DISH IS MADE WITH CHOPPED HAZELNUTS AND PINE
NUTS, WHICH NOT ONLY ADD FLAVOUR, BUT ALSO THICKEN THE TOMATO AND HERB MIXTURE.*

SERVES FOUR

INGREDIENTS

45ml/3 tbsp sunflower oil
4 small red mullet or snapper, gutted
    and cleaned
1 large onion, finely chopped
75g/3oz/½ cup hazelnuts, chopped
75g/3oz/½ cup pine nuts
3–4 tomatoes, sliced
45–60ml/3–4 tbsp finely chopped
    fresh parsley
250ml/8fl oz/1 cup fish stock
salt and ground black pepper
fresh parsley sprigs, to garnish
cooked new potatoes or rice, and
    vegetables or salad, to serve

1 Preheat the oven to 190°C/375°F/
Gas 5. Heat 30ml/2 tbsp of the oil in a
frying pan and fry the fish, two at a
time, until crisp on both sides.

2 Meanwhile, heat the remaining oil in a
large pan or flameproof casserole and
fry the onion for 3–4 minutes, until
golden. Add the chopped hazelnuts and
pine nuts and stir-fry for a few minutes.

3 Stir in the tomatoes, cook for a few
minutes and then add the chopped
parsley, seasoning and stock and
simmer for 10–15 minutes, stirring
occasionally.

4 Place the fish in an ovenproof dish
and spoon the sauce over. Bake in the
oven for 20 minutes, until the fish is
cooked through and flakes easily when
tested with a knite.

5 Serve the fish immediately,
accompanied by cooked new potatoes
or rice, and vegetables or salad.

VARIATION
Other small whole fish, such as snapper
or trout, can be used for this recipe if
mullet is unavailable.

Energy 470Kcal/1952kJ; Protein 25.8g; Carbohydrate 10.4g, of which sugars 8.3g; Fat 36.4g, of which saturates 2.9g; Cholesterol 0mg; Calcium 166mg; Fibre 4.9g; Sodium 108mg.

LEBANESE FISH WITH RICE

THIS IS A FINE EXAMPLE OF SAADIYEH, WHICH MEANS A PLAIN FISH DISH WITH RICE. IT IS IMPORTANT TO USE A GOOD QUALITY FISH STOCK, PREFERABLY ONE WHICH YOU HAVE MADE YOURSELF FROM SCRAPS PURCHASED FROM THE FISHMONGER AT THE SAME TIME AS YOU BOUGHT THE COD.

SERVES FOUR TO SIX

INGREDIENTS
   juice of 1 lemon
   45ml/3 tbsp olive oil
   900g/2lb cod steaks
   4 large onions, chopped
   5ml/1 tsp ground cumin
   2–3 saffron threads
   1 litre/1¾ pints/4 cups fish stock
   450g/1lb/2¼ cups basmati or other
     long grain rice
   50g/2oz/⅓ cup pine nuts,
     lightly toasted
   salt and ground black pepper
   fresh flat leaf parsley sprigs,
     to garnish

1 Whisk together the lemon juice and 15ml/1 tbsp of the oil in a shallow, non-metallic dish. Add the fish, turn to coat well, then cover and leave to marinate for 30 minutes.

2 Heat the remaining oil in a large pan or flameproof casserole and fry the onions for 5–6 minutes, until golden, stirring occasionally.

3 Drain the fish, reserving the marinade, and add to the pan. Fry for 1–2 minutes each side until golden, then add the cumin and saffron.

4 Pour in the fish stock, the reserved marinade and a little salt and pepper. Bring to the boil and then simmer very gently over a low heat for 5–10 minutes, until the fish is nearly done.

5 Transfer the fish to a plate and keep warm, then add the rice to the stock. Bring to the boil and then reduce the heat and simmer very gently for 15 minutes, until nearly all the stock has been absorbed.

6 Arrange the fish over the rice and cover the pan. Cook over a low heat for a further 15–20 minutes.

7 Transfer the fish to a plate, then spoon the rice on to a large, warmed, flat dish and arrange the fish steaks on top. Sprinkle the fish with toasted pine nuts and garnish with parsley sprigs. Serve immediately.

COOK'S TIP
Take care when cooking the rice that the pan does not boil dry. Check it occasionally and add more stock or water if it becomes necessary.

Energy 834Kcal/3483kJ; Protein 54.3g; Carbohydrate 110g, of which sugars 14.5g; Fat 19.5g, of which saturates 2g; Cholesterol 104mg; Calcium 106mg; Fibre 3.7g; Sodium 143mg.

TURKISH COLD FISH

WHOLE FISH, COOKED IN A FLAVOURSOME SAUCE AND SERVED COLD, OFTEN FORM THE CENTREPIECE OF A MIDDLE EASTERN MEAL. THIS VERSION FROM TURKEY CAN ALSO BE MADE USING MACKEREL.

SERVES FOUR

INGREDIENTS
    60ml/4 tbsp olive oil
    900g/2lb red mullet or snapper
    2 onions, sliced
    1 green (bell) pepper, seeded
      and sliced
    1 red (bell) pepper, seeded and sliced
    3 garlic cloves, crushed
    15ml/1 tbsp tomato purée (paste)
    50ml/2fl oz/¼ cup fish stock
      or water
    5–6 tomatoes, skinned and sliced or
      400g/14oz can chopped tomatoes
    30ml/2 tbsp chopped fresh parsley
    30ml/2 tbsp lemon juice
    5ml/1 tsp paprika
    15–20 green and black olives
    salt and ground black pepper
    fresh bread and salad, to serve

1 Heat 30ml/2 tbsp of the oil in a large, flameproof roasting pan or frying pan and fry the fish on both sides, until golden brown. Remove from the pan, cover and keep warm.

2 Heat the remaining oil in the roasting pan or frying pan and fry the onions for 2–3 minutes, until slightly softened. Add the sliced peppers and continue cooking for 3–4 minutes, then add the garlic and stir-fry for a further minute.

3 Blend the tomato purée with the fish stock or water and stir into the pan with the tomatoes, chopped parsley, lemon juice, paprika and seasoning. Simmer gently without boiling for 15 minutes, stirring occasionally.

4 Return the fish to the roasting pan or frying pan and cover with the sauce. Cook for 10 minutes, then add the olives and cook for a further 5 minutes, until just cooked through.

5 Transfer the fish to a serving dish and pour the sauce over the top. Allow to cool, then cover and chill until completely cold. Serve cold with bread and salad.

VARIATION
One large fish looks spectacular, but it is tricky to both cook and serve. If you prefer, buy four smaller fish and cook for a shorter time, until just tender and cooked through but not overdone.

Energy 352Kcal/1466kJ; Protein 25g; Carbohydrate 15.8g, of which sugars 13.7g; Fat 21.5g, of which saturates 2.5g; Cholesterol 0mg; Calcium 158mg; Fibre 5.3g; Sodium 1124mg.

RED MULLET WITH CHERMOULA

THE CORIANDER AND CHILLI CHERMOULA MARINADE GIVES THIS DISH ITS DISTINCT FLAVOUR. THE OLIVES AND PRESERVED LEMON ADD A TOUCH OF EXCITEMENT. ON THEIR OWN, THESE MULLET MAKE A DELICIOUS APPETIZER. SERVED WITH SAFFRON COUSCOUS AND A CRISP, HERB-FILLED SALAD, THEY ARE DELICIOUS AS A MAIN COURSE. CHOOSE LARGER FISH IF YOU WISH.

SERVES FOUR

INGREDIENTS
  30–45ml/2–3 tbsp olive oil, plus
    extra for brushing
  1 onion, chopped
  1 carrot, chopped
  ½ preserved lemon, finely chopped
  4 plum tomatoes, skinned
    and chopped
  600ml/1 pint/2½ cups fish stock
    or water
  3–4 new potatoes, peeled and diced
  4 small red mullet or snapper, gutted
    and filleted
  handful of black olives, pitted
    and halved
  small bunch of fresh coriander
    (cilantro), chopped
  small bunch of fresh mint, chopped
  salt and ground black pepper
For the chermoula
  small bunch of fresh coriander
    (cilantro), finely chopped
  2–3 garlic cloves, chopped
  5–10ml/1–2 tsp ground cumin
  pinch of saffron threads
  60ml/4 tbsp olive oil
  juice of 1 lemon
  1 hot red chilli, seeded and chopped
  5ml/1 tsp salt

1 To make the chermoula, pound the ingredients in a mortar with a pestle, or process them together in a food processor, then set aside.

2 Heat the olive oil in a pan. Add the onion and carrot and cook until softened but not browned. Stir in half the preserved lemon, along with 30ml/ 2 tbsp of the chermoula, the tomatoes and the stock or water.

3 Bring to the boil, then reduce the heat, cover and simmer gently for about 30 minutes. Add the potatoes and simmer for a further 10 minutes, until they are tender.

4 Preheat the grill (broiler) on the hottest setting and brush a baking sheet or grill pan with oil. Brush the fish fillets with olive oil and a little chermoula. Season with salt and pepper, then place skin side up, on the sheet or pan and cook under the grill for 5–6 minutes.

5 Meanwhile, stir in the olives, the remaining chermoula and preserved lemon into the sauce and check the seasoning. Serve the fish fillets in wide bowls, spoon the sauce over and sprinkle liberally with chopped coriander and mint.

Energy 374Kcal/1558kJ; Protein 24.7g; Carbohydrate 13.8g, of which sugars 7.2g; Fat 24.9g, of which saturates 2.9g; Cholesterol 0mg; Calcium 193mg; Fibre 4.7g; Sodium 704mg.

FISH IN VINE LEAVES WITH DIPPING SAUCE

ALMOST ANY TYPE OF FIRM WHITE FISH CAN BE USED TO MAKE THESE KEBABS. THE FISH IS FIRST MARINATED IN CHERMOULA AND THEN WRAPPED IN VINE LEAVES TO SEAL IN THE FLAVOURS. WHEN COOKED, THE VINE LEAF WRAPPER BECOMES CRISP, CONTRASTING BEAUTIFULLY WITH ITS SUCCULENT AND AROMATIC CONTENTS. THE SWEET AND SOUR SAUCE IS PERFECT FOR DIPPING.

SERVES FOUR

INGREDIENTS
   about 30 preserved vine leaves
   4–5 large white fish fillets, skinned,
      such as haddock, ling or monkfish
For the chermoula
   small bunch of fresh coriander
      (cilantro), finely chopped
   2–3 garlic cloves, chopped
   5–10ml/1–2 tsp ground cumin
   60ml/4 tbsp olive oil
   juice of 1 lemon
   salt
For the dipping sauce
   50ml/2fl oz/¼ cup white wine
      vinegar or lemon juice
   115g/4oz/generous ½ cup caster
      (superfine) sugar
   15–30ml/1–2 tbsp water
   pinch of saffron threads
   1 onion, finely chopped
   2 garlic cloves, finely chopped
   2–3 spring onions (scallions),
      thinly sliced
   25g/1oz fresh root ginger, peeled
      and grated
   2 hot fresh red or green chillies,
      seeded and thinly sliced
   small bunch of fresh coriander
      (cilantro), finely chopped
   small bunch of mint, finely chopped

1 To make the chermoula, pound the ingredients in a mortar with a pestle, or process in a food processor.

2 Rinse the vine leaves in a bowl, then soak them in cold water. Remove any bones from the fish and cut each fillet into about eight bitesize pieces. Coat the pieces of fish in the chermoula, cover and chill for 1 hour.

3 Meanwhile, prepare the dipping sauce. Heat the vinegar or lemon juice with the sugar and water until the sugar has dissolved. Bring to the boil and boil for about 1 minute, then leave to cool. Add the remaining ingredients and mix well to combine. Spoon the sauce into small individual bowls and set aside until ready to serve.

4 Drain the vine leaves and pat dry on kitchen paper. Lay a vine leaf flat on the work surface and place a piece of marinated fish in the centre. Fold the edges of the leaf over the fish, then wrap up the fish and leaf into a small parcel. Repeat with the remaining pieces of fish and vine leaves. Thread the parcels on to kebab skewers and brush with any leftover marinade.

5 Heat the grill (broiler) on the hottest setting and cook the kebabs for 2–3 minutes on each side. Serve immediately, with the sweet and sour chilli sauce for dipping.

Energy 295Kcal/1232kJ; Protein 40.7g; Carbohydrate 3.8g, of which sugars 2.3g; Fat 13g, of which saturates 1.8g; Cholesterol 98mg; Calcium 111mg; Fibre 1.6g; Sodium 139mg.

CHICKEN DISHES

In the Middle East, chicken is second only to lamb in popularity, and a similar situation exists in Africa. This chapter shows the very different approaches adopted by cooks on either side of the Mediterranean divide. From Morocco come sweet and fruity tagines and a roast with a spicy rub. Senegal contributes a tangy lemon chicken dish, while Sierra Leone's Palaver Chicken is well worth making a fuss about. Crossing to Iran, we discover khoresh, a soup-like stew served over rice, together with a delicious chicken and yogurt dish.

CHICKEN KDRA WITH CHICKPEAS AND ALMONDS

A KDRA IS A TYPE OF TAGINE THAT IS TRADITIONALLY COOKED WITH SMEN, A STRONGLY FLAVOURED CLARIFIED BUTTER, AND PLENTY OF ONIONS. THE ALMONDS IN THIS RECIPE ARE PRE-COOKED UNTIL SOFT, ADDING AN INTERESTING TEXTURE AND FLAVOUR TO THE LIGHTLY SPICED CHICKEN.

SERVES FOUR

INGREDIENTS
  75g/3oz/½ cup blanched almonds
  75g/3oz/½ cup chickpeas,
    soaked overnight and drained
  4 part-boned chicken breast
    portions, skinned
  50g/2oz/¼ cup butter
  2.5ml/½ tsp saffron threads
  2 Spanish onions, thinly sliced
  900ml/1½ pints/3¾ cups
    chicken stock
  1 small cinnamon stick
  60ml/4 tbsp chopped fresh flat leaf
    parsley, plus extra to garnish
  lemon juice, to taste
  salt and ground black pepper

1 Place the almonds in a pan of water and simmer for 1½–2 hours until fairly soft, then drain and set aside.

2 Cook the chickpeas in a pan of boiling water for 1–1½ hours until they are completely soft. Drain the chickpeas, then place in a bowl of cold water and rub with your fingers to remove the skins. Discard the skins and drain.

3 Place the chicken portions in a pan, together with the butter, half of the saffron, salt and plenty of black pepper. Heat gently, stirring, until the butter has melted.

4 Add the onions and stock, bring to the boil and then add the chickpeas and cinnamon stick. Cover and cook very gently for 45–60 minutes.

5 Transfer the chicken to a serving plate and keep warm. Bring the sauce to the boil and simmer until reduced, stirring frequently. Add the almonds, parsley and remaining saffron and cook for 2–3 minutes. Sharpen the sauce with a little lemon juice, then pour over the chicken and serve, garnished with extra parsley.

CHICKEN WITH TOMATOES AND HONEY

COOKING THE TOMATOES VERY SLOWLY WITH THE AROMATIC SPICES GIVES THE SAUCE FOR THIS CHICKEN DISH A WONDERFULLY INTENSE FLAVOUR, WHICH MELLOWS WHEN THE HONEY IS STIRRED IN.

SERVES FOUR

INGREDIENTS
  30ml/2 tbsp sunflower oil
  25g/1oz/2 tbsp butter
  4 chicken quarters or 1 whole
    chicken, quartered
  1 onion, grated or very
    finely chopped
  1 garlic clove, crushed
  5ml/1 tsp ground cinnamon
  good pinch of ground ginger
  1.3–1.6kg/3–3½lb tomatoes,
    skinned, cored and roughly chopped
  30ml/2 tbsp clear honey
  50g/2oz/⅓ cup blanched almonds
  15ml/1 tbsp sesame seeds
  salt and ground black pepper
  Moroccan corn bread, to serve

1 Heat the oil and butter in a large, flameproof casserole. Add the chicken quarters and cook over a medium heat for about 3 minutes, until browned.

2 Add the onion, garlic, cinnamon, ginger, tomatoes and seasoning, and heat gently until the tomatoes begin to bubble.

3 Lower the heat, cover and simmer very gently for 1 hour, stirring and turning the chicken occasionally, until it is completely cooked through.

4 Transfer the chicken pieces to a plate and then increase the heat and cook the tomatoes until the sauce is reduced to a thick purée, stirring frequently. Stir in the honey, cook for 1 minute and then return the chicken to the pan and cook for 2–3 minutes to heat through. Dry-fry the almonds and sesame seeds or toast under the grill (broiler).

5 Transfer the chicken and sauce to a warmed serving dish and sprinkle with the almonds and sesame seeds. Serve with Moroccan corn bread.

TOP Energy 477Kcal/1994kJ; Protein 46g; Carbohydrate 21g, of which sugars 8.7g; Fat 23.9g, of which saturates 7.9g; Cholesterol 132mg; Calcium 146mg; Fibre 5.9g; Sodium 185mg.
BOTTOM Energy 610Kcal/2539kJ; Protein 37.7g; Carbohydrate 16.8g, of which sugars 16.4g; Fat 44g, of which saturates 11.4g; Cholesterol 206mg; Calcium 92mg; Fibre 4.5g; Sodium 211mg.

EAST AFRICAN ROAST CHICKEN

RUBBING THE SKIN ON THE CHICKEN WITH A SPICY HERB BUTTER AND THEN MARINATING IT OVERNIGHT GIVES IT A WONDERFUL FLAVOUR. BASTE IT FREQUENTLY WHILE IT COOKS.

SERVES SIX

INGREDIENTS
  1.8–2kg/4–4½lb chicken
  30ml/2 tbsp softened butter, plus
    extra for basting
  3 garlic cloves, crushed
  5ml/1 tsp ground black pepper
  5ml/1 tsp ground turmeric
  2.5ml/½ tsp ground cumin
  5ml/1 tsp dried thyme
  15ml/1 tbsp finely chopped fresh
    coriander (cilantro)
  60ml/4 tbsp thick coconut milk
  60ml/4 tbsp medium-dry sherry
  5ml/1 tsp tomato purée (paste)
  salt and chilli powder

1 Remove and discard the giblets from the chicken, if necessary, rinse out the cavity and pat the skin dry. Put the butter and all the remaining ingredients in a bowl and mix together well to form a thick paste.

2 Ease the skin of the chicken away from the flesh and push in some of the herb and butter mixture. Rub more of the mixture over the skin, legs and wings of the chicken.

3 Place the chicken in a roasting pan, cover loosely with foil and marinate overnight in the fridge.

VARIATION
Use ground coriander instead of ground cumin or dried thyme.

4 Preheat the oven to 190°C/375°F/ Gas 5. Cover the chicken with clean foil and roast for 1 hour, then turn the chicken over and baste with the pan juices. Cover again with foil and roast for a further 30 minutes.

5 Remove the foil and place the chicken breast side up. Rub with a little extra butter and roast for a further 10–15 minutes, until the meat juices run clear and the skin is golden brown. Serve with a rice dish or a salad.

YASSA CHICKEN

OFTEN DESCRIBED AS THE NATIONAL DISH OF SENEGAL, YASSA CAN BE MADE WITH CHICKEN, TURKEY OR FISH. THE LEMON JUICE MARINADE GIVES THE SAUCE ITS TYPICALLY TANGY TASTE.

SERVES FOUR

INGREDIENTS
  150ml/¼ pint/⅔ cup lemon juice
  60ml/4 tbsp malt vinegar
  3 onions, sliced
  60ml/4 tbsp groundnut (peanut) or
    vegetable oil
  1kg/2¼lb chicken pieces
  1 fresh thyme sprig
  1 fresh green chilli, seeded and
    finely chopped
  2 bay leaves
  450ml/¾ pint/scant 2 cups
    chicken stock

VARIATION
For a less tangy flavour, you can add less lemon juice, although it does mellow after cooking.

1 Mix the lemon juice, vinegar, onions and 30ml/2 tbsp of the oil together, place the chicken pieces in a dish and pour over the lemon mixture. Cover and leave in a cool place for 3 hours.

2 Heat the remaining oil in a large pan and fry the chicken pieces for 4–5 minutes, until browned.

3 Add the marinated onions to the chicken. Fry for 3 minutes, then add the marinade, thyme, chilli, bay leaves and half the stock.

4 Reduce the heat, cover the pan and simmer for about 35 minutes, until the chicken is cooked, add more stock as the sauce evaporates. Serve hot.

TOP Energy 439Kcal/1824kJ; Protein 43.3g; Carbohydrate 1.2g, of which sugars 1.2g; Fat 27.9g, of which saturates 10.7g; Cholesterol 206mg; Calcium 23mg; Fibre 0g; Sodium 211mg.
BOTTOM Energy 462Kcal/1918kJ; Protein 37.4g; Carbohydrate 8.9g, of which sugars 6.3g; Fat 31g, of which saturates 8g; Cholesterol 163mg; Calcium 43mg; Fibre 1.6g; Sodium 141mg.

PALAVER CHICKEN

IT IS SAID THAT THIS STEW GAINED ITS INTRIGUING NAME BECAUSE OF THE ARGUMENTS THAT SURROUNDED THE RIGHT WAY TO COOK IT. CONTROVERSY STILL RAGES, WITH VARIATIONS EXISTING IN GHANA, LIBERIA AND SIERRA LEONE. PALAVER CAN BE MADE WITH BEEF, CHICKEN OR FISH AND ALWAYS INCLUDES A GREEN VEGETABLE SUCH AS BITTERLEAF. SPINACH IS SUBSTITUTED HERE.

SERVES FOUR

INGREDIENTS

675g/1½lb skinless, boneless chicken breast fillets
2 garlic cloves, crushed
30ml/2 tbsp butter or margarine
30ml/2 tbsp palm or vegetable oil
1 onion, finely chopped
4 tomatoes, skinned and chopped
30ml/2 tbsp peanut butter
600ml/1 pint/2½ cups chicken stock or water
1 fresh thyme sprig or 5ml/1 tsp dried thyme
225g/8oz frozen leaf spinach, defrosted and chopped
1 fresh red or green chilli, seeded and chopped
salt and ground black pepper

1 Cut the chicken breast fillets into thin slices, place in a bowl and stir in the garlic and a little salt and pepper.

2 Melt the butter or margarine in a large frying pan and fry the chicken over a medium heat, turning once or twice to brown evenly. Transfer to a plate using a slotted spoon and set aside.

3 Heat the oil in a large pan and fry the onion and tomatoes over a high heat for 5 minutes, until soft.

4 Reduce the heat, add the peanut butter and half of the stock or water and blend together well.

5 Cook for 4–5 minutes, stirring all the time to prevent the peanut butter burning, then add the remaining stock or water, thyme, spinach, chilli and seasoning. Stir in the chicken slices and cook over a medium heat for about 10–15 minutes, until the chicken is cooked through.

6 Pour the chicken mixture into a warmed serving dish and serve with boiled yams, rice or ground rice.

COOK'S TIPS

If you're short of time, frozen spinach is more convenient, but chopped fresh spinach, adds a fresher flavour to this recipe. Egusi – ground melon seed – can be used instead of peanut butter.

Energy 387Kcal/1615kJ; Protein 41.1g; Carbohydrate 7.2g, of which sugars 5.8g; Fat 21.7g, of which saturates 7.3g; Cholesterol 89mg; Calcium 131mg; Fibre 2.9g; Sodium 280mg.

KHORESH FESENJAN

A KHORESH IS A THICK STEW-LIKE SAUCE WHICH IS SERVED OVER RICE IN IRAN. THIS FAMOUS VERSION OWES ITS SUPERB FLAVOUR TO POMEGRANATES AND WALNUTS. KHORESH FESENJAN IS OFTEN SERVED ON FESTIVE OCCASIONS, WHEN WILD DUCK IS USED INSTEAD OF CHICKEN.

SERVES FOUR

INGREDIENTS

30ml/2 tbsp vegetable oil
4 chicken portions (leg or breast)
1 large onion, grated
250ml/8fl oz/1 cup water
115g/4oz/1 cup finely
 chopped walnuts 石榴
75ml/5 tbsp pomegranate purée
15ml/1 tbsp tomato purée (paste)
30ml/2 tbsp lemon juice
15ml/1 tbsp granulated sugar
3–4 saffron threads dissolved in
 15ml/1 tbsp boiling water
salt and ground black pepper
Persian rice and salad leaves,
 to serve

1 Heat 15ml/1 tbsp of the oil in a large pan or flameproof casserole and sauté the chicken portions until golden brown.

2 Add half of the grated onion to the chicken and fry until slightly softened, then add the water and seasoning and bring to the boil. Cover the pan, reduce the heat and simmer for 15 minutes.

3 Meanwhile, heat the remaining oil in a small pan or frying pan and fry the remaining onion for 2–3 minutes, until soft.

4 Add the chopped walnuts to the onion and fry for a further 2–3 minutes over a low heat, stirring frequently and taking great care that the walnuts do not burn.

5 Stir in the pomegranate and tomato purées, lemon juice, sugar and the saffron liquid. Season to taste and then simmer over a low heat for 5 minutes.

6 Pour the walnut sauce over the chicken, ensuring all the pieces are well covered. Cover and simmer for 30–35 minutes, until the meat is cooked and the oil of the walnuts has risen to the surface.

7 Serve immediately with Persian rice and salad leaves.

COOK'S TIP
Pomegranate purée is available from Middle Eastern delicatessens.

Energy 460Kcal/1918kJ; Protein 42.1g; Carbohydrate 12.8g, of which sugars 11.2g; Fat 27g, of which saturates 2.7g; Cholesterol 105mg; Calcium 60mg; Fibre 2.5g; Sodium 148mg.

CHICKEN AND PRESERVED LEMON TAGINE

MOROCCAN TAGINES ARE SUBTLY FLAVOURED STEWS WHICH ARE COOKED IN THE CONICAL-LIDDED DISHES FROM WHICH THEY GET THEIR NAME. THIS IS THE MOST FAMOUS TAGINE RECIPE, IN WHICH THE PRESERVED LEMON'S MELLOW FLAVOUR CONTRASTS WITH THE EARTHINESS OF THE OLIVES.

SERVES FOUR

INGREDIENTS

    30ml/2 tbsp olive oil
    1 Spanish onion, chopped
    3 garlic cloves
    1cm/½in fresh root ginger, peeled
      and grated, or 2.5ml/½ tsp
      ground ginger
    2.5–5ml/½–1 tsp ground cinnamon
    pinch of saffron threads
    4 chicken quarters, preferably
      breasts, halved if liked
    750ml/1¼ pints/3 cups
      chicken stock
    30ml/2 tbsp chopped fresh
      coriander (cilantro)
    30ml/2 tbsp chopped fresh parsley
    1 preserved lemon
    115g/4oz/⅔ cup Moroccan tan olives
    salt and ground black pepper
    lemon wedges and fresh coriander
      (cilantro) sprigs, to garnish

1 Heat the oil in a large flameproof casserole and fry the onion for 6–8 minutes over a moderate heat until lightly golden, stirring occasionally.

2 Meanwhile, crush the garlic and blend with the ginger, cinnamon, saffron and a little salt and pepper. Stir into the pan and fry for 1 minute.

3 Add the chicken quarters to the pan, in batches if necessary, and fry over a medium heat for 2–3 minutes, until lightly browned.

4 Add the stock, chopped coriander and parsley, bring to the boil and then cover and simmer very gently for 45 minutes, until the chicken is tender.

5 Rinse the preserved lemon, discard the flesh and cut the peel into small pieces. Stir into the pan with the olives and simmer for a further 15 minutes, until the chicken is very tender.

6 Transfer the chicken to a plate and keep warm. Bring the sauce to the boil and bubble for 3–4 minutes, until reduced and fairly thick.

7 Pour the sauce over the chicken and serve, garnished with lemon wedges and coriander sprigs.

Energy 474Kcal/1967kJ; Protein 36.3g; Carbohydrate 5.3g, of which sugars 3.8g; Fat 34.3g, of which saturates 8.1g; Cholesterol 209mg; Calcium 83mg; Fibre 2.6g; Sodium 807mg.

MARRAKESH ROAST CHICKEN

MOROCCANS INVENTED THE SPICE RUB LONG BEFORE IT BECAME A TRENDY DELI ITEM. FOR THIS TRADITIONAL DISH, A PASTE MADE FROM SHALLOTS, GARLIC, FRESH HERBS AND SPICES IS RUBBED INTO THE CHICKEN SKIN A FEW HOURS BEFORE ROASTING, SO THE FLAVOUR PERMEATES THE FLESH.

SERVES FOUR TO SIX

INGREDIENTS
- 1.8–2kg/4–4½lb chicken
- 2 small shallots
- 1 garlic clove
- 1 fresh parsley sprig
- 1 fresh coriander (cilantro) sprig
- 5ml/1 tsp salt
- 7.5ml/1½ tsp paprika
- pinch of cayenne pepper
- 5–7.5ml/1–1½ tsp ground cumin
- about 40g/1½oz/3 tbsp butter, at room temperature
- ½–1 lemon (optional)
- sprigs of fresh parsley or coriander (cilantro), to garnish

VARIATION
If you are unable to buy shallots, use one small onion instead.

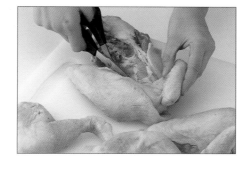

1 Remove and discard the chicken giblets, if necessary, and rinse out the cavity with cold running water. Unless cooking it whole, cut the chicken in half or into quarters using poultry shears or a sharp knife.

2 Place the shallots, garlic, herbs, salt and spices in a blender or food processor and process until the shallots are finely chopped. Add the butter and process to make a smooth paste.

3 Thoroughly rub the paste over the skin of the chicken and then allow it to stand in a cool place for 1–2 hours.

4 Preheat the oven to 200°C/400°F/ Gas 6 and place the chicken in a roasting pan. If using, quarter the lemon and place one or two quarters around the chicken pieces (or in the body cavity if the chicken is whole) and squeeze a little juice over the skin.

5 Roast the chicken in the oven for 1–1¼ hours (2–2¼ hours for a whole bird), until the chicken is cooked through and the meat juices run clear. Baste occasionally during cooking with the juices in the roasting pan. If the skin browns too quickly, cover the chicken loosely with foil or greaseproof (waxed) paper.

6 Allow the chicken to stand for 5–10 minutes, covered in foil, before serving, and then serve garnished with sprigs of fresh parsley or coriander.

Energy 559Kcal/2323kJ; Protein 54.1g; Carbohydrate 0.2g, of which sugars 0.2g; Fat 37.9g, of which saturates 15.3g; Cholesterol 265mg; Calcium 25mg; Fibre 0.1g; Sodium 759mg.

JOLOFF CHICKEN AND RICE

FEW VISITORS TO WEST AFRICA FAIL TO TRY THIS FESTIVE CHICKEN AND RICE DISH. IT IS RICHLY FLAVOURED WITH TOMATOES AND CAN BE MADE WITH CHICKEN, BEEF OR JUST WITH VEGETABLES.

SERVES FOUR

INGREDIENTS

1kg/2¼lb chicken, cut into
  4–6 pieces
2 garlic cloves, crushed
5ml/1 tsp dried thyme
30ml/2 tbsp palm or vegetable oil
400g/14oz can chopped tomatoes
15ml/1 tbsp tomato purée (paste)
1 onion, chopped
450ml/¾ pint/scant 2 cups
  chicken stock
30ml/2 tbsp dried shrimps, ground
1 fresh green chilli, seeded and
  finely chopped
350g/12oz/1¾ cups long grain
  rice, washed

1 Rub the chicken with the garlic and thyme and set aside.

2 Heat the oil in a pan and brown the chicken pieces. Add the tomatoes, tomato purée and onion. Cook over a medium-high heat for about 5 minutes, stirring occasionally at first then more frequently as it thickens.

3 Add the stock and stir well. Bring to the boil, then reduce the heat, cover and simmer for 40 minutes. Add the shrimps and chilli. Cook for 5 minutes.

4 Put the rice in a pan. Scoop 300ml/½ pint/1¼ cups of tomato stock from the chicken into a measuring jug (cup), top up with water to 450ml/¾ pint/scant 2 cups and add to the rice. Cook for 10 minutes to partly absorb the liquid

5 Place a piece of foil on top of the rice, cover and cook over a low heat for 10 minutes, adding a little more water if necessary. Transfer the chicken pieces to a serving plate. Simmer the sauce until reduced by half. Pour over the chicken and serve with the rice.

Energy 719Kcal/2998kJ; Protein 44.1g; Carbohydrate 76.3g, of which sugars 5.4g; Fat 25.9g, of which saturates 7.4g; Cholesterol 163mg; Calcium 54mg; Fibre 1.3g; Sodium 187mg.

KUKU

THIS DELICIOUS TANGY CHICKEN STEW COMES FROM KENYA. THE SAUCE IS THICKENED WITH MASHED MUNG BEANS, AND FLAVOURED WITH CHILLI AND COCONUT MILK.

SERVES FOUR TO SIX

INGREDIENTS

6 chicken thighs or pieces
2.5–4ml/½–¾ tsp ground ginger
50g/2oz dried mung beans
60ml/4 tbsp corn oil
2 onions, finely chopped
2 garlic cloves, crushed
5 tomatoes, skinned and chopped
1 fresh green chilli, seeded and
  finely chopped
30ml/2 tbsp lemon juice
300ml/½ pint/1¼ cups coconut milk
300ml/½ pint/1¼ cups water
15ml/1 tbsp chopped fresh
  coriander (cilantro)
salt and ground black pepper

1 Season the chicken pieces with the ginger and a little salt and pepper and set aside in a cool place. Boil the mung beans in plenty of water for 35 minutes until soft. Drain and mash.

2 Heat the oil in a large pan over a medium heat and fry the chicken pieces, in batches if necessary, until evenly browned. Transfer to a plate and set aside. Reserve the juices in the pan.

3 In the same pan, fry the onions and garlic for 5 minutes, then add the chopped tomatoes and green chilli and cook for a further 1–2 minutes, stirring all the time. Add the mashed mung beans and lemon juice.

4 Pour the coconut milk in to the pan. Simmer for 5 minutes, then add the chicken pieces and a little water if the sauce is too thick. Stir in the chopped coriander and simmer for about 35 minutes, until the chicken is cooked through. Serve with a green vegetable and rice or chapatis.

Energy 257Kcal/1089kJ; Protein 41.1g; Carbohydrate 18.7g, of which sugars 11.3g; Fat 2.6g, of which saturates 0.8g; Cholesterol 105mg; Calcium 81mg; Fibre 3.7g; Sodium 188mg.

BISTILLA

ONE OF THE MOST ELABORATE DISHES IN MOROCCAN CUISINE, BISTILLA OFTEN FORMS THE CENTREPIECE AT A FEAST OR BANQUET. IT IS TRADITIONALLY MADE USING PIGEON, COOKED WITH SPICES AND LAYERED WITH THE WAFER-THIN PASTRY KNOWN AS OUARKA. THE PIE IS THEN COOKED OVER HOT COALS. THIS IS A SIMPLIFIED VERSION, USING FILO PASTRY, WHICH IS MUCH EASIER TO HANDLE THAN OUARKA. THE DUSTING OF CINNAMON AND ICING SUGAR ON TOP OF THE PIE IS A TYPICAL NORTH AFRICAN REFINEMENT, ALSO USED ON BRIOUATES.

SERVES FOUR

INGREDIENTS
30ml/2 tbsp sunflower oil, plus extra
   for brushing
25g/1oz/2 tbsp butter
3 chicken quarters, preferably breasts
1½ Spanish onions, grated or very
   finely chopped
good pinch of ground ginger
good pinch of saffron threads
10ml/2 tsp ground cinnamon, plus
   extra for dusting
40g/1½oz/4 tbsp flaked
   (sliced) almonds
1 large bunch of fresh coriander
   (cilantro), finely chopped
1 large bunch of fresh parsley,
   finely chopped
3 eggs, beaten
about 175g/6oz filo pastry sheets
5–10ml/1–2 tsp icing (confectioners')
   sugar (optional), plus extra
   for dusting
salt and ground black pepper

1 Heat the oil and butter in a large flameproof casserole or pan until the butter is melted. Add the chicken pieces and brown for about 4 minutes.

2 Add the onions, ginger, saffron, 2.5ml/½ tsp of the cinnamon and enough water (about 300ml/½ pint/1¼ cups) so that the chicken braises, rather than boils. Season well with salt and pepper.

3 Bring to the boil and then cover and simmer very gently for 45–55 minutes, until the chicken is tender and completely cooked. Meanwhile, dry-fry the almonds in a separate small pan until golden and then set aside.

4 Transfer the chicken to a plate and, when cool enough to handle, remove and discard the skin and bones and cut the flesh into pieces.

5 Stir the chopped coriander and parsley into the pan and simmer the sauce until well reduced and thick. Add the beaten eggs and cook over a very gentle heat until the eggs are lightly scrambled.

6 Preheat the oven to 180°C/350°F/ Gas 4. Oil a shallow round ovenproof dish, about 25cm/10in in diameter.

7 Place one or two sheets of filo pastry in a single layer over the bottom of the dish (it will depend on the size of your filo pastry sheets), so that it is completely covered and the edges of the pastry sheets hang over the sides. Brush lightly with oil and make two more layers of filo, brushing with oil between the layers.

8 Place the chicken on the pastry and then spoon the egg and herb mixture on top and spread evenly.

9 Place a single layer of filo pastry on top of the filling (you may need to use more than one sheet of filo pastry).

10 Scatter the almonds over the layer of filo pastry. Sprinkle with some of the remaining cinnamon and the icing sugar, if using.

11 Fold the edges of the filo over the almonds and then make four further layers of filo (using one or two sheets of filo per layer, depending on size), brushing each layer with a little oil. Tuck the filo edges under the pie (as if you were making a bed!) and brush the top layer with oil.

12 Bake in the oven for 40–45 minutes, until golden. Dust the top with icing sugar and use the extra cinnamon to make criss-cross or diagonal lines. Serve immediately.

VARIATIONS
Use standard large onions instead of Spanish onions. Use flaked hazelnuts or whole pine nuts instead of flaked almonds.

Energy 653Kcal/2720kJ; Protein 39.2g; Carbohydrate 33.6g, of which sugars 7.1g; Fat 41.3g, of which saturates 11g; Cholesterol 321mg; Calcium 176mg; Fibre 4.4g; Sodium 224mg.

KHORESH BADEMJAN

THIS CLASSIC PERSIAN DISH, BELIEVED TO HAVE BEEN A FAVOURITE OF KINGS, IS OFTEN SERVED ON FESTIVE OCCASIONS. THE WORD BADEMJAN MEANS AUBERGINES AND THIS IS A WONDERFUL VEHICLE FOR THE DELICIOUS PURPLE VEGETABLE. CUBES OF BEEF CAN BE USED INSTEAD OF CHICKEN.

SERVES FOUR

INGREDIENTS
  30ml/2 tbsp sunflower oil
  1 whole chicken or 4 large
    chicken portions
  1 large onion, chopped
  2 garlic cloves, crushed
  400g/14oz can chopped tomatoes
  250ml/8fl oz/1 cup water
  3 aubergines (eggplants), sliced
  3 (bell) peppers, preferably red,
    green and yellow, seeded and sliced
  30ml/2 tbsp lemon juice
  15ml/1 tbsp ground cinnamon
  salt and ground black pepper
  Persian rice, to serve

1 Heat 15ml/1 tbsp of the oil in a large pan or flameproof casserole and fry the chicken or chicken portions on both sides for about 10 minutes until the skin is a golden brown.

2 Remove the chicken from the pan, and set aside on a warm plate. Add the chopped onion and fry for 4–5 minutes, until golden brown. Return the chicken to the pan.

3 Add the garlic, chopped tomatoes, water and seasoning to the chicken and onion. Bring to the boil, then reduce the heat and simmer slowly, covered, for 10 minutes.

VARIATION
Substitute 1 large red onion or 5–6 shallots instead of standard onion.

4 Meanwhile, heat the remaining oil in a frying pan and fry the aubergines in batches until lightly golden. Transfer to a plate using a slotted spoon. Add the sliced peppers to the pan and fry for a few minutes, until slightly softened.

5 Place the aubergine slices over the chicken or chicken portions and then add the peppers. Sprinkle over the lemon juice and cinnamon, then cover and continue to cook over a low heat for about 45 minutes, until the chicken is cooked.

6 Transfer the chicken to a warmed serving plate and spoon the aubergines and peppers around the edge. Reheat the sauce, if necessary, adjust the seasoning and pour over the chicken. Serve the khoresh with Persian rice.

Energy 467Kcal/1945kJ; Protein 39.9g; Carbohydrate 18.4g, of which sugars 16.2g; Fat 26.4g, of which saturates 7.7g; Cholesterol 163mg; Calcium 63mg; Fibre 5.7g; Sodium 186mg.

TAH CHIN

IRANIANS LOVE THIS RICE DISH AND OFTEN MAKE IT WITH LAMB INSTEAD OF CHICKEN. THE NAME MEANS "ARRANGED AT THE BOTTOM OF THE POT" AND REFERS TO THE WAY THE INGREDIENTS ARE LAYERED. THE YOGURT MARINADE FLAVOURS THE CHICKEN AND MAKES IT BEAUTIFULLY TENDER.

SERVES SIX

INGREDIENTS
  40g/1½oz/3 tbsp butter
  1.3–1.6kg/3–3½lb chicken
  1 large onion, chopped
  250ml/8fl oz/1 cup chicken stock
  2 eggs
  475ml/16fl oz/2 cups natural
    (plain) yogurt
  2–3 saffron threads, dissolved in
    15ml/1 tbsp boiling water
  5ml/1 tsp ground cinnamon
  450g/1lb/scant 2⅓ cups basmati
    rice, rinsed
  75g/3oz zereshk (see Cook's Tips)
  salt and ground black pepper
  herb salad, to serve

1 Melt 25g/1oz/2 tbsp of the butter in a large pan and fry the chicken and onion for 4–5 minutes, until the onion is softened and the chicken is browned.

2 Add the chicken stock and salt and pepper, bring to the boil then reduce the heat and simmer for 45 minutes, until the stock is reduced by half.

3 Remove the pan from the heat. Remove the chicken to a plate, and when cool enough to handle, skin and bone the chicken. Cut the flesh into large pieces and place in a large bowl. Discard the bones and reserve the stock.

COOK'S TIPS
Zereshk is a small sour berry that grows on trees by the waterside in the warmer part of Iran.

4 Beat the eggs and blend with the yogurt. Add the saffron liquid and ground cinnamon and season with salt and pepper. Pour over the chicken and leave to marinate for up to 2 hours.

5 Drain the rice and boil it in salted water for 5 minutes. Reduce the heat and simmer for 5 minutes until almost cooked. Drain and rinse in warm water.

6 Transfer the chicken from the yogurt mixture to a dish and mix half the rice into the yogurt.

7 Preheat the oven to 160°C/325°F/ Gas 3 and grease a large, 10cm/4in deep, ovenproof dish.

8 Place the rice and yogurt mixture in the bottom of the dish, arrange the chicken pieces in a layer on top and then add the plain rice. Sprinkle with the zereshk.

9 Mix the remaining butter with the reserved stock and pour over the rice. Cover tightly with foil and cook in the oven for 35–45 minutes.

10 Leave the dish to cool for a few minutes. Place on a cold, damp cloth which will help lift the rice from the bottom of the dish, then run a knife around the edges of the dish. Place a large flat plate over the dish and turn out. You should have a rice "cake" which can be cut into wedges. Serve hot with a herb salad.

Energy 682Kcal/2843kJ; Protein 43.4g; Carbohydrate 69g, of which sugars 8.2g; Fat 25.7g, of which saturates 10.2g; Cholesterol 220mg; Calcium 198mg; Fibre 0.6g; Sodium 250mg.

LEBANESE CHICKEN KEBABS

CHICKEN KEBABS ARE PREPARED IN MUCH THE SAME WAY ALL OVER THE MIDDLE EAST AND ARE A GREAT FAVOURITE EVERYWHERE. KEEP THE CHICKEN PIECES QUITE LARGE, SO THEY STAY MOIST.

SERVES SIX TO EIGHT

INGREDIENTS
  2 small chickens
  1 large onion, grated
  2 garlic cloves, crushed
  120ml/4fl oz/½ cup olive oil
  juice of 1 lemon
  5ml/1 tsp paprika
  2–3 saffron threads, dissolved in
    15ml/1 tbsp boiling water
  salt and ground black pepper
  naan bread or pitta bread, to serve

1 Cut the chickens into small pieces, removing the bones if preferred, and place the portions in a shallow non-metallic bowl.

2 Mix the onion, garlic, olive oil, lemon juice, paprika and saffron liquid together, and season with salt and pepper.

3 Pour the marinade over the chicken, turning the chicken so that all the pieces are coated evenly.

4 Cover the bowl loosely with clear film (plastic wrap) and leave to marinate in a cool place for at least 2 hours.

5 Thread the chicken on to long, metal skewers. If barbecuing, once the coals are ready, cook for 10–15 minutes each side. Or, if you prefer, cook under a medium-hot grill (broiler) for about 10–15 minutes each side.

6 Serve with rice and salad. Or remove boneless chicken from the skewers and serve it in pitta as a sandwich, with a garlicky yogurt sauce.

BAKED POUSSINS WITH YOGHURT AND SAFFRON

IN MIDDLE EASTERN MARKETS, CHICKENS ARE OFTEN ON THE SMALL SIDE, AND ARE OFTEN SPLIT AND SPATCHCOCKED BEFORE BEING COOKED OVER THE COALS. POUSSINS CAN BE TREATED IN THE SAME WAY, AND TASTE PARTICULARLY GOOD WHEN MARINATED IN YOGURT, SAFFRON AND OTHER SPICES.

SERVES FOUR

INGREDIENTS
  475ml/16fl oz/2 cups natural
    (plain) yogurt
  60ml/4 tbsp olive oil
  1 large onion, grated
  2 garlic cloves, crushed
  2.5ml/½ tsp paprika
  2–3 saffron threads, dissolved in
    15ml/1 tbsp boiling water
  juice of 1 lemon
  4 poussins, halved
  salt and ground black pepper
  cos or romaine lettuce salad,
    to serve

1 Blend together the yogurt, olive oil, onion, garlic, paprika, saffron liquid and lemon juice, and season with salt and pepper.

2 Place the poussin halves in a shallow, non-metallic dish, pour over the marinade and then cover and allow to marinate overnight in a cool place or for at least 4 hours in the fridge.

3 Preheat the oven to 180°C/350°F/Gas 4. Arrange the poussins in a greased ovenproof dish and bake in the oven for 30–45 minutes, basting frequently, until cooked. Serve with a lettuce salad.

COOK'S TIP
The poussins can also be cooked on a barbecue, for an authentic and even more delicious taste.

POUSSINS WITH COURGETTES AND APRICOT STUFFING

COUSCOUS ABSORBS THE LIQUID FROM THE COURGETTES AND MAKES A SUPERB STUFFING. QUAIL AND PARTRIDGE ARE POPULAR IN THE MIDDLE EAST, AND CAN BE USED INSTEAD OF BABY POUSSINS.

SERVES FOUR

INGREDIENTS
    4 small poussins
    about 40g/1½oz/3 tbsp butter,
        at room temperature
    5–10ml/1–2 tsp ground coriander
    1 large red (bell) pepper
    1 fresh red chilli
    15–30ml/1–2 tbsp olive oil
    120ml/4fl oz/½ cup chicken stock
    30ml/2 tbsp cornflour (cornstarch)
    salt and ground black pepper
    fresh flat leaf parsley, to garnish
For the stuffing
    525ml/17fl oz/2¼ cups chicken or
        vegetable stock
    275g/10oz/generous 1½ cups
        couscous
    2 small courgettes (zucchini)
    8 ready-to-eat dried apricots
    15ml/1 tbsp chopped fresh flat
        leaf parsley
    15ml/1 tbsp chopped fresh
        coriander (cilantro)
    juice of ½ lemon

1 First make the stuffing. Bring the stock to the boil and pour it over the couscous in a large bowl. Stir once and then set aside for 10 minutes.

2 Meanwhile, top and tail the courgettes and then grate coarsely. Roughly chop the apricots and add to the courgettes. Preheat the oven to 200°C/400°F/Gas 6.

3 When the couscous has swollen, fluff it up with a fork and then spoon 90ml/6 tbsp into a separate bowl and add the courgettes and chopped apricots to this. Add the chopped herbs, lemon juice and seasoning and stir to make a fairly loose stuffing. Set aside the remaining couscous for serving (see Cook's Tips).

4 Spoon the stuffing loosely into the body cavities of the poussins and secure with string or cocktail sticks. Place the birds in a medium or large flameproof roasting pan so that they fit comfortably but not too closely. Rub the butter into the skins and sprinkle with ground coriander and a little salt and pepper.

COOK'S TIPS
You can reheat the couscous in two ways: either cover the bowl with clear film (plastic wrap) and microwave on High for 2–3 minutes, stirring once or twice, or place in a colander or steamer and set over a pan of simmering water. If liked, finely chopped herbs can be added to the couscous to give colour.

5 Cut the red pepper into medium-sized strips and thinly slice the chilli, discarding the seeds and core. Place in the roasting pan around the poussins and then spoon over the olive oil.

6 Roast in the oven for 20 minutes, then reduce the oven temperature to 180°C/350°F/Gas 4. Pour the stock around the poussins and baste each one with the stock and red pepper/chilli mixture. Return the pan to the oven and roast for a further 30–35 minutes, until the poussins are cooked through and the meat juices run clear, basting occasionally with the stock.

7 When the poussins are cooked, transfer to a warmed serving plate. Blend the cornflour with 45ml/3 tbsp cold water, stir into the stock and peppers in the roasting pan and heat gently, stirring all the time, until the sauce is slightly thickened. Taste, and adjust the seasoning, and then pour into a jug or pour over the poussins. Garnish with flat leaf parsley and serve at once with the reserved couscous.

Energy 593Kcal/2477kJ; Protein 28.1g; Carbohydrate 59.4g, of which sugars 10.2g; Fat 28.5g, of which saturates 10.1g; Cholesterol 137mg; Calcium 64mg; Fibre 2.5g; Sodium 156mg.

MEAT DISHES

In the Middle East, lamb is the dominant meat. A similar situation exists in Morocco and Tunisia, but elsewhere in Africa beef is often the preferred option. Food is often cooked over an open fire, and kebabs are universally enjoyed. Stews range from the lightly spiced tagines of North Africa, which are cooked in distinctive dishes with conical lids, to the rib-sticking ragouts favoured by Nigerian cooks. One of the most unusual dishes featured here is Lebanese Kibbeh, in which two meat mixtures, one with bulgur wheat, are layered in a roasting pan.

COUSCOUS WITH LAMB CUTLETS AND FENNEL

THIS STYLE OF COUSCOUS DISH IS OFTEN SERVED WITH SOUR PICKLES, SUCH AS CABBAGE AND HOT PEPPERS. BUTCHERS IN THE MIDDLE EAST AND AFRICA PREPARE THIN LAMB CUTLETS, SOMETIMES DESCRIBED AS RIB CHOPS, FOR GRILLING OR FRYING. ASK YOUR BUTCHER TO DO THE SAME FOR YOU.

SERVES FOUR

INGREDIENTS
   45ml/3 tbsp olive oil
   2 onions, quartered
   4 garlic cloves, chopped
   30–45ml/2–3 tbsp tomato
      purée (paste)
   10ml/2 tsp harissa
   4 fennel bulbs, stalks removed and
      quartered (feathery fronds reserved)
   50g/2oz/¼ cup butter
   8 thin lamb cutlets (US rib chops)
   salt and ground black pepper
For the couscous
   2.5ml/½ tsp salt
   400ml/14fl oz/1⅔ cups warm water
   350g/12oz/2 cups medium couscous
   30ml/2 tbsp sunflower oil
   knob (pat) of butter, diced

1 Heat the olive oil in a heavy pan, add the onions and garlic and cook for 15 minutes, until softened. Mix the tomato purée with the harissa and dilute with a little water. Pour it into the pan with 600ml/1 pint/2½ cups water. Bring to the boil and add the fennel. Reduce the heat, cover and cook for about 10 minutes, until tender.

2 Meanwhile, prepare the couscous. Stir the salt into the warm water. Place the couscous in a bowl and cover with the water, stirring. Set aside for 10 minutes. Using your fingers, rub the sunflower oil into the couscous. Set aside.

3 Use a slotted spoon to lift the vegetables from the cooking liquid and transfer to a covered dish; keep warm. Boil the liquid to reduce it. Melt the butter in a heavy frying pan, add the lamb cutlets and brown on both sides. Add the cutlets to the reduced liquid and simmer for 15 minutes, until tender.

4 Preheat the oven to 180°C/350°F/ Gas 4. Tip the couscous into an ovenproof dish and arrange the diced butter on top. Chop the fennel fronds and sprinkle over the couscous. Cover with foil and bake in the oven for about 20 minutes.

5 Put the vegetables in the pan with the lamb and heat through. Fluff up the couscous then mound it on to a serving dish. Place the cutlets around the edge and spoon the vegetables over. Moisten with the cooking liquid and serve.

COOK'S TIP
Crunchy pickles make a delicious accompaniment to serve with this dish and are easy to make. Simply combine whole or chopped raw vegetables with white wine vinegar mixed with a little salt and leave to soak for about 3 weeks. The most popular pickled vegetables enjoyed in Morocco are green tomatoes, hot peppers, white cabbage and garlic.

Energy 688Kcal/2862kJ; Protein 35.6g; Carbohydrate 54.5g, of which sugars 7.7g; Fat 37.7g, of which saturates 14.3g; Cholesterol 137mg; Calcium 95mg; Fibre 5.9g; Sodium 421mg.

TAGINE OF SPICED KEFTA WITH LEMON

This North African dish knows no boundaries. It can be found in the tiniest rural villages, in street stalls in the towns and cities, and in the finest restaurants of Casablanca, Fez and Marrakesh. Kefta are lamb meatballs, flavoured with onion, herbs and spices. Poached in a buttery ginger and lemon sauce, with plenty of coriander, they taste wonderful. Bread for mopping up the juices is essential.

SERVES FOUR

INGREDIENTS
450g/1lb finely minced
  (ground) lamb
3 large onions, grated
small bunch of fresh flat leaf
  parsley, chopped
5–10ml/1–2 tsp ground cinnamon
5ml/1 tsp ground cumin
pinch of cayenne pepper
40g/1½oz/3 tbsp butter
25g/1oz fresh root ginger, peeled
  and finely chopped
1 fresh hot chilli, seeded and
  finely chopped
pinch of saffron threads
small bunch of fresh coriander
  (cilantro), finely chopped
juice of 1 lemon
300ml/½ pint/1¼ cups water
1 lemon, quartered
salt and ground black pepper

1 To make the kefta, pound the minced lamb in a bowl by using your hand to lift it up and slap it back down into the bowl. Knead in half the grated onions, the parsley, cinnamon, cumin and cayenne pepper. Season with salt and pepper, and continue pounding the mixture by hand for a few minutes. Break off pieces of the mixture and shape them into walnut-size balls.

2 In a lidded heavy frying pan, melt the butter and add the remaining onions with the ginger, chilli and saffron. Cook until the onions just begin to colour, stirring frequently, then stir in the chopped coriander and lemon juice.

3 Pour in the water, season with salt and bring to the boil. Drop in the kefta, reduce the heat and cover the pan. Poach the kefta gently, turning them occasionally, for about 20 minutes.

4 Remove the lid, tuck the lemon quarters around the kefta, raise the heat a little and cook, uncovered, for a further 10 minutes to reduce the liquid slightly.

5 Garnish with parsley and serve the kefka hot, straight from the pan with lots of fresh crusty bread to mop up the delicious juices.

Energy 362Kcal/1503kJ; Protein 24.5g; Carbohydrate 12.9g, of which sugars 9.3g; Fat 24g, of which saturates 12.2g; Cholesterol 108mg; Calcium 134mg; Fibre 4g; Sodium 155mg.

LAMB WITH BLACK-EYED BEANS AND PUMPKIN

BLACK-EYED BEANS ARE POPULAR THROUGHOUT AFRICA, AND VERSIONS OF THIS DISH ARE TO BE FOUND FROM MOROCCO TO MALAWI. IT IS IN WEST AFRICA, HOWEVER, THAT THE BEANS ARE MOST WIDELY USED, WHICH EXPLAINS WHY THEY CROP UP IN THE CARIBBEAN, COURTESY OF SLAVES WHO PLANTED THEM TO PROVIDE MEALS WITH A FLAVOUR OF HOME. THE PUMPKIN ADDS A SWEET NOTE.

SERVES FOUR

INGREDIENTS

450g/1lb boneless lean lamb or
    mutton, cubed
1 litre/1¾ pints/4 cups chicken or
    lamb stock or water
75g/3oz/scant ½ cup black-eyed
    beans (peas), soaked for 6 hours,
    or overnight
1 onion, chopped
2 garlic cloves, crushed
40ml/2½ tbsp tomato purée (paste)
7.5ml/1½ tsp dried thyme
7.5ml/1½ tsp palm or vegetable oil
5ml/1 tsp mixed spice (apple pie
    spice)
2.5ml/½ tsp ground black pepper
115g/4oz pumpkin flesh, chopped
salt and a little hot pepper sauce

1 Put the lamb or mutton in a large pan with the stock or water and bring to the boil. Skim off any foam, then reduce the heat, cover and simmer for 1 hour.

2 Stir in the drained black-eyed beans and continue to cook for about 35 minutes.

VARIATIONS
Mutton is a mature meat with a very good flavour and texture, ideal for stews and casseroles. If mutton is not available, lamb makes a good substitute. Any dried white beans can be used instead of black-eyed beans (peas). If a firmer texture is preferred, cook the pumpkin for about 5 minutes only, until just tender.

3 Add the onion, garlic, tomato purée, thyme, oil, mixed spice, black pepper and salt and hot pepper sauce and cook for a further 15 minutes, until the beans are tender.

4 Add the pumpkin and simmer for 10 minutes, until the pumpkin is very soft or almost mushy. Serve with boiled yam, plantains or sweet potatoes.

Energy 294Kcal/1231kJ; Protein 27.6g; Carbohydrate 15.2g, of which sugars 4.6g; Fat 14.1g, of which saturates 6.1g; Cholesterol 86mg; Calcium 46mg; Fibre 2.6g; Sodium 125mg.

AWAZE TIBS

AN ETHIOPIAN DISH, AWAZE TIBS IS FLAVOURED WITH BERBERE, A POWERFUL BLEND OF CHILLIES WITH LOCAL HERBS AND SPICES. THIS VERSION OFFERS ALTERNATIVE FLAVOURINGS THAT ARE MORE READILY AVAILABLE, BUT FOR A TRULY AUTHENTIC TASTE, LOOK OUT FOR THE PACKAGED SPICE MIX.

SERVES FOUR

INGREDIENTS
  450g/1lb lamb fillet
  45ml/3 tbsp olive oil
  1 red onion, sliced
  2.5ml/½ tsp peeled, grated fresh
    root ginger
  2 garlic cloves, crushed
  ½ fresh green chilli, seeded and
    finely chopped (optional)
  15ml/1 tbsp clarified butter or ghee
  salt and ground black pepper
For the berbere
  2.5ml/½ tsp each chilli powder,
    paprika, ground ginger, ground
    cinnamon, ground cardamom seeds
    and dried basil
  5ml/1 tsp garlic powder

1 To make the berbere, combine all the ingredients in a small bowl and tip into an airtight container. Berbere will keep for several months if stored in a cool, dry place.

2 Trim the lamb of any fat and then cut the meat into 2cm/¾in cubes.

3 Heat the oil in a large frying pan and fry the meat and onion for 5–6 minutes, until the meat is browned on all sides, stirring occasionally.

4 Add the ginger and garlic to the pan, together with 10ml/2 tsp of the berbere, then stir-fry over a brisk heat for a further 5–10 minutes.

5 Add the chilli, if using, and season well with salt and pepper. Just before serving, add the butter or ghee and stir well.

COOK'S TIPS
Clarified butter is traditionally used for this recipe. It can be made by gently heating butter, preferably unsalted (sweet) butter, up to boiling point and then scooping off and discarding the milk solids that rise to the surface. You are then left with clarified butter, which is a clear yellow liquid. Ghee is an Indian version of clarified butter which is made by simmering butter until all the moisture has evaporated and the butter caramelises. This results in a stronger, sweeter and quite nutty flavour.

Energy 336Kcal/1392kJ; Protein 22g; Carbohydrate 1.2g, of which sugars 0.9g; Fat 27g, of which saturates 10.3g; Cholesterol 92mg; Calcium 9mg; Fibre 0.2g; Sodium 92mg.

PERSIAN LAMB <u>WITH</u> SPLIT PEAS

THIS DISH — KHORESH GHAIMEH — IS TRADITIONALLY SERVED AT PARTIES AND RELIGIOUS FESTIVALS IN IRAN. THE RECIPE IS ANCIENT, AND ORIGINALLY USED PRESERVED MEAT.

SERVES FOUR

INGREDIENTS
    25g/1oz/2 tbsp butter or margarine
    1 large onion, chopped
    450g/1lb lean lamb, cut into
      small cubes
    5ml/1 tsp ground turmeric
    5ml/1 tsp ground cinnamon
    5ml/1 tsp curry powder
    300ml/½ pint/1¼ cups water
    2–3 saffron threads
    90g/3½oz/½ cup yellow split peas
    3 dried limes
    3–4 tomatoes, chopped
    30ml/2 tbsp olive oil
    2 large potatoes, diced
    salt and ground black pepper
    cooked rice, to serve

1 Melt the butter or margarine in a large pan or flameproof casserole and fry the onion for 3–4 minutes, until golden, stirring occasionally. Add the meat and cook over a high heat for a further 3–4 minutes, until it has browned.

2 Add the turmeric, cinnamon and curry powder and cook for about 2 minutes, stirring frequently.

3 Stir in the water, season well and bring to the boil, then cover and simmer over a low heat for about 30–35 minutes. Stir the saffron into about 15ml/1 tbsp boiling water.

4 Add the saffron liquid to the meat with the split peas, dried limes and tomatoes. Stir well and then simmer, covered, for a further 35 minutes, until the meat is completely tender.

5 Meanwhile, heat the oil in a frying pan and sauté the potatoes for 10–15 minutes, until cooked and golden.

6 Lift out the dried lime and discard. Spoon the meat on to a warmed, large serving dish and scatter the sautéed potatoes on top. Serve the khoresh with cooked rice.

COOK'S TIPS
Dried limes (*Limu amani*) are available in all Middle Eastern shops. However, if you have difficulty obtaining them, use the juice of either 2 limes or 1 lemon instead. If you prefer, you can use beef in place of the lamb in this khoresh.

Energy 463Kcal/1941kJ; Protein 30.3g; Carbohydrate 35.1g, of which sugars 7g; Fat 23.4g, of which saturates 10g; Cholesterol 99mg; Calcium 45mg; Fibre 3.6g; Sodium 162mg.

TURKISH SAUTÉED LAMB WITH YOGURT

IN THE MIDDLE EAST MEAT IS USUALLY STEWED OR COOKED ON THE BARBECUE. THIS DELICIOUS EXCEPTION COMES FROM TURKEY. LAMB IS MARINATED IN YOGURT, PAN-FRIED, AND LAYERED WITH COOKED TOMATOES OVER TOASTED BREAD. IT MUST BE SERVED QUICKLY, WHILE THE TOAST IS CRISP.

SERVES FOUR

INGREDIENTS
- 450g/1lb lean lamb, preferably boned leg, cubed
- 40g/1½oz/3 tbsp butter
- 4 tomatoes, skinned and chopped
- 4 thick slices of white or brown bread, crusts removed
- 250ml/8fl oz/1 cup Greek (US strained plain) yogurt
- 2 garlic cloves, crushed
- salt and ground black pepper
- paprika and fresh mint leaves, to garnish

For the marinade
- 120ml/4fl oz/½ cup Greek (US strained plain) yogurt
- 1 large onion, grated

1 First make the marinade: blend together the yogurt, onion and a little seasoning in a large bowl. Add the cubed lamb, toss to coat all over, and then cover loosely with clear film (plastic wrap) and leave to marinate in a cool place for at least 1 hour.

2 Melt half the butter in a frying pan and fry the meat for 5–10 minutes, until cooked and tender, but still moist. Transfer to a plate using a slotted spoon and keep warm while cooking the tomatoes.

VARIATION
You can also use lean beef or skinless chicken breast fillets, instead of lamb, for this recipe.

3 Melt the remaining butter in the same pan and fry the tomatoes for 4–5 minutes, until soft. Meanwhile, toast the bread and arrange in the bottom of a shallow serving dish.

4 Season the tomatoes and then spread over the toasted bread in an even layer.

5 Blend the yogurt and garlic together and season with salt and pepper. Spoon evenly over the tomatoes.

6 Arrange the pan-fried lamb in a layer on top. Sprinkle with paprika and mint leaves and serve at once.

Energy 463Kcal/1939kJ; Protein 30.3g; Carbohydrate 25.2g, of which sugars 4.8g; Fat 28.3g, of which saturates 14.4g; Cholesterol 107mg; Calcium 158mg; Fibre 1.4g; Sodium 436mg.

KEBAB BAHRG

THESE KEBABS ARE SO POPULAR IN THEIR NATIVE IRAN THAT MANY RESTAURANTS SERVE NOTHING ELSE. THE MEAT IS NOT CUBED, AS IN AFRICA, BUT INSTEAD IS CUT INTO STRIPS BEFORE BEING MARINATED AND THREADED ONTO SKEWERS. TOMATOES ARE GRILLED ON SEPARATE SKEWERS.

SERVES FOUR

INGREDIENTS
    450g/1lb lean lamb or beef fillet
    2–3 saffron threads
    1 large onion, grated
    4–6 tomatoes, halved
    15ml/1 tbsp butter, melted
    salt and ground black pepper
    45ml/3 tbsp sumac (see Cook's Tip),
        to garnish (optional)
    cooked rice, to serve

1 Using a sharp knife remove and discard any excess fat from the meat and cut the meat into strips, 1cm/½in thick and 4cm/1½in long.

COOK'S TIP
Sumac are red berries that are dried and crushed to a powder.

2 Soak the saffron in 15ml/1 tbsp boiling water, pour into a small bowl and mix with the grated onion. Add to the meat and stir a few times so that the meat is thoroughly coated. Cover loosely with clear film (plastic wrap) and leave to marinate in the fridge overnight.

3 Season the meat with salt and pepper and then thread it on to flat skewers, aligning the strips in neat rows. Thread the tomatoes on to two separate skewers.

4 Grill the kebabs and tomatoes over hot charcoal for 10–12 minutes, basting with butter and turning occasionally. Serve with cooked rice, sprinkled with sumac, if you like.

SHISH KEBAB

ONE OF THE FIRST MIDDLE EASTERN DISHES TO ACHIEVE GLOBAL POPULARITY, SHISH KEBAB IS BELIEVED TO DATE FROM THE DAYS OF THE OTTOMAN EMPIRE, WHEN SOLDIERS GRILLED MEAT ON THEIR SWORDS OVER OPEN FIRES. THE LAMB CUBES ARE ALTERNATED WITH COLOURFUL VEGETABLES.

SERVES FOUR

INGREDIENTS
    450g/1lb boned leg of lamb, cubed
    1 large green (bell) pepper, seeded
        and cut into squares
    1 large yellow (bell) pepper, seeded
        and cut into squares
    8 baby onions, halved
    225g/8oz button (white) mushrooms
    4 tomatoes, halved
    15ml/1 tbsp melted butter
    bulgur wheat, to serve
For the marinade
    45ml/3 tbsp olive oil
    juice of 1 lemon
    2 garlic cloves, crushed
    1 large onion, grated
    15ml/1 tbsp chopped fresh oregano
    salt and ground black pepper

1 First make the marinade: blend together the oil, lemon juice, garlic, onion, chopped oregano and seasoning. Place the meat in a shallow, non-metallic dish and pour over the marinade.

2 Cover with clear film (plastic wrap) and leave to marinate in the fridge for 2–3 hours, or overnight.

3 Thread the cubes of lamb on to skewers, alternating with pieces of green and yellow pepper, onions and mushrooms. Thread the tomatoes on to separate skewers.

4 Grill the kebabs and tomatoes over hot charcoal for 10–12 minutes, basting with butter and turning occasionally. Serve with bulgur wheat.

TOP Energy 268Kcal/1119kJ; Protein 23.5g; Carbohydrate 7.9g, of which sugars 6.5g; Fat 16.1g, of which saturates 7.9g; Cholesterol 94mg; Calcium 32mg; Fibre 1.9g; Sodium 130mg.
BOTTOM Energy 340Kcal/1417kJ; Protein 25g; Carbohydrate 11.7g, of which sugars 10.3g; Fat 21.8g, of which saturates 7.3g; Cholesterol 86mg; Calcium 36mg; Fibre 3.4g; Sodium 111mg.

LEBANESE KIBBEH

LAMB PLAYS A DUAL ROLE IN THIS, LEBANON'S NATIONAL DISH. THE GROUND MEAT IS MIXED WITH BULGUR WHEAT AND THEN WRAPPED AROUND A SECOND LAMB MIXTURE, THIS TIME WITH SPICES AND NUTS. KIBBEH IS OFTEN MADE INTO MEATBALLS, BUT THIS TRAY VERSION IS POPULAR, TOO.

SERVES SIX

INGREDIENTS
   115g/4oz/²⁄₃ cup bulgur wheat
   450g/1lb finely minced (ground)
     lean lamb
   1 large onion, grated
   15ml/1 tbsp melted butter
   salt and ground black pepper
   sprigs of fresh mint, to garnish
   cooked rice, to serve
For the filling
   30ml/2 tbsp oil
   1 onion, finely chopped
   225g/8oz minced (ground) lamb
     or veal
   50g/2oz/¹⁄₃ cup pine nuts
   2.5ml/½ tsp ground allspice
For the yogurt dip
   600ml/1 pint/2½ cups Greek
     (US strained plain) yogurt
   2–3 garlic cloves, crushed
   15–30ml/1–2 tbsp chopped
     fresh mint

1 Preheat the oven to 190°C/375°F/ Gas 5. Rinse the bulgur wheat in a sieve and squeeze out the excess moisture.

2 Mix the lamb, onion and seasoning in a bowl, kneading the mixture to make a thick paste. Add the bulgur wheat and mix well. Set aside.

VARIATION
Use finely minced (ground) lean beef instead of lamb.

3 To make the filling, heat the oil in a frying pan and fry the onion until golden. Add the lamb or veal and cook, stirring, until evenly browned and then add the pine nuts, allspice and salt and pepper.

4 Oil a large baking dish and spread half of the meat and bulgur wheat mixture over the bottom. Spoon over the filling and top with a second layer of the remaining meat and bulgur wheat, pressing down firmly with the back of a spoon.

5 Pour the melted butter over the top and then bake in the oven for 40–45 minutes, until browned on top.

6 Meanwhile make the yogurt dip: blend together the yogurt and garlic, spoon into a serving bowl and sprinkle with the chopped mint.

7 Cut the cooked kibbeh into squares or rectangles and serve garnished with mint sprigs and accompanied by cooked rice and the yogurt dip.

Energy 452Kcal/1883kJ; Protein 29.7g; Carbohydrate 22.8g, of which sugars 11.5g; Fat 27.7g, of which saturates 9.7g; Cholesterol 93mg; Calcium 230mg; Fibre 1.1g; Sodium 178mg.

SHISH BARAK

THIS LEBANESE SPECIALITY IS A FAVOURITE LUNCHTIME DISH IN THE RESTAURANTS OF BEIRUT. DUMPLINGS FILLED WITH LAMB, ONION AND NUTS ARE SIMMERED IN A YOGURT AND EGG SAUCE.

SERVES FOUR

INGREDIENTS
    30ml/2 tbsp olive oil
    1 large onion, chopped
    60ml/4 tbsp pine nuts or
        chopped walnuts
    450g/1lb minced (ground) lamb
    25g/1oz/2 tbsp butter
    3 garlic cloves, crushed
    15ml/1 tbsp chopped fresh mint
    salt and ground black pepper
    fresh mint leaves, to garnish
    cooked rice and green salad, to serve
For the dough
    5ml/1 tsp salt
    225g/8oz/2 cups plain
        (all-purpose) flour
For the yogurt sauce
    2 litres/3½ pints/8 cups natural
        (plain) yogurt
    1 egg, beaten
    15ml/1 tbsp cornflour (cornstarch),
        blended with 15ml/1 tbsp
        cold water
    salt and white pepper

1 First make the dough: mix the salt and the flour together and then stir in enough water for the dough to hold together. Cover and leave to rest for 1 hour.

2 Heat the oil in a large frying pan and fry the onion for 3–4 minutes, until soft. Add the pine nuts or walnuts and fry until golden. Stir in the meat and cook until brown. Season, then remove the pan from the heat.

3 Roll out the dough thinly on a floured board. Cut into small rounds 5–6cm/ 2–2½in in diameter. Place 5ml/1 tsp of filling on each one, fold the pastry over and firmly press the edges together to seal. Bring the ends together to form a handle.

4 Meanwhile, make the yogurt sauce: pour the yogurt into a pan and beat in the egg and cornflour mixture. Season with salt and white pepper and slowly bring to the boil, stirring constantly.

5 Cook over a gentle heat until the sauce thickens and then carefully drop in the dumplings and simmer for about 20 minutes.

6 Spoon the dumplings and sauce on to warmed serving plates. Melt the butter in a small frying pan and fry the garlic until golden. Stir in the chopped mint, cook briefly and then pour over the dumplings. Garnish with mint leaves and serve with rice and a green salad.

Energy 820Kcal/3441kJ; Protein 55.4g; Carbohydrate 86.1g, of which sugars 41.8g; Fat 31.5g, of which saturates 13g; Cholesterol 153mg; Calcium 1061mg; Fibre 2.6g; Sodium 1062mg.

LAMB AND VEGETABLE PILAU

ALTHOUGH MANY PEOPLE ASSOCIATE THE PILAU WITH INDIA, THIS METHOD OF COOKING RICE HAS A CLOSE ASSOCIATION WITH THE MIDDLE EAST. ANCIENT PERSIANS CALLED THE DISH PULAW, AND INVENTED EXCITING VARIATIONS, INTRODUCING FRUIT AS WELL AS VEGETABLES AND SPICES.

SERVES FOUR

INGREDIENTS
For the meat curry
  450g/1lb boned shoulder of
    lamb, cubed
  2.5ml/½ tsp dried thyme
  2.5ml/½ tsp paprika
  5ml/1 tsp garam masala
  1 garlic clove, crushed
  25ml/1½ tbsp vegetable oil
  900ml/1½ pints/3¾ cups lamb stock
    or water
  salt and ground black pepper
For the rice
  30ml/2 tbsp butter or margarine
  1 onion, chopped
  175g/6oz potato, diced
  1 carrot, sliced
  ½ red (bell) pepper, seeded
    and chopped
  115g/4oz green cabbage, sliced
  1 fresh green chilli, seeded and
    finely chopped
  60ml/4 tbsp natural (plain) yogurt
  2.5ml/½ tsp ground cumin
  5 green cardamom pods
  2 garlic cloves, crushed
  350g/12oz/1¾ cups basmati rice
  about 50g/2oz/⅓ cup cashew nuts

1 To make the curry, place the lamb in a large bowl and add the thyme, paprika, garam masala, garlic and salt and pepper. Mix, then cover and set aside to marinate for 2–3 hours.

2 Heat the oil in a large pan and fry the lamb, in batches if necessary, over a medium heat for 5–6 minutes, until browned.

3 Add the stock or water, stir well and then cook, covered, for 35–40 minutes, until the lamb is just tender. Transfer the lamb to a plate or bowl and pour the liquid into a measuring jug (cup), topping up with water if necessary, to make 600ml/1 pint/2½ cups. Set aside.

4 To make the rice, melt the butter or margarine and fry the onion, potato and carrot for 5 minutes.

5 Add the red pepper, cabbage, chilli, yogurt, spices, garlic and the reserved meat stock. Stir well, cover, and then simmer gently for 5–10 minutes, until the cabbage has wilted.

6 Stir in the rice and lamb, cover and simmer over a low heat for 20 minutes, until the rice is cooked. Sprinkle in the cashew nuts and season to taste with salt and pepper. Serve hot.

VARIATIONS
If you prefer, fewer vegetables can be used for this dish and cubed chicken or minced lamb substituted for the cubed lamb. Basmati rice is ideal, but long grain rice may be used instead. The amount of liquid can be varied, depending on whether firm, or well-cooked rice is preferred.

Energy 751Kcal/3135kJ; Protein 33.7g; Carbohydrate 86.3g, of which sugars 7.3g; Fat 30.1g, of which saturates 11.6g; Cholesterol 102mg; Calcium 88mg; Fibre 2.3g; Sodium 200mg.

STUFFED LEG OF LAMB, MOROCCAN STYLE

THROUGHOUT NORTH AFRICA, AND IN PARTS OF SPAIN SETTLED BY THE MOORS, THIS IS A FAVOURITE WAY OF COOKING LAMB. THE SPICY RICE STUFFING COMPLEMENTS THE SWEETNESS OF THE MEAT.

SERVES SIX

INGREDIENTS
  1.3–1.6kg/3–3½lb leg of
    lamb, boned
  2 garlic cloves, crushed
  40g/1½oz/3 tbsp butter
  175ml/6fl oz/¾ cup chicken or
    lamb stock
  15ml/1 tbsp cornflour (cornstarch)
  15ml/1 tbsp apricot jam
  salt and ground black pepper
For the stuffing
  1 fresh green chilli, seeded
  2 shallots
  1 garlic clove
  1 bunch of fresh coriander (cilantro)
  sprig of fresh parsley
  25g/1oz/2 tbsp butter
  10ml/2 tsp ground cumin
  2.5ml/½ tsp ground cinnamon
  150g/5oz/¾ cup cooked long
    grain rice
  30ml/2 tbsp pine nuts

1 Preheat the oven to 200°C/400°F/ Gas 6 and then make the stuffing. Place the chilli, shallots, garlic, coriander and parsley in a blender or food processor and process until very finely chopped.

2 Melt the butter in a small frying pan and fry the shallot and herb mixture for 2–3 minutes over a gentle heat to soften the shallots. Add the cumin and cinnamon and stir well.

3 Place the cooked rice in a bowl, add the pine nuts and then stir in the contents of the pan. Season well with salt and pepper. Set aside.

4 Season the meat on both sides with salt and pepper and rub the outside with the crushed garlic and butter. Place the meat, skin side down, on a work surface and spread the stuffing evenly over it. Roll the meat up, secure with a skewer and then tie with cooking string at even intervals.

5 Place in a flameproof roasting pan and roast in the oven for 20 minutes, then reduce the oven temperature to 180°C/ 350°F/Gas 4 and continue to roast for 1½–2 hours, basting occasionally with the juices from the pan.

6 To make the sauce, pour away the excess fat from the roasting pan and then add the chicken stock. Heat gently, stirring all the time, to deglaze the pan.

7 Blend the cornflour with 30ml/ 2 tbsp water and add to the roasting pan together with the apricot jam. Gradually bring to the boil, stirring all the time. Strain the sauce into a serving jug and serve with the stuffed lamb.

Energy 414Kcal/1726kJ; Protein 28.1g; Carbohydrate 13.7g, of which sugars 1.1g; Fat 27.8g, of which saturates 12.9g; Cholesterol 124mg; Calcium 46mg; Fibre 0.9g; Sodium 188mg.

BEEF TAGINE WITH SWEET POTATOES

FEZ IS CREDITED WITH MOROCCO'S FINEST TAGINES. THIS IS A PARTICULARLY GOOD ONE, THE SWEET POTATOES AND WARM SPICES PROVIDING A MELLOW COUNTERPOINT TO THE ROBUST FLAVOUR OF THE BEEF. USE A CASSEROLE WITH A TIGHT-FITTING LID TO MIRROR AS CLOSELY AS POSSIBLE THE EFFECT OF COOKING IN THE TRADITIONAL POT THAT GAVE ITS NAME TO THIS TYPE OF STEW.

SERVES FOUR

INGREDIENTS

675–900g/1½–2lb braising or
    stewing beef
30ml/2 tbsp sunflower oil
good pinch of ground turmeric
1 large onion, chopped
1 fresh red or green chilli, seeded
    and finely chopped
7.5ml/1½ tsp paprika
good pinch of cayenne pepper
2.5ml/½ tsp ground cumin
450g/1lb sweet potatoes
15ml/1 tbsp chopped fresh parsley
15ml/1 tbsp chopped fresh
    coriander (cilantro)
15g/½oz/1 tbsp butter
salt and ground black pepper

1 Trim the meat and cut into 2cm/¾in cubes. Heat the oil in a flameproof casserole and fry the meat, together with the turmeric and seasoning, over a medium heat for 3–4 minutes, until the meat is evenly browned, stirring frequently.

2 Cover the pan tightly and cook for 15 minutes over a fairly gentle heat, without lifting the lid. Preheat the oven to 180°C/350°F/Gas 4.

3 Add the onion, chilli, paprika, cayenne pepper and cumin to the pan together with just enough water to cover the meat. Cover tightly and cook in the oven for 1–1½ hours, until the meat is very tender, checking occasionally and adding a little extra water, if necessary, to keep the stew fairly moist.

4 Meanwhile, peel the sweet potatoes and slice them straight into a bowl of salted water to avoid discolouring. Transfer to a pan, bring to the boil, simmer for 2–3 minutes. Drain.

5 Stir the chopped herbs into the meat, adding a little extra water if the stew appears dry. Arrange the potato slices over the meat and dot with the butter. Cover and cook in the oven for a further 10 minutes, until the potatoes feel very tender. Increase the oven temperature to 200°C/400°F/Gas 6 or preheat the grill (broiler) to its hottest setting.

6 Remove the lid of the casserole and cook in the oven or under the grill for a further 5–10 minutes, until the potatoes are golden. Serve at once.

VARIATIONS
You can use lean lamb instead of beef. Use swede (rutabaga) in place of the sweet potatoes.

Energy 434Kcal/1819kJ; Protein 39.1g; Carbohydrate 28.9g, of which sugars 10g; Fat 18.8g, of which saturates 6.8g; Cholesterol 114mg; Calcium 66mg; Fibre 3.9g; Sodium 180mg.

TAGINE OF BEEF WITH PEAS AND SAFFRON

EVER SINCE THE PERSIANS DISCOVERED THAT THE BRILLIANT ORANGE STIGMAS OF A TINY WILD FLOWER COULD BE USED TO COLOUR AND FLAVOUR FOOD, SAFFRON HAS BEEN HIGHLY PRIZED, NOT ONLY IN THE MIDDLE EAST, BUT ALSO IN MEDITERRANEAN COUNTRIES. THE SPICE IS CULTIVATED COMMERCIALLY IN MOROCCO AND IS A FAVOURITE INGREDIENT IN DISHES LIKE THIS CLASSIC FRESH PEA AND PRESERVED LEMON TAGINE.

SERVES SIX

INGREDIENTS

1.2kg/2½lb chuck steak or stewing
    beef, trimmed and cubed
30ml/2 tbsp olive oil
1 onion, chopped
25g/1oz fresh root ginger, peeled and
    finely chopped
5ml/1 tsp ground ginger
pinch of cayenne pepper
pinch of saffron threads
1.2kg/2½lb shelled fresh peas
2 tomatoes, skinned and chopped
1 preserved lemon, chopped
a handful of brown kalamata olives
salt and ground black pepper
bread or couscous, to serve

1 Put the cubed meat in a tagine, flameproof casserole or heavy pan with the olive oil, onion, fresh and ground ginger, cayenne and saffron and season with salt and pepper. Pour in enough water to cover the meat completely and then bring to the boil. Reduce the heat and then cover and simmer for about 1½ hours, until the meat is very tender. Cook for a little longer, if necessary.

2 Add the peas, tomatoes, preserved lemon and olives. Stir well and cook, uncovered, for about 10 minutes, or until the peas are tender and the sauce has reduced. Check the seasoning and serve with bread or plain couscous.

Energy 492Kcal/2049kJ; Protein 57.9g; Carbohydrate 25.6g, of which sugars 7g; Fat 18.2g, of which saturates 6g; Cholesterol 126mg; Calcium 61mg; Fibre 10.1g; Sodium 134mg.

SPICY BEEF KOFTAS WITH CHICKPEA PURÉE

Wherever you go in the Middle East you will encounter these tasty kebabs, as street food, on barbecues, at beach bars and at family meals. The task of pounding the meat — traditionally performed by hand using a mortar and pestle — is much easier in a food processor. It takes just a few minutes to mould the mixture around the skewers, and they don't take long to cook. Chickpea purée is the traditional accompaniment.

SERVES SIX

INGREDIENTS

500g/1¼lb finely minced
   (ground) beef
1 onion, grated
10ml/2 tsp ground cumin
10ml/2 tsp ground coriander
10ml/2 tsp paprika
4ml/¾ tsp cayenne pepper
5ml/1 tsp salt
small bunch of fresh flat leaf parsley,
   finely chopped
small bunch of fresh coriander
   (cilantro), finely chopped
For the chickpea purée
225g/8oz/1¼ cups dried chickpeas,
   soaked overnight, drained
   and cooked
50ml/2fl oz/¼ cup olive oil
juice of 1 lemon
2 garlic cloves, crushed
5ml/1 tsp cumin seeds
30ml/2 tbsp light tahini paste
60ml/4 tbsp thick Greek (US strained
   plain) yogurt
40g/1½oz/3 tbsp butter, melted
salt and ground black pepper
salad and bread, to serve

1 Mix the minced beef with the onion, cumin, ground coriander, paprika, cayenne, salt, chopped parsley and fresh coriander. Knead the mixture well, then pound it until smooth in a mortar with a pestle or in a blender or food processor. Place in a dish, cover and leave to stand in a cool place for 1 hour.

2 Meanwhile, make the chickpea purée. Preheat the oven to 200°C/400°F/Gas 6. In a blender or food processor, process the chickpeas with the olive oil, lemon juice, garlic, cumin seeds, tahini and yogurt until well mixed. Season with salt and pepper, tip the purée into an ovenproof dish, cover with foil and heat through in the oven for 20 minutes.

3 Divide the meat mixture into six portions and mould each on to a metal skewer, so that the meat resembles a fat sausage. Preheat the grill (broiler) on the hottest setting and cook the kebabs for 4–5 minutes on each side.

4 Melt the butter and pour it over the hot chickpea purée. Serve the kebabs with the hot chickpea purée. Serve with salad and bread.

Energy 456Kcal/1898kJ; Protein 26.6g; Carbohydrate 21.8g, of which sugars 3.5g; Fat 29.8g, of which saturates 10.7g; Cholesterol 64mg; Calcium 153mg; Fibre 5.4g; Sodium 463mg.

PERSIAN TANGY BEEF AND HERB KHORESH

IN MODERN-DAY IRAN, AS IN ANCIENT PERSIA, RICE IS EATEN AT ALMOST EVERY MEAL. THAT THE DIET IS NEVER DULL IS THANKS TO THE KHORESH. THIS IS A DELICATELY SPICED SAUCE OR STEW THAT SERVES AS A TOPPING, AND PERSIAN COOKS KNOW DOZENS OF RECIPES. THIS IS A CLASSIC MEAT KHORESH, BUT THERE ARE ALSO VEGETARIAN VERSIONS, OFTEN WITH FRUIT AND FRESH HERBS.

SERVES FOUR

INGREDIENTS
45ml/3 tbsp olive oil
1 large onion, chopped
450g/1lb lean stewing beef, cubed
15ml/1 tbsp fenugreek leaf
10ml/2 tsp ground turmeric
2.5ml/½ tsp ground cinnamon
600ml/1 pint/2½ cups water
25g/1oz fresh parsley, chopped
25g/1oz fresh chives, chopped
400g/14oz can red kidney beans
juice of 1 lemon
salt and ground black pepper
cooked rice, to serve

1 Heat 30ml/2 tbsp of the oil in a large pan or flameproof casserole and fry the onion for about 3–4 minutes, until lightly golden. Add the beef and fry for a further 10 minutes until browned on all sides.

2 Add the fenugreek, turmeric and cinnamon and cook for about 1 minute, then add the water and bring to the boil. Cover and simmer over a gentle heat for 45 minutes, stirring occasionally.

3 Heat the remaining oil in a small frying pan and fry the parsley and chives over a medium heat for 2–3 minutes, stirring frequently.

4 Rinse and drain the kidney beans and then stir them into the beef with the fried herbs and lemon juice. Season with salt and pepper. Simmer the stew for a further 30–35 minutes, until the meat is tender. Serve on a bed of cooked rice.

Energy 357Kcal/1491kJ; Protein 32.5g; Carbohydrate 22.9g, of which sugars 7.3g; Fat 15.5g, of which saturates 4g; Cholesterol 71mg; Calcium 117mg; Fibre 7.7g; Sodium 468mg.

NIGERIAN MEAT STEW

LIFT THE LID ON A NIGERIAN COOKING POT AND YOU WILL GENERALLY FIND A STEW INSIDE, WHICH WILL HAVE BEEN INSPIRED BY WHATEVER INGREDIENTS WERE AVAILABLE AT MARKET THAT DAY — A SINGLE TYPE OF MEAT OR A MIXTURE, PLUS VEGETABLES. OCCASIONALLY NIGERIAN WOMEN WILL ADD DRIED FISH OR SNAILS TO MEAT STEWS.

SERVES FOUR TO SIX

INGREDIENTS
675g/1½lb oxtail, chopped
450g/1lb stewing beef, cubed
450g/1lb skinless, chicken breast
  fillets, diced
2 garlic cloves, crushed
1½ onions
30ml/2 tbsp palm or vegetable oil
30ml/2 tbsp tomato purée (paste)
400g/14oz can plum tomatoes
2 bay leaves
5ml/1 tsp dried thyme
5ml/1 tsp mixed spice (apple pie
  spice)
salt and ground black pepper

5 Meanwhile, place the plum tomatoes and the remaining half onion in a blender or food processor and process to a purée. Stir into the chicken mixture with the bay leaves, thyme, mixed spice and seasoning.

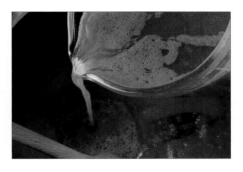

6 Add about 600ml/1 pint/2½ cups of stock from the cooked oxtail and beef and simmer for 35 minutes.

7 Add the oxtail and beef to the chicken. Heat gently, adjust the seasoning and serve hot.

1 Place the oxtail in a large pan, cover with water and bring to the boil. Skim the surface of any froth, then cover and cook for 1½ hours, adding more water as necessary. Add the beef and continue to cook for a further 1 hour.

2 Meanwhile, season the chicken with the crushed garlic and roughly chop one of the onions.

3 Heat the oil in a large pan over a medium heat and fry the chopped onion for about 5 minutes, until soft.

4 Stir the tomato purée in to the onions, cook briskly for a few minutes, then add the chicken. Stir well and cook gently for 5 minutes.

Energy 588Kcal/2472kJ; Protein 88.3g; Carbohydrate 8.8g, of which sugars 7.2g; Fat 22.5g, of which saturates 9g; Cholesterol 281mg; Calcium 56mg; Fibre 1.8g; Sodium 390mg.

BEEF KOFTA CURRY

KOFTAS COME IN VARIOUS SHAPES AND SIZES. THE BASIC MINCED MEAT MIXTURE CAN BE MOULDED AROUND A SKEWER, SAUSAGE-STYLE, OR SHAPED INTO MEATBALLS. IN THIS VARIATION, THE MORE COMMONLY USED LAMB IS REPLACED BY BEEF, WHICH WORKS WELL WITH THE HOT CURRY SAUCE.

SERVES FOUR

INGREDIENTS

For the meatballs
    450g/1lb minced (ground) beef
    45ml/3 tbsp finely chopped onion
    15ml/1 tbsp chopped fresh
        coriander (cilantro)
    15ml/1 tbsp natural (plain) yogurt
    about 60ml/4 tbsp plain
        (all-purpose) flour
    10ml/2 tsp ground cumin
    5ml/1 tsp garam masala
    5ml/1 tsp ground turmeric
    5ml/1 tsp ground coriander
    1 fresh green chilli, seeded and
        finely chopped
    2 garlic cloves, crushed
    1.5ml/¼ tsp black mustard seeds
    1 egg (optional)
    salt and ground black pepper
For the curry sauce
    30ml/2 tbsp butter
    1 onion, finely chopped
    2 garlic cloves, crushed
    45ml/3 tbsp curry powder
    4 green cardamom pods
    600ml/1 pint/2½ cups hot beef stock
        or water
    15ml/1 tbsp tomato purée (paste)
    30ml/2 tbsp natural (plain) yogurt
    15ml/1 tbsp chopped fresh
        coriander (cilantro)

1 To make the meatballs, put the beef into a large bowl, add all the remaining meatball ingredients and mix well with your hands. Roll the mixture into small balls or koftas and then put aside on a floured plate until required.

2 To make the curry sauce, heat the butter in a pan over a medium heat and fry the onion and garlic for about 10 minutes, until the onion is soft.

3 Reduce the heat and then add the curry powder and cardamon pods and cook for a few minutes, stirring well.

4 Slowly stir in the stock or water and then add the tomato purée, yogurt and chopped coriander and stir well.

5 Simmer gently for 10 minutes. Add the koftas a few at a time, allow to cook briefly and then add a few more, until all of the koftas are in the pan. Simmer, uncovered, for about 20 minutes, until the koftas are cooked through. Avoid stirring, but gently shake the pan occasionally to move the koftas around. The curry should thicken slightly but if it becomes too dry, add a little more stock or water. Serve hot.

Energy 313Kcal/1301kJ; Protein 25.8g; Carbohydrate 4.9g, of which sugars 3.7g; Fat 21.3g, of which saturates 11.3g; Cholesterol 90mg; Calcium 42mg; Fibre 1g; Sodium 192mg.

GAMBIAN BEEF IN AUBERGINE SAUCE

BEEF IS POPULAR IN THE GAMBIA. IT IS RELATIVELY EXPENSIVE, THOUGH, SO IS USUALLY RESERVED FOR SPECIAL OCCASION DISHES LIKE THIS MILDLY SPICED AUBERGINE AND BEEF STEW.

SERVES FOUR

INGREDIENTS

    450g/1lb stewing beef, cubed
    5ml/1 tsp dried thyme
    45ml/3 tbsp palm or vegetable oil
    1 large onion, finely chopped
    2 garlic cloves, crushed
    4 canned plum tomatoes, chopped,
      plus the juice
    15ml/1 tbsp tomato purée (paste)
    2.5ml/½ tsp mixed spice (apple pie
      spice)
    1 fresh red chilli, seeded and
      finely chopped
    900ml/1½ pints/3¾ cups beef stock
    1 large aubergine (eggplant), about
      350g/12oz
    salt and ground black pepper

1 Season the cubed beef with 2.5ml/½ tsp thyme, salt and pepper.

2 Heat 15ml/1 tbsp of the oil in a pan and fry the meat for 8–10 minutes, until browned. Transfer to a bowl and set aside. Add the remaining oil to the pan.

3 Fry the onion and garlic for a few minutes, then add the tomatoes.

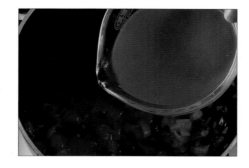

4 Simmer for 5–10 minutes, stirring occasionally. Stir in the tomato purée, mixed spice, chilli and remaining thyme, and then add the reserved beef and stock. Bring to the boil, cover and simmer for 30 minutes.

5 Cut the aubergine into 1cm/½in dice. Stir into the beef mixture and cook, covered, for a further 30 minutes, until the beef is completely tender. Adjust the seasoning and serve hot.

Energy 251Kcal/1050kJ; Protein 27.2g; Carbohydrate 7.2g, of which sugars 6.2g; Fat 12.8g, of which saturates 2.9g; Cholesterol 75mg; Calcium 29mg; Fibre 3g; Sodium 87mg.

VEGETARIAN DISHES

When it comes to appetizers and mezzes, vegetarians visiting Africa and the Middle East are spoilt for choice. Main courses are a little more challenging, as there is a tendency in both regions to use meat stock in vegetable dishes. There are, however, some exciting vegetarian dishes to be had. Try a tempting tagine of artichoke hearts, a Turkish spinach and cheese filo pie, summer vegetable kebabs with harissa and yogurt dip, Kenyan mung bean stew, or spinach with ground melon seed.

CLASSIC CASABLANCAN COUSCOUS WITH ROASTED SUMMER VEGETABLES

THIS DISH IS BASED ON THE TRADITION THAT A STEW SERVED WITH COUSCOUS SHOULD INCLUDE SEVEN VEGETABLES. THE NUMBER SEVEN IS SAID TO BRING GOOD LUCK, AND ANY SUITABLE COMBINATION OF VEGETABLES CAN BE USED, AS LONG AS THE TOTAL ADDS UP TO THE MAGIC NUMBER. TO ADD A FLICKER OF FIRE TO THIS DISH, SERVE IT WITH A SPOONFUL OF HARISSA. TO COOL THE PALATE, OFFER A BOWL OF THICK AND CREAMY YOGURT.

SERVES SIX

INGREDIENTS
    3 red onions, peeled and quartered
    2–3 courgettes (zucchini), halved
      lengthways and cut across into
      2–3 pieces
    2–3 red, green or yellow (bell)
      peppers, seeded and quartered
    2 aubergines (eggplants), cut into
      6–8 long segments
    2–3 leeks, trimmed and cut into
      long strips
    2–3 sweet potatoes, peeled,
      halved lengthways and cut
      into long strips
    4–6 tomatoes, quartered
    6 garlic cloves, crushed
    25g/1oz fresh root ginger, sliced
    a few large fresh rosemary sprigs
    about 150ml/¼ pint/⅔ cup olive oil
    10ml/2 tsp clear honey
    salt and ground black pepper
    natural (plain) yogurt or harissa and
      bread, to serve
For the couscous
    500g/1¼lb/3 cups couscous
    5ml/1 tsp salt
    600ml/1 pint/2½ cups warm water
    45ml/3 tbsp sunflower oil
    about 25g/1oz/2 tbsp butter, diced

1 Preheat the oven to 200°C/400°F/ Gas 6. Arrange all the vegetables in a roasting pan. Tuck the garlic, ginger and rosemary around the vegetables.

2 Pour lots of olive oil over the vegetables, drizzle with the honey, add salt and pepper, and then roast for about 1½ hours until they are extremely tender and slightly caramelized. The cooking time will depend on the size of the vegetable pieces. Turn them in the oil occasionally.

3 When the vegetables are nearly ready, put the couscous in a bowl. Stir the salt into the water, then pour it over the couscous, stirring to make sure it is absorbed evenly. Leave to stand for 10 minutes to plump up then, using your fingers, rub the sunflower oil into the grains to air them and break up any lumps. Tip the couscous into an ovenproof dish, arrange the butter over the top, cover with foil and heat in the oven for about 20 minutes.

4 To serve, use your fingers to work the melted butter into the grains of couscous and fluff it up, then pile it on a large dish and shape into a mound with a little pit at the top. Spoon some vegetables into the pit and arrange the rest around the dish. Pour the oil from the pan over the couscous or serve separately. Serve immediately with yogurt, or harissa if you prefer, and bread for mopping up the juices.

Energy 561Kcal/2340kJ; Protein 10.4g; Carbohydrate 78.8g, of which sugars 18.7g; Fat 24.6g, of which saturates 3.5g; Cholesterol 0mg; Calcium 101mg; Fibre 7.3g; Sodium 51mg.

TAGINE OF ARTICHOKE HEARTS, POTATOES, PEAS AND SAFFRON

ARTICHOKES ARE A DELICACY IN BOTH THE MIDDLE EAST AND NORTH AFRICA, AND WHEN THE SEASON STARTS, COOKS COMPETE FOR THE PICK OF THE CROP. IN SOME MARKETS IT IS POSSIBLE TO BUY JUST THE ARTICHOKE HEARTS, WHICH SAVES THE SOMEWHAT TEDIOUS TASK OF PREPARATION AT HOME. IF YOU DO NEED TO DO THIS YOURSELF, REMOVE THE OUTER LEAVES, CUT OFF THE STEMS AND SCOOP OUT THE CHOKE AND HAIRY BITS WITH A TEASPOON.

SERVES FOUR TO SIX

INGREDIENTS
6 fresh globe artichoke hearts
juice of 1 lemon
30–45ml/2–3 tbsp olive oil
1 onion, chopped
675g/1½lb potatoes, peeled
  and quartered
small bunch of fresh flat leaf
  parsley, chopped
small bunch of fresh coriander
  (cilantro), chopped
small bunch of fresh mint, chopped
pinch of saffron threads
5ml/1 tsp ground turmeric
about 350ml/12fl oz/1½ cups
  vegetable stock
finely chopped rind of
  ½ preserved lemon
250g/9oz/2¼ cups shelled peas
salt and ground black pepper
couscous or bread, to serve

COOK'S TIP
When preparing artichokes, once cut, the flesh of artichokes will blacken. To prevent this from happening, put the artichokes into acidulated water – you can use lemon juice or white wine vinegar.

1 Poach the artichoke hearts very gently in plenty of simmering water with half the lemon juice, for 10–15 minutes, until tender. Drain and refresh under cold water, then drain again.

2 Heat the olive oil in a tagine or heavy pan. Add the onion and cook over a low heat for about 15 minutes, until softened but not browned. Add the potatoes, most of the chopped parsley, the chopped coriander and mint, the remaining lemon juice, and the saffron and turmeric to the pan.

3 Pour in the stock, bring to the boil, then reduce the heat. Cover the pan and cook for about 15 minutes, until the potatoes are almost tender.

4 Stir the preserved lemon, artichoke hearts and peas into the stew, and cook, uncovered, for a further 10 minutes. Season to taste, sprinkle with the remaining parsley, and serve with couscous or chunks of fresh bread.

Energy 260Kcal/1089kJ; Protein 8.6g; Carbohydrate 42g, of which sugars 10.6g; Fat 7.5g, of which saturates 1.2g; Cholesterol 0mg; Calcium 96mg; Fibre 7.9g; Sodium 47mg.

TAGINE OF YAM, CARROTS AND PRUNES

THE YAMS IN THIS MOROCCAN DISH REVEAL A WEST AFRICAN INFLUENCE. IT COMES FROM THE ATLAS MOUNTAINS, WHERE THE TEMPERATURE OFTEN DROPS TO BELOW ZERO IN WINTER, AND WARMING STEWS ARE VERY WELCOME. THIS IS QUITE A SWEET-TASTING DISH, THANKS TO THE CARAMELIZED VEGETABLES AND THE PRUNES. SERVE IT WITH COUSCOUS AND A GREEN SALAD THAT INCLUDES SOME BITTER LEAVES, PREFERABLY WITH A SHARP LEMON AND OIL DRESSING.

SERVES FOUR TO SIX

INGREDIENTS
   45ml/3 tbsp olive oil
   a little butter
   25–30 button (pearl) onions,
     blanched and peeled
   900g/2lb yam or sweet potatoes,
     peeled and cut into bitesize chunks
   2–3 carrots, cut into bitesize chunks
   150g/5oz/generous ½ cup ready-to-
     eat pitted prunes
   5ml/1 tsp ground cinnamon
   2.5ml/½ tsp ground ginger
   10ml/2 tsp clear honey
   450ml/¾ pint/scant 2 cups
     vegetable stock
   small bunch of fresh coriander
     (cilantro), finely chopped
   small bunch of fresh mint,
     finely chopped
   salt and ground black pepper

COOK'S TIP
Yams have a brown skin and cream-coloured flesh; sweet potatoes have dark red or orange skin and orange flesh. Buy firm specimens that do not "give".

1 Preheat the oven to 200°C/400°F/ Gas 6. Heat the olive oil in a flameproof casserole with the butter and stir in the onions. Cook for about 5 minutes until the onions are tender, then remove half of the onions from the pan and set aside.

2 Add the yam or sweet potatoes and carrots to the pan and cook until lightly browned. Stir in the prunes with the cinnamon, ginger and honey, then pour in the stock. Season well, cover the casserole and transfer to the oven for about 45 minutes.

3 Stir in the reserved onions and bake for a further 10 minutes. Gently stir in the chopped coriander and mint, and serve the tagine immediately.

Energy 454Kcal/1922kJ; Protein 6.2g; Carbohydrate 91.8g, of which sugars 27.1g; Fat 9.5g, of which saturates 1.5g; Cholesterol 0mg; Calcium 111mg; Fibre 7.9g; Sodium 32mg.

BUTTER BEAN, TOMATO AND OLIVE TAGINE

VEGETARIANS SOMETIMES STRUGGLE TO FIND SOMETHING HOT AND SUBSTANTIAL TO EAT WHEN TRAVELLING IN AFRICA AND THE MIDDLE EAST, AS EVEN VEGETABLE STEWS ARE OFTEN MADE WITH MEAT STOCK. THIS TAGINE TAKES ITS MOISTURE FROM TOMATOES AND OLIVE OIL, HOWEVER, SO FITS THE BILL PERFECTLY. IT IS HEARTY ENOUGH TO BE SERVED ON ITS OWN, WITH FRESH, CRUSTY BREAD AND PERHAPS A SALAD. IF YOU ARE SERVING IT TO NON-VEGETARIANS, ADD SOME SLICED CHORIZO.

SERVES FOUR

INGREDIENTS
    115g/4oz/⅔ cup butter (lima) beans,
      soaked overnight
    30–45ml/2–3 tbsp olive oil
    1 onion, chopped
    2–3 garlic cloves, crushed
    25g/1oz fresh root ginger, peeled
      and finely chopped
    pinch of saffron threads
    16 cherry tomatoes
    generous pinch of granulated sugar
    handful of fleshy black olives, pitted
    5ml/1 tsp ground cinnamon
    5ml/1 tsp paprika
    small bunch of fresh flat leaf parsley
    salt and ground black pepper

1 Rinse the beans and place them in a large pan with plenty of water. Bring to the boil and boil for about 10 minutes, and then reduce the heat and simmer gently for 1–1½ hours until tender. Drain the beans and refresh under cold running water, then drain again.

COOK'S TIP
If you are in a hurry, you could use two 400g/14oz cans of butter (lima) beans for this tagine. Make sure you rinse the them well before adding, as canned beans tend to be salty.

2 Heat the olive oil in a heavy pan. Add the onion, garlic and ginger, and cook for about 10 minutes, until softened but not browned. Stir in the saffron threads, followed by the cherry tomatoes and a sprinkling of sugar.

3 As the tomatoes begin to soften, stir in the butter beans. When the tomatoes have heated through, stir in the olives, ground cinnamon and paprika. Season to taste and sprinkle over the chopped parsley. Serve immediately.

Energy 146Kcal/615kJ; Protein 7.4g; Carbohydrate 16.2g, of which sugars 3.8g; Fat 6.3g, of which saturates 0.9g; Cholesterol 0mg; Calcium 62mg; Fibre 6g; Sodium 16mg.

OKRA AND TOMATO TAGINE

ALTHOUGH THIS VEGETABLE STEW IS A NORTH AFRICAN SPECIALITY, SIMILAR DISHES EXIST THROUGHOUT THE MIDDLE EAST. OKRA IS PARTICULARLY POPULAR IN EGYPT, WHERE IT IS CULTIVATED COMMERCIALLY ON A GRAND SCALE. THE VEGETABLE IS ALSO KNOWN AS "LADIES' FINGERS", A REFERENCE TO THEIR TAPERED SHAPE. WHEN CUT BEFORE BEING COOKED, AS IN THIS RECIPE, THE PODS OOZE A GLUE-LIKE SUBSTANCE WHICH GIVES THE DISH A DISTINCTIVE TEXTURE.

SERVES FOUR

INGREDIENTS
    350g/12oz okra
    5–6 tomatoes
    2 small onions
    2 garlic cloves, crushed
    1 fresh green chilli, seeded
    5ml/1 tsp paprika
    small handful of fresh
      coriander (cilantro)
    30ml/2 tbsp sunflower oil
    juice of 1 lemon

1 Trim the okra and then cut it into 1cm/½in lengths. Skin and seed the tomatoes and roughly chop the flesh.

2 Roughly chop one of the onions and place it in a blender or food processor with the garlic, chilli, paprika, coriander and 60ml/4 tbsp water. Process to make a paste.

VARIATION
Use 3–4 shallots instead of onions.

3 Thinly slice the second onion and fry it in the oil in a pan for 5–6 minutes, until golden brown. Transfer to a plate and set aside. Reduce the heat and pour the onion and coriander paste into the pan. Cook for 1–2 minutes, stirring frequently.

4 Add the okra, tomatoes, lemon juice and about 120ml/4fl oz/½ cup water. Stir well to mix, cover tightly and simmer over a low heat for about 15 minutes, until the okra is tender. Transfer to a serving dish, sprinkle with the fried onion rings and serve.

Energy 113Kcal/471kJ; Protein 4.1g; Carbohydrate 9.2g, of which sugars 8g; Fat 7g, of which saturates 1.1g; Cholesterol 0mg; Calcium 181mg; Fibre 5.8g; Sodium 23mg.

CHICKPEA TAGINE

THE PRESERVED LEMON IN THIS RECIPE TELLS YOU THAT IT COMES FROM NORTH AFRICA, PROBABLY MOROCCO, WHERE THE DISTINCTIVE YELLOW GLOBES IN GLASS JARS GLIMMER LIKE MINIATURE SUNS IN THE MARKETS. THE FLAVOUR OF PRESERVED — OR PICKLED — LEMON IS WONDERFUL. SLIGHTLY SALTY, LESS TART THAN THE FRESH FRUIT, IT ADDS A REAL ZING TO THE BLANDNESS OF THE CHICKPEAS.

SERVES FOUR

INGREDIENTS
150g/5oz/¾ cup chickpeas, soaked
    overnight, or 2 x 400g/14oz cans
    chickpeas, rinsed and drained
30ml/2 tbsp sunflower oil
1 large onion, chopped
1 garlic clove, crushed (optional)
400g/14oz can chopped tomatoes
5ml/1 tsp ground cumin
350ml/12fl oz/1½ cups
    vegetable stock
¼ preserved lemon
30ml/2 tbsp chopped fresh
    coriander (cilantro)

1 If using dried chickpeas, cook them in plenty of boiling water for 1–1½ hours until tender. Drain well.

2 Place the chickpeas in a bowl of cold water and rub them between your fingers to remove the skins.

3 Heat the oil in a pan or flameproof casserole and fry the onion and garlic, if using, for 8–10 minutes, until golden.

4 Add the chickpeas, tomatoes, cumin and stock and stir well. Bring to the boil and simmer, uncovered, for 30–40 minutes, until the chickpeas are very soft and most of the liquid has evaporated.

5 Rinse the preserved lemon and cut away the flesh and pith. Cut the peel into slivers and stir it into the chickpeas together with the chopped coriander. Serve immediately with Moroccan bread.

Energy 207Kcal/871kJ; Protein 9.7g; Carbohydrate 26.4g, of which sugars 7.1g; Fat 7.8g, of which saturates 0.9g; Cholesterol 0mg; Calcium 87mg; Fibre 5.6g; Sodium 56mg.

SUMMER VEGETABLE KEBABS
WITH HARISSA AND YOGURT DIP

THERE'S NOTHING NEW ABOUT THREADING VEGETABLE CHUNKS ON SKEWERS, BUT THIS METHOD OF TOSSING THEM IN A SPICY OIL AND LEMON JUICE MARINADE MAKES ALL THE DIFFERENCE. SERVE THEM WITH THE HOT AND CREAMY DIP AND YOU'LL HAVE VEGETARIAN GUESTS EATING OUT OF YOUR HANDS — OR THEIRS. THE KEBABS CAN ALSO BE COOKED ON THE BARBECUE, PREFERABLY ON A DEDICATED PORTION OF THE GRILL, WELL AWAY FROM ANY MEAT JUICES.

SERVES FOUR

INGREDIENTS
   2 aubergines (eggplants), part peeled
   and cut into chunks
   2 courgettes (zucchini), cut
   into chunks
   2–3 red or green (bell) peppers,
   seeded and cut into chunks
   12–16 cherry tomatoes
   4 small red onions, quartered
   60ml/4 tbsp olive oil
   juice of ½ lemon
   1 garlic clove, crushed
   5ml/1 tsp ground coriander
   5ml/1 tsp ground cinnamon
   10ml/2 tsp clear honey
   5ml/1 tsp salt
For the harissa and yogurt dip
   450g/1lb/2 cups Greek (US strained
   plain) yogurt
   30–60ml/2–4 tbsp harissa
   small bunch of fresh coriander
   (cilantro), finely chopped
   small bunch of mint, finely chopped
   salt and ground black pepper

1 Preheat the grill (broiler) on the hottest setting. Put all the vegetables in a bowl. Mix together the olive oil, lemon juice, garlic, ground coriander, cinnamon, honey and salt and pour the mixture over the vegetables.

2 Using your hands, turn the vegetables gently in the marinade, then thread them on to metal skewers. Cook the kebabs under the grill, turning them occasionally, until the vegetables are nicely browned all over.

3 To make the dip, put the yogurt in a bowl and beat in the harissa, making it as fiery in taste as you like by adding more harissa. Add most of the chopped coriander and mint, reserving a little to garnish, and season well with salt and pepper. While they are still hot, slide the vegetables off the skewers and dip them into the yogurt dip before eating. Garnish with the reserved herbs.

COOK'S TIP
Make sure you cut the aubergines, courgettes and peppers into fairly even-size chunks, so they will all cook at the same rate.

Energy 274Kcal/1144kJ; Protein 11.1g; Carbohydrate 28.8g, of which sugars 26.2g; Fat 13.7g, of which saturates 2.5g; Cholesterol 1mg; Calcium 303mg; Fibre 5.9g; Sodium 111mg.

COUSCOUS WITH DRIED FRUIT NUTS AND CINNAMON

IN MOROCCO, THIS DISH OF COUSCOUS WITH DATES, RAISINS AND NUTS FREQUENTLY FORMS PART OF A CELEBRATION MEAL. THE DISH IS OFTEN SERVED AS A COURSE ON ITS OWN, JUST BEFORE THE DESSERT. IT ALSO TASTES GOOD WITH A SPICY TAGINE, OR AS A SIDE DISH WITH ROASTED OR GRILLED MEAT OR POULTRY. THE SUGAR AND CINNAMON MIXTURE IS TRADITIONALLY SPRINKLED IN STRIPES.

SERVES SIX

INGREDIENTS
- 500g/1¼lb/3 cups couscous
- 600ml/1 pint/2½ cups warm water
- 5ml/1 tsp salt
- pinch of saffron threads
- 45ml/3 tbsp sunflower oil
- 30ml/2 tbsp olive oil
- a little butter or smen
- 115g/4oz/½ cup dried apricots, cut into slivers
- 75g/3oz/½ cup dried dates, chopped
- 75g/3oz/generous ½ cup seedless raisins
- 115g/4oz/⅔ cup blanched almonds, cut into slivers
- 75g/3oz/½ cup pistachio nuts
- 10ml/2 tsp ground cinnamon
- 45ml/3 tbsp caster (superfine) sugar

1 Preheat the oven to 180°C/350°F/ Gas 4. Put the couscous in a bowl. Mix together the water, salt and saffron and pour it over the couscous, stirring. Leave to stand for 10 minutes. Add the sunflower oil and, using your fingers, rub it through the grains. Set aside.

2 In a heavy pan, heat the olive oil and butter or smen and stir in the apricots, dates, raisins, most of the almonds (reserve some for garnish) and pistachio nuts.

3 Cook until the raisins plump up, then tip the nuts and fruit into the couscous and toss together to mix. Tip the couscous into an ovenproof dish and cover with foil. Place in the oven for about 20 minutes, until heated through.

4 Toast the reserved slivered almonds. Pile the hot couscous in a mound on a large serving dish and sprinkle with the cinnamon and sugar – these are usually sprinkled in stripes down the mound. Scatter the toasted almonds over the top and serve hot.

Energy 567Kcal/2367kJ; Protein 11.9g; Carbohydrate 71.5g, of which sugars 27.9g; Fat 27.7g, of which saturates 3g; Cholesterol 0mg; Calcium 94mg; Fibre 3.3g; Sodium 79mg.

CAMEROONIAN COCONUT RICE

THIS SPICY RICE AND VEGETABLE MEDLEY COMES FROM BUEA, WHICH IS A SMALL TOWN CLOSE TO MOUNT CAMEROON IN THE NORTH WEST OF THE COUNTRY. USE THIN COCONUT MILK, WHICH WILL CONTRIBUTE PLENTY OF FLAVOUR WITHOUT DOMINATING THE OTHER INGREDIENTS.

SERVES FOUR

INGREDIENTS
    30ml/2 tbsp vegetable oil
    1 onion, chopped
    30ml/2 tbsp tomato purée (paste)
    600ml/1 pint/2½ cups coconut milk
    2 carrots, diced
    1 yellow (bell) pepper, seeded
      and chopped
    5ml/1 tsp dried thyme
    2.5ml/½ tsp mixed spice (apple pie
      spice)
    1 fresh green chilli, seeded
      and chopped
    350g/12oz/1¾ cups long grain rice
    salt

1 Heat the oil in a large pan and fry the onion for 2 minutes. Add the tomato purée and cook over a medium heat for 5–6 minutes, stirring all the time. Add the coconut milk, stir well and bring to the boil.

2 Stir the carrots, pepper, thyme, mixed spice, chilli and rice into the onion mixture, season with salt and bring to the boil. Cover and cook over a low heat, until the rice has absorbed most of the liquid, stirring occasionally. Cover the rice with foil, secure with the lid and steam very gently until the rice is cooked. Serve hot.

CHICKPEA AND OKRA STIR-FRY

THIS MODERN TREATMENT OF MIDDLE EASTERN INGREDIENTS TYPIFIES WHAT YOUNG PROFESSIONALS PREPARE WHEN TIME IS SHORT. THEIR MOTHERS WOULD HAVE COOKED THE CHICKPEAS THEMSELVES.

SERVES FOUR

INGREDIENTS
    450g/1lb okra
    15ml/1 tbsp vegetable oil
    15ml/1 tbsp mustard oil
    15g/½oz/1 tbsp butter
    1 onion, finely chopped
    1 garlic clove, crushed
    2 tomatoes, finely chopped
    1 fresh green chilli, seeded and
      finely chopped
    2 slices of fresh root ginger, peeled
    5ml/1 tsp ground cumin
    15ml/1 tbsp chopped fresh coriander
      (cilantro)
    400g/14oz can chickpeas, rinsed
      and drained

VARIATION
Use other canned beans such as black-eyed beans (peas) instead of chickpeas.

1 Wash and dry the okra, trim the ends and roughly chop the flesh.

2 Heat the vegetable and mustard oils and the butter in a large frying pan.

3 Fry the onion and garlic for 5 minutes, until the onion is slightly softened. Add the chopped tomatoes, chilli and ginger stir well, then add the okra, cumin and chopped coriander. Simmer for 5 minutes, stirring frequently, and then stir in the chickpeas and seasoning.

4 Cook gently for a few minutes until the chickpeas are heated through, then spoon the mixture into a serving bowl and serve at once.

TOP Energy 448Kcal/1876kJ; Protein 8.6g; Carbohydrate 87.8g, of which sugars 17g; Fat 6.9g, of which saturates 1.1g; Cholesterol 0mg; Calcium 82mg; Fibre 2.6g; Sodium 194mg.
BOTTOM Energy 241Kcal/1010kJ; Protein 10.9g; Carbohydrate 22.2g, of which sugars 5.6g; Fat 12.8g, of which saturates 3.3g; Cholesterol 8mg; Calcium 231mg; Fibre 9.3g; Sodium 257mg.

FATAYER

THIS SPINACH AND CHEESE FILO PIE IS THE TURKISH VERSION OF THAT GREEK FAVOURITE,
SPANAKOPITA. SIMILAR RECIPES ARE FOUND THROUGHOUT THE MIDDLE EAST, THE MEDITERRANEAN
AND NORTH AFRICA, THE DIFFERENCES BEING IN THE SPICING AND THE TYPE OF PASTRY USED.

SERVES SIX

INGREDIENTS
  900g/2lb fresh spinach, chopped
  25g/1oz/2 tbsp butter or margarine
  2 onions, chopped
  2 garlic cloves, crushed
  275g/10oz feta cheese, crumbled
  115g/4oz/⅔ cup pine nuts
  5 eggs, beaten
  2 saffron threads, soaked in 30ml/
    2 tbsp boiling water
  5ml/1 tsp paprika
  1.5ml/¼ tsp ground cumin
  1.5ml/¼ tsp ground cinnamon
  14 sheets of filo pastry
  about 60ml/4 tbsp olive oil
  salt and ground black pepper
  lettuce leaves, to serve

1 Place the spinach in a large colander, sprinkle with a little salt, rub it into the leaves and leave for 30 minutes to drain the excess liquid.

2 Preheat the oven to 180°C/350°F/ Gas 4. Melt the butter or margarine in a large pan and fry the onions, until golden. Stir in the garlic, feta cheese and pine nuts.

3 Remove the pan from the heat and stir in the eggs, spinach, saffron water and spices. Season with salt and pepper and mix well.

VARIATION
Grated Cheddar, fresh Parmesan or any hard cheese can be added to this dish as well as the feta.

4 Grease a large rectangular baking dish. Take seven of the sheets of filo pastry and brush one side of each with a little olive oil. Place on the bottom of the dish, overlapping the sides.

5 Spoon all of the spinach mixture over the pastry and carefully drizzle 30ml/ 2 tbsp of the remaining olive oil over the top.

6 Fold the overlapping pastry over the filling. Cut the remaining pastry sheets to the dish size and brush each one with more olive oil. Arrange on top of the filling.

7 Brush with water to prevent curling and then bake in the oven for about 30 minutes, until the pastry is golden brown. Serve with the lettuce leaves.

Energy 565Kcal/2349kJ; Protein 22.7g; Carbohydrate 31.8g, of which sugars 5.6g; Fat 39.5g, of which saturates 11.9g; Cholesterol 200mg; Calcium 500mg; Fibre 4.9g; Sodium 956mg.

KUKU SABZI

THE TRADITIONAL WAY OF CELEBRATING THE NEW YEAR IN IRAN IS TO INVITE SOME FRIENDS OVER TO SHARE IN THIS BAKED EGG AND HERB DISH. IT RESEMBLES A LARGE OVEN-BAKED OMELETTE AND IS FILLED WITH FRESH VEGETABLES. THESE WILL USUALLY BE WHATEVER GREENS ARE IN SEASON AT THE TIME. CHOPPED LETTUCE IS OFTEN INCLUDED, AS IS SPINACH AND FRESH MIXED HERBS.

SERVES FOUR TO SIX

INGREDIENTS

2–3 saffron threads
8 eggs
2 leeks, trimmed and washed
115g/4oz fresh spinach
½ iceberg lettuce
4 spring onions (scallions)
45ml/3 tbsp chopped fresh parsley
45ml/3 tbsp chopped fresh chives
45ml/3 tbsp chopped fresh
  coriander (cilantro)
1 garlic clove, crushed
30ml/2 tbsp chopped walnuts
  (optional)
25g/1oz/2 tbsp butter
salt and ground black pepper
natural (plain) yogurt and pitta bread,
  to serve

1 Preheat the oven to 180°C/350°F/ Gas 4. Soak the saffron threads in 15ml/1 tbsp boiling water in a bowl.

2 Beat the eggs in a large bowl. Finely chop the leeks, spinach, lettuce and spring onions.

3 Add the chopped greens to the eggs together with the herbs, garlic, and walnuts, if using. Season with salt and pepper, add the saffron water and stir thoroughly to mix. Melt the butter in a large flameproof, ovenproof dish and pour in the vegetable and egg mixture.

4 Bake in the oven for 35–40 minutes, until the egg mixture is set and the top is golden. Serve warm or cold, cut into wedges, with yogurt and bread.

Energy 230Kcal/955kJ; Protein 15.5g; Carbohydrate 4.2g, of which sugars 3.4g; Fat 17.2g, of which saturates 6.5g; Cholesterol 394mg; Calcium 162mg; Fibre 3.5g; Sodium 225mg.

EGUSI SPINACH AND EGG

THIS IS A SUPERBLY BALANCED DISH FOR THOSE WHO DON'T EAT MEAT. EGUSI, OR GROUND MELON SEED, IS WIDELY USED IN WEST AFRICAN COOKING AND ADDS A CREAMY TEXTURE AND A NUTTY FLAVOUR TO MANY RECIPES. IT IS ESPECIALLY GOOD WITH FRESH SPINACH AND TOMATOES.

SERVES FOUR

INGREDIENTS
    900g/2lb fresh spinach
    115g/4oz egusi
    90ml/6 tbsp groundnut (peanut)
      or vegetable oil
    4 tomatoes, skinned and chopped
    1 onion, chopped
    2 garlic cloves, crushed
    1 slice of fresh root ginger, peeled
      and finely chopped
    150ml/¼ pint/⅔ cup vegetable stock
    1 fresh red chilli, seeded and
      finely chopped
    6 eggs
    salt

1 Roll the spinach into bundles and cut into strips. Place in a bowl.

2 Cover with boiling water, then drain through a sieve. Press with your fingers to remove excess water. Set aside.

3 Place the egusi in a bowl and gradually add enough water to form a paste, stirring all the time. Set aside.

4 Heat the oil in a pan, add the tomatoes, onion, garlic and ginger and fry over a medium heat for about 10 minutes, stirring frequently.

5 Add the egusi paste, stock, chilli and salt, cook for 10 minutes, then add the spinach and stir it into the sauce. Cook for 15 minutes, uncovered, stirring frequently.

6 Meanwhile hard-boil the eggs, and then stand them in cold water for a few minutes to cool. Shell the eggs and then cut them in half. Arrange the eggs in a shallow serving dish and pour the egusi spinach over the top. Serve hot.

VARIATION
Instead of using boiled eggs, you could make an omelette flavoured with chopped herbs and garlic. Serve it either whole, or sliced, with the egusi sauce. If you can't find egusi, use ground almonds as a substitute.

Energy 436Kcal/1803kJ; Protein 21.5g; Carbohydrate 12.6g, of which sugars 7.5g; Fat 33.3g, of which saturates 5.1g; Cholesterol 285mg; Calcium 464mg; Fibre 7.3g; Sodium 428mg.

GHANIAN BEAN AND GARI LOAF

KIDNEY BEANS AND CAPSICUMS ARE USED TO MAKE THIS TASTY LOAF, WHICH IS THICKENED WITH EGGS AND GROUND CASSAVA. THIS RECIPE IS TYPICAL OF THE CREATIVE DISHES MADE IN GHANA.

SERVES FOUR TO SIX

INGREDIENTS

225g/8oz/1¼ cups red kidney beans, soaked overnight
15g/½oz/1 tbsp butter or margarine
1 onion, finely chopped
2 garlic cloves, crushed
½ red (bell) pepper, seeded and chopped
½ green (bell) pepper, seeded and chopped
1 fresh green chilli, seeded and finely chopped
5ml/1 tsp chopped fresh mixed herbs
2 eggs, beaten
15ml/1 tbsp lemon juice
75ml/5 tbsp gari (see Cook's Tip)
salt and ground black pepper

COOK'S TIP
Gari is a course-grained flour, made from a starchy root vegetable, cassava, which is first dried, then ground. Gari is used in a similar way to ground rice.

1 Drain the kidney beans, then place them in a pan, cover with water and boil rapidly for 15 minutes. Reduce the heat and continue boiling for about 1 hour, until the beans are tender, adding more water, if necessary. Drain, reserving the cooking liquid. Preheat the oven to 190°C/375°F/Gas 5 and grease a 900g/2lb loaf tin (pan).

2 Melt the butter or margarine in a large frying pan and fry the onion, garlic and peppers for 5 minutes. Add the chilli, mixed herbs and a little salt and pepper and stir to mix.

3 Place the cooked kidney beans in a large bowl or in a blender or food processor and mash or process to a pulp. Add the onion and pepper mixture and stir well to mix. Cool slightly, then stir in the eggs and lemon juice.

4 Place the gari in a separate bowl and sprinkle generously with warm water. The gari should become soft and fluffy after about 5 minutes.

5 Pour the gari into the bean and onion mixture and stir together thoroughly. If the consistency is too stiff, add a little of the bean cooking liquid. Spoon the mixture evenly into the prepared loaf tin and bake in the oven for 35–45 minutes, until firm to the touch.

6 Cool the loaf in the tin and then turn it out on to a plate. Cut into thick slices and serve.

Energy 303Kcal/1275kJ; Protein 18g; Carbohydrate 42.5g, of which sugars 5g; Fat 7.5g, of which saturates 2.9g; Cholesterol 103mg; Calcium 79mg; Fibre 10.2g; Sodium 70mg.

BLACK-EYED BEAN STEW WITH SPICY PUMPKIN

GOURDS OF ALL SHAPES AND SIZES ARE A FAMILIAR SIGHT AT AFRICAN MARKETS. PUMPKIN MAKES A TASTY AND COLOURFUL CONTRASTING DISH TO SERVE WITH A SIMPLE BEAN STEW.

SERVES THREE TO FOUR

INGREDIENTS
225g/8oz/1¼ cups black-eyed beans
    (peas), soaked for 4 hours
    or overnight
1 onion, chopped
1 green or red (bell) pepper, seeded
    and chopped
2 garlic cloves, chopped
1 vegetable stock (bouillon) cube
1 fresh thyme sprig or 5ml/1 tsp
    dried thyme
5ml/1 tsp paprika
2.5ml/½ tsp mixed spice (apple pie
    spice)
2 carrots, sliced
15–30ml/1–2 tbsp palm oil
salt, pepper and hot pepper sauce
For the spicy pumpkin
675g/1½lb pumpkin
1 onion
25g/1oz/2 tbsp butter or margarine
2 garlic cloves, crushed
3 tomatoes, skinned and chopped
2.5ml/½ tsp ground cinnamon
10ml/2 tsp curry powder
pinch of freshly grated nutmeg
300ml/½ pint/1¼ cups water
ground black pepper, to taste

1 Drain the beans, place them in a pan and cover generously with water. Bring the beans to the boil.

2 Add the onion, green or red pepper, garlic, stock cube, thyme and spices. Simmer for 45 minutes, until the beans are just tender. Season to taste with salt and a little hot pepper sauce.

3 Add the carrots and palm oil and continue to cook for about 10–12 minutes, until the carrots are tender, adding a little more water, if necessary. Remove the pan from the heat and set aside.

4 To make the spicy pumpkin, cut the pumpkin into cubes and finely chop the onion.

5 Melt the butter or margarine in a frying pan or heavy pan, and add the pumpkin, onion, garlic, tomatoes, spices and water. Stir well to combine, bring to the boil and simmer until the pumpkin is soft, stirring occasionally.

6 Season with salt, hot pepper sauce and black pepper, to taste. Serve with the black-eyed bean stew.

Energy 420Kcal/1772kJ; Protein 21.5g; Carbohydrate 58.4g, of which sugars 16.9g; Fat 12.9g, of which saturates 6.9g; Cholesterol 18mg; Calcium 165mg; Fibre 12.1g; Sodium 84mg.

KENYAN MUNG BEAN STEW

THE LOCAL NAME FOR THIS VEGETARIAN STEW IS DENGU. IT IS A GOOD EXAMPLE OF HOW AFRICAN COOKS ADD VARIETY AND NUTRITION TO A DIET THAT DEPENDS LARGELY ON SEASONAL PRODUCE.

SERVES FOUR

INGREDIENTS
225g/8oz/1¼ cups mung beans,
   soaked overnight
25g/1oz/2 tbsp ghee or butter
2 garlic cloves, crushed
1 red onion, chopped
30ml/2 tbsp tomato purée (paste)
½ green (bell) pepper, seeded and
   cut into small cubes
½ red (bell) pepper, seeded and cut
   into small cubes
1 fresh green chilli, seeded and
   finely chopped
300ml/½ pint/1¼ cups water

1 Put the mung beans in a large pan, cover with water, bring to the boil and boil until the beans are very soft and the water has evaporated. Remove the pan from the heat and mash the beans with a fork or potato masher until smooth. Set aside.

2 Heat the ghee or butter in a separate pan, add the garlic and onion and fry for 4–5 minutes, until golden, then add the tomato purée and cook for a further 2–3 minutes, stirring all the time.

3 Stir in the mashed beans, then add the green and red peppers and chilli.

COOK'S TIP
Mung beans can be found in most Asian shops. If unavailable, use whole green lentils instead.

4 Add the water, stirring well to mix all the ingredients together.

5 Pour the mixture into a clean pan and simmer for about 10 minutes, then spoon into a serving dish and serve immediately.

Energy 224Kcal/944kJ; Protein 14.3g; Carbohydrate 30.2g, of which sugars 4g; Fat 6g, of which saturates 3.5g; Cholesterol 13mg; Calcium 64mg; Fibre 6.9g; Sodium 48mg.

SIDE DISHES AND SALADS

The concept of side dishes is not as clearly defined in the Middle East and Africa as it is in Europe and America. Although a vegetable such fresh green beans might be served solo, with just a simple oil and lemon juice dressing, it is far more common to find composite vegetable dishes. Rice is served at many meals, either plain or with extra ingredients, as in the Persian pilaff or West African Joloff. Breads, especially of the flatbread variety such as chapati, are present at almost every meal, while salads are intriguing, often introducing elements that are relatively unknown outside the country of origin.

CHELO WITH TAHDIG

IN IRAN, STEAMED RICE — CHELO — IS SERVED ALMOST EVERY DAY. THE TRADITIONAL METHOD INVOLVES SOAKING THE RICE, THEN STEAMING IT VERY SLOWLY, SO IT BECOMES SOFT AND FLUFFY, AND A CRISP GOLDEN RICE CRUST OR "TAHDIQ" FORMS ON THE BOTTOM OF THE PAN.

SERVES FOUR

INGREDIENTS
350g/12oz/1¾ cups long grain rice
5ml/1 tsp salt
45ml/3 tbsp melted butter
2–3 saffron threads, soaked in 15ml/
    1 tbsp boiling water (optional)

1 Soak the rice in lukewarm water, salted with 15ml/1 tbsp salt for a minimum of 2 hours.

2 When the rice has soaked, and you are ready to cook, fill a non-stick pan with fresh water, add a little salt and bring to the boil.

3 Drain the rice and stir it into the boiling water. Boil for 5 minutes, then reduce the heat and simmer for about 10 minutes, until the rice is almost cooked. Drain the rice and rinse in lukewarm water. Wash and dry the pan.

4 Heat 30ml/2 tbsp of the melted butter in the pan. Make sure it does not burn. Add about 15ml/1 tbsp water and stir in the rice. Cook the rice over a very low heat for 10 minutes, and then pour over the remaining butter.

5 Cover the pan with a clean dishtowel and secure with a tightly fitting lid, lift the corners of the cloth over the lid.

6 Steam the rice for 30–40 minutes. The cloth will absorb the excess steam and the bottom of the rice will turn into a crisp, golden crust called tahdiq. This is regarded by many as the best part of the rice. To serve, if you like, mix 30–45ml/2–3 tbsp of the rice with the saffron water and sprinkle over the top of the rice.

PLAIN PERSIAN RICE

THIS IS A QUICKER, EASIER METHOD OF COOKING CHELO. DON'T SKIMP ON THE SOAKING TIME, THOUGH, AS IT SOFTENS THE GRAINS AND IMPROVES THE FLAVOUR OF THE FINISHED DISH.

SERVES FOUR

INGREDIENTS
750ml/1¼ pints/3 cups water
5ml/1 tsp salt
350g/12oz/1¾ cups basmati rice
40g/1½oz/3 tbsp butter

1 Place the water and salt in a pan and pour in the rice. Set aside to soak for at least 30 minutes and up to 2 hours.

2 Bring the water and rice to the boil, and then reduce the heat and simmer for 10–15 minutes, until the water is absorbed.

3 Add the butter to the rice, cover the pan with a tight-fitting lid and steam over a very low heat for about 30 minutes. Serve with Khoresh, or any other meat dish.

TOP Energy 398Kcal/1659kJ; Protein 6.6g; Carbohydrate 69.9g, of which sugars 0.1g; Fat 9.7g, of which saturates 5.9g; Cholesterol 24mg; Calcium 19mg; Fibre 0g; Sodium 552mg.
BOTTOM Energy 389Kcal/1620kJ; Protein 6.5g; Carbohydrate 69.9g, of which sugars 0.1g; Fat 8.7g, of which saturates 5.2g; Cholesterol 21mg; Calcium 19mg; Fibre 0g; Sodium 552mg.

BULGUR AND PINE NUT PILAFF

A VARIATION ON RICE PILAFF, THIS IS PARTICULARLY POPULAR IN SYRIA, JORDAN AND TURKEY. THE PINE NUTS ACCENTUATE THE NUTTY FLAVOUR OF THE BULGUR WHEAT.

SERVES FOUR

INGREDIENTS
30ml/2 tbsp olive oil
1 onion, chopped
1 garlic clove, crushed
5ml/1 tsp ground saffron or turmeric
2.5ml/½ tsp ground cinnamon
1 fresh green chilli, seeded and
   finely chopped
600ml/1 pint/2½ cups
   vegetable stock
150ml/¼ pint/⅔ cup white wine
225g/8oz/1⅓ cups bulgur wheat
15g/½oz/1 tbsp butter or margarine
30–45ml/2–3 tbsp pine nuts
30ml/2 tbsp chopped fresh parsley

1 Heat the oil in a pan and fry the onion, until soft. Add the garlic, saffron or turmeric, ground cinnamon and chopped chilli, and fry for a few seconds more.

2 Add the stock and wine, bring to the boil, then reduce the heat and simmer for 8 minutes.

3 Rinse the bulgur wheat under cold running water, drain and add to the stock mixture. Cover and simmer gently for about 15 minutes until the stock is absorbed.

4 Melt the butter or margarine in a separate small pan, add the pine nuts and fry for a few minutes, until golden. Add to the bulgur wheat with the chopped parsley and fork through.

5 Spoon into a warmed serving dish and serve with a vegetable stew.

VARIATION
You can replace the wine with water or stock, if you prefer.

JOLOFF RICE

SOMETIMES REFERRED TO AS WEST AFRICAN PAELLA, THIS MIXED RICE DISH IS MADE USING LOCALLY PRODUCED PALM OIL, WHICH GIVES IT A RICH FLAVOUR AND A REDDISH COLOUR.

SERVES FOUR

INGREDIENTS
30ml/2 tbsp vegetable oil
1 large onion, chopped
2 garlic cloves, crushed
30ml/2 tbsp tomato purée (paste)
350g/12oz/1¾ cups long grain rice
1 fresh green chilli, seeded
   and chopped
pinch of salt
600ml/1 pint/2½ cups vegetable or
   chicken stock

1 Heat the oil in a pan and fry the onion and garlic for 4–5 minutes, until soft. Add the tomato purée and fry over a medium heat for about 3 minutes, stirring all the time.

2 Rinse the rice in cold water, drain well and add to the pan with the chilli and a pinch of salt. Cook for 2–3 minutes, stirring all the time to prevent the rice sticking to the base of the pan.

3 Add the stock, bring to the boil, then cover and simmer over a low heat for about 15 minutes.

4 When the liquid is nearly absorbed, cover the rice with a piece of foil, cover the pan and steam, over a low heat, until the rice is cooked. Serve immediately.

TOP Energy 295Kcal/1225kJ; Protein 4.8g; Carbohydrate 32.4g, of which sugars 2.7g; Fat 14.4g, of which saturates 3.1g; Cholesterol 8mg; Calcium 25mg; Fibre 0.7g; Sodium 26mg.
BOTTOM Energy 392Kcal/1637kJ; Protein 7.8g; Carbohydrate 75.7g, of which sugars 4.5g; Fat 6.1g, of which saturates 0.7g; Cholesterol 0mg; Calcium 36mg; Fibre 1.1g; Sodium 20mg.

GARI FOTO

THE NAME SUGGESTS THIS DISH MIGHT INSPIRE GUESTS TO GET OUT THEIR CAMERAS. IT IS A WEST AFRICAN SPECIALITY, THICKENED WITH A COARSE GROUND FLOUR MADE FROM GROUND CASSAVA ROOT.

SERVES FOUR

INGREDIENTS

25g/1oz/2 tbsp butter or margarine
1 onion, chopped
3 tomatoes, skinned and chopped
15ml/1 tbsp tomato purée (paste)
175g/6oz carrots, chopped
115g/4oz/⅔ cup corn
175g/6oz red (bell) peppers, seeded
  and chopped
300ml/½ pint/1¼ cups vegetable
  stock or water
1 fresh green chilli, seeded
  and chopped
115g/4oz gari

COOK'S TIP
Gari, used in many African recipes, is a
coarse flour made from cassava.

1 Melt the butter or margarine in a non-stick pan and fry the onion and tomatoes until pulpy, stirring frequently.

2 Add the tomato purée and carrots and fry for a few minutes, then stir in the corn, red peppers, stock or water and chilli. Bring to the boil, and then cover and simmer for 5 minutes.

3 Slowly mix the gari into the sauce, stirring constantly, until it is well mixed with the vegetables.

4 Cover the pan and cook over a low heat for 5–8 minutes. Transfer the mixture to a serving dish and serve hot.

FUFU

EVERY AFRICAN COUNTRY HAS A VERSION OF THIS PORRIDGE-LIKE SIDE DISH, DESIGNED TO MOP UP THE LIQUID FROM A STEW. IN SOUTHERN AFRICA IT IS CALLED PUTU AND IS MADE WITH CORN MEAL. WEST AFRICANS PREFER TO USE GROUND RICE, SOMETIMES WITH SEMOLINA.

SERVES FOUR

INGREDIENTS

300ml/½ pint/1¼ cups milk
300ml/½ pint/1¼ cups water
25g/1oz/2 tbsp butter
  or margarine
2.5ml/½ tsp salt
15ml/1 tbsp chopped
  fresh parsley
275g/10oz/1½ cups ground rice

COOK'S TIP
Ground rice is creamy white and when cooked it has a slightly grainy texture. Although often used in sweet dishes, it is a tasty grain to serve with savoury dishes too. The addition of milk makes it creamier, but it can be replaced with water, if preferred.

1 Place the milk, water and butter or margarine and salt in a pan, bring to the boil and then turn the heat to low.

2 Add the chopped parsley. Then gradually add the ground rice, stirring vigorously with a wooden spoon to prevent the rice becoming lumpy.

3 Cover the pan and cook over a low heat for about 15 minutes, beating the mixture regularly every 2 minutes to prevent lumps forming.

4 To test if the rice is cooked, rub a pinch of the mixture between your fingers; if it feels smooth and fairly dry, it is ready; if not, continue cooking for a few more minutes and then test again. Serve hot.

TOP Energy 211Kcal/880kJ; Protein 4.6g; Carbohydrate 33.1g, of which sugars 10.9g; Fat 6.7g, of which saturates 3.4g; Cholesterol 13mg; Calcium 32mg; Fibre 3.8g; Sodium 68mg.
BOTTOM Energy 319Kcal/1333kJ; Protein 7.1g; Carbohydrate 56.9g, of which sugars 3.6g; Fat 7.2g, of which saturates 4.1g; Cholesterol 18mg; Calcium 105mg; Fibre 0g; Sodium 316mg.

TANZANIAN VEGETABLE RICE

KERNELS OF CORN AND SMALL PIECES OF CARROT AND PEPPER MAKE THIS A COLOURFUL ACCOMPANIMENT. IT TASTES GREAT WITH GRILLED OR BAKED CHICKEN, AND CAN ALSO BE USED AS A FILLING FOR BAKED FISH. IN TANZANIA THE RICE IS OFTEN SERVED WITH A DELICIOUS FRESH RELISH CALLED KACHUMBALI.

SERVES FOUR

INGREDIENTS

- 350g/12oz/1¾ cups basmati rice
- 45ml/3 tbsp vegetable oil
- 1 onion, chopped
- 2 garlic cloves, crushed
- 750ml/1¼ pints/3 cups vegetable stock or water
- 115g/4oz/⅔ cup corn
- ½ red or green (bell) pepper, chopped
- 1 large carrot, grated

1 Wash the rice in a sieve under cold running water, then leave to drain for about 15 minutes.

2 Heat the oil in a large pan and fry the onion for a few minutes over a medium heat, until just soft.

3 Add the rice and stir-fry for about 10 minutes, taking care to keep stirring all the time so that the rice doesn't stick to the pan.

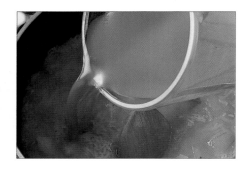

4 Add the garlic and the stock or water and stir well. Bring to the boil and cook over a high heat for 5 minutes, then reduce the heat, cover and cook the rice for 20 minutes.

5 Scatter the corn over the rice, then scatter the pepper on top and lastly sprinkle over the grated carrot.

6 Cover tightly and steam over a low heat until the rice is cooked, then mix the ingredients together with a fork and serve immediately.

Energy 455Kcal/1902kJ; Protein 8.3g; Carbohydrate 84.2g, of which sugars 8.5g; Fat 9.3g, of which saturates 1.1g; Cholesterol 0mg; Calcium 34mg; Fibre 1.9g; Sodium 84mg.

ZERESHK POLO

THE ZERESHK, OR BARBERRIES, THAT FLAVOUR THIS DISH ARE VERY SMALL DRIED BERRIES THAT ARE DELICIOUS WITH RICE. THEY ARE AVAILABLE FROM MOST PERSIAN AND MIDDLE EASTERN FOOD STORES.

SERVES FOUR

INGREDIENTS
50g/2oz zereshk
45ml/3 tbsp melted butter
50g/2oz/⅓ cup raisins
30ml/2 tbsp granulated sugar
5ml/1 tsp ground cinnamon
5ml/1 tsp ground cumin
350g/12oz/1¾ cups basmati rice,
soaked in salted water for
2 hours
2–3 saffron threads, soaked in 15ml/
1 tbsp boiling water
salt

1 Thoroughly wash the zereshk in cold water at least 4–5 times to rinse off any bits of grit.

2 Heat 15ml/1 tbsp of the butter in a small frying pan and stir-fry the raisins for 1–2 minutes.

3 Add the zereshk, stir-fry for a few seconds and then add the sugar, and half of the cinnamon and cumin. Cook briefly and then set aside.

4 Drain the rice and then boil it in a pan of salted water for 5 minutes, reduce the heat and simmer for 10 minutes, until almost cooked.

5 Drain and rinse the rice in lukewarm water, and wash and dry the pan. Heat half of the remaining butter in the pan, add 15ml/1 tbsp water and stir in half of the rice.

6 Sprinkle with half of the raisin and zereshk mixture and top with all but 45ml/3 tbsp of the rice. Sprinkle over the remaining raisin mixture.

7 Blend the reserved rice with the remaining cinnamon and cumin and sprinkle over the top of the rice mixture.

8 Dribble the remaining butter over and then cover the pan with a clean dishtowel and secure with a tightly fitting lid, lifting the corners of the cloth back over the lid. Steam the rice over a very low heat for about 30–40 minutes.

9 Just before serving, mix 45ml/3 tbsp of the rice with the saffron water. Spoon the rice on to a large, flat serving dish and sprinkle the saffron rice over the top to garnish.

Energy 465Kcal/1943kJ; Protein 7g; Carbohydrate 87g, of which sugars 17.2g; Fat 9.8g, of which saturates 5.9g; Cholesterol 24mg; Calcium 32mg; Fibre 0.6g; Sodium 77mg.

SHIRIN POLO

ALSO KNOWN AS SWEET RICE, THIS COLOURFUL DISH IS TRADITIONALLY SERVED AT IRANIAN WEDDING BANQUETS. FOR A MAIN COURSE, CHICKEN MAY BE ADDED TO THE RICE MIXTURE.

SERVES EIGHT TO TEN

INGREDIENTS
  3 oranges
  90ml/6 tbsp granulated sugar
  45ml/3 tbsp melted butter
  5–6 carrots, cut into julienne strips
  50g/2oz/½ cup mixed chopped
    pistachios, almonds and pine nuts
  675g/1½lb/3⅓ cups basmati rice,
    soaked in salted water for 2 hours
  2–3 saffron threads, soaked in
    15ml/1 tbsp boiling water
  salt

COOK'S TIP
Take care to cook this rice over a very low heat as it can burn easily owing to the added sugar and the natural sugar in the carrots.

1 Cut the peel from the oranges in wide strips using a potato peeler, and cut the peel into thin shreds.

2 Place the strips of peel in a pan cover with water and bring to the boil. Simmer for a few minutes, and then drain and repeat this process, until you have removed the bitter flavour of the peel.

3 Place the peel back in the pan with 45ml/3 tbsp sugar and 60ml/4 tbsp water. Bring to the boil then simmer, until reduced by half. Set aside.

4 Heat 15ml/1 tbsp of the butter in a pan and fry the carrots for 2–3 minutes. Add the remaining sugar and 60ml/4 tbsp water and simmer for 10 minutes, until the liquid has almost evaporated.

5 Stir the carrots and half of the nuts into the orange peel and set aside. Drain the rice, boil it in a pan of salted water for 5 minutes, then reduce the heat and simmer very gently for 10 minutes, until almost cooked. Drain and rinse.

6 Heat 15ml/1 tbsp of the remaining butter in the pan and add 45ml/3 tbsp water. Fork a little of the rice into the pan and spoon on some of the orange mixture. Make layers until all the mixture has been used.

7 Cook gently for 10 minutes. Pour over the remaining butter and cover with a clean dishtowel. Secure the lid and steam for 30–45 minutes. Garnish with nuts, and drizzle over the saffron water.

RICE WITH FRESH HERBS

CORIANDER, CHIVES AND DILL LOOK PRETTY SCATTERED AMONG THE RICE GRAINS IN THIS POPULAR MIDDLE EASTERN ACCOMPANIMENT. SERVE IT WITH A HIGHLY SPICED MAIN COURSE.

SERVES FOUR

INGREDIENTS
  350g/12oz/1¾ cups basmati rice,
    soaked in salted water for 2 hours
  30ml/2 tbsp finely chopped
    fresh parsley
  30ml/2 tbsp finely chopped fresh
    coriander (cilantro)
  30ml/2 tbsp chopped fresh chives
  15ml/1 tbsp chopped fresh dill
  3–4 spring onions (scallions),
    finely chopped
  60ml/4 tbsp butter
  5ml/1 tsp ground cinnamon
  2–3 saffron threads, soaked in
    15ml/1 tbsp boiling water
  salt

1 Drain the rice, and then boil it in a pan of salted water for 5 minutes, reduce the heat and simmer for 10 minutes.

2 Stir in the chopped herbs and spring onions and mix well with a fork. Simmer for a few minutes more, then drain but do not rinse. Wash and dry the pan.

3 Heat half of the butter in the pan, add 15ml/1 tbsp water, then stir in the rice. Cook over a very low heat for 10 minutes, till almost cooked, then add the remaining butter, the cinnamon and saffron water and cover the pan with a clean towel. Secure a tight-fitting lid, and steam for 30–40 minutes. Serve.

TOP Energy 460Kcal/1924kJ; Protein 8.3g; Carbohydrate 87.2g, of which sugars 19.6g; Fat 8.7g, of which saturates 3.4g; Cholesterol 12mg; Calcium 66mg; Fibre 2.2g; Sodium 79mg.
BOTTOM Energy 435Kcal/1809kJ; Protein 7.3g; Carbohydrate 70.7g, of which sugars 0.8g; Fat 13.1g, of which saturates 7.8g; Cholesterol 32mg; Calcium 61mg; Fibre 1.1g; Sodium 98mg.

ETHIOPIAN COLLARD GREENS

ALSO KNOWN AS ABESHA GOMEN, THIS SPICY DISH CAN BE MADE WITH COLLARD GREENS, SPRING GREENS OR KALE. ETHIOPIANS SERVE IT ON A LARGE FLAT PANCAKE-LIKE BREAD CALLED INJERA.

SERVES FOUR

INGREDIENTS
  450g/1lb collard greens
  60ml/4 tbsp olive oil
  2 small red onions, finely chopped
  1 garlic clove, crushed
  2.5ml/½ tsp grated fresh root ginger
  2 fresh green chillies, seeded
    and sliced
  150ml/¼ pint/⅔ cup vegetable stock
    or water
  1 red (bell) pepper, seeded
    and sliced
  salt and ground black pepper

1 Wash the collard greens, then strip the leaves from the stalks and steam the leaves over a pan of boiling water for about 5 minutes, until slightly wilted.

2 Set the greens aside on a plate to cool, then place in a sieve or colander and press out the excess water.

3 Using a large sharp knife, slice the collard greens very thinly.

4 Heat the oil in a pan and fry the onions, until browned. Add the garlic and ginger and fry for a few minutes, then add the chillies and a little of the stock or water and cook for 2 minutes.

5 Add the collard greens, red pepper and the remaining stock or water. Season with salt and pepper, mix well, then cover and cook over a low heat for about 15 minutes. Serve immediately.

COOK'S TIPS
Traditionally this dish is cooked with more liquid and for longer. The cooking time has been reduced from 45 minutes to 15 minutes. However, if you fancy a more authentic taste, cook for longer and increase the amount of liquid. Green cabbage or spring greens are a good substitute for collard greens.

GREEN LENTIL SALAD

ANOTHER ETHIOPIAN SPECIALITY, THIS GREEN LENTIL AND TOMATO SALAD IS TRADITIONALLY FLAVOURED WITH SENAFITCH, WHICH IS A PEPPERY HERB FROM WHICH A TYPE OF MUSTARD IS MADE. THIS RECIPE USES ENGLISH MUSTARD INSTEAD.

SERVES FOUR

INGREDIENTS
  225g/8oz/1 cup green lentils, rinsed
  2 tomatoes, skinned and chopped
  1 red onion, finely chopped
  1 fresh green chilli, seeded
    and chopped
  60ml/4 tbsp lemon juice
  75ml/5 tbsp olive oil
  2.5ml/½ tsp prepared mustard
  salt and ground black pepepr

1 Place the lentils in a pan, cover with water and bring to the boil. Simmer for 45 minutes until soft, drain, then turn into a bowl and mash lightly.

2 Add the tomatoes, onion, chilli, lemon juice, olive oil, mustard and seasoning. Mix well, adjust the seasoning if necessary, then cool and chill before serving as an accompaniment to meat or fish dishes.

TOP Energy 149Kcal/615kJ; Protein 4.1g; Carbohydrate 6g, of which sugars 4.8g; Fat 12.3g, of which saturates 1.7g; Cholesterol 0mg; Calcium 248mg; Fibre 4.3g; Sodium 24mg.
BOTTOM Energy 192Kcal/816kJ; Protein 14.2g; Carbohydrate 30.2g, of which sugars 3.1g; Fat 2.5g, of which saturates 0.4g; Cholesterol 0mg; Calcium 47mg; Fibre 5.7g; Sodium 12mg.

SESE PLANTAIN AND YAM

THE WORD "SESE" REFERS TO THE WRIST ACTION USED IN TOSSING THE PLANTAIN AND YAM MIXTURE WITH THE OIL. THERE'S A DEFINITE TRICK TO IT, IF YOU WISH TO AVOID SPLASHES. THIS RECIPE SUGGESTS STIRRING THE INGREDIENTS TOGETHER, WHICH IS MORE DECOROUS AND LESS DANGEROUS.

SERVES FOUR

INGREDIENTS
    2 green plantains
    450g/1lb white yam
    2 tomatoes, skinned and chopped
    1 fresh red chilli, seeded and chopped
    1 onion, chopped
    ½ vegetable stock (bouillon) cube
    15ml/1 tbsp palm oil
    15ml/1 tbsp tomato purée (paste)
    salt

1 Peel the plantains by cutting them in half, slitting the skin along the natural ridges, and then lifting off the skin in sections. Cut each of the plantain halves into three sections.

2 Prepare the yam, then place the plantains and yam in a large pan with 600ml/1 pint/2½ cups water, bring to the boil and cook for 5 minutes.

3 Add the tomatoes, chilli and onion and simmer for a further 10 minutes, then crumble in the stock cube, stir well, cover and simmer for 5 minutes.

4 Stir in the oil and tomato purée and continue cooking for about 5 minutes, until the plantains are tender. Season with salt and pour into a warmed serving dish. Serve immediately.

MAKANDE

THIS SIMPLE CORN AND RED BEAN STEW IS THE STANDARD LUNCH FOR MANY TANZANIANS, ESPECIALLY THOSE WHO LIVE IN THE KILIMANJARO REGION. WHEN TIMES ARE GOOD, MEAT IS ADDED.

SERVES THREE TO FOUR

INGREDIENTS
    225g/8oz/1¼ cups dried red kidney
        beans, soaked overnight
    1 onion, chopped
    2 garlic cloves, crushed
    75g/3oz creamed coconut or
        175ml/6fl oz/¾ cup coconut cream
    225g/8oz/1⅓ cups frozen corn
    300ml/½ pint/1¼ cups vegetable
        stock or water
    salt and ground black pepper

1 Drain the beans and place them in a pan, cover with water and boil rapidly for 15 minutes. Reduce the heat and continue boiling for 1 hour, until the beans are tender, adding more water, if necessary. Drain.

2 Place the beans in a clean pan with the onion, garlic, creamed coconut or coconut cream, corn and salt and pepper.

3 Add the stock or water, bring to the boil and simmer for 20 minutes, stirring occasionally to dissolve or combine the coconut.

4 Adjust the seasoning and spoon into a warmed serving dish. Serve with an onion and tomato salad.

TOP Energy 258Kcal/1097kJ; Protein 3.2g; Carbohydrate 57.1g, of which sugars 8g; Fat 3.5g, of which saturates 1.6g; Cholesterol 0mg; Calcium 32mg; Fibre 3.3g; Sodium 19mg.
BOTTOM Energy 465Kcal/1959kJ; Protein 20.5g; Carbohydrate 56.4g, of which sugars 11.9g; Fat 19.2g, of which saturates 15.1g; Cholesterol 0mg; Calcium 89mg; Fibre 13.1g; Sodium 224mg.

GHANAIAN PRAWN AND PLANTAIN SALAD

USUALLY SERVED AS A SIDE DISH, BUT SUBSTANTIAL ENOUGH FOR LUNCH, THIS FRESH-TASTING SALAD IS A COLOURFUL BLEND OF FRUITS, VEGETABLES, HARD-BOILED EGGS AND FISH.

SERVES FOUR

INGREDIENTS

115g/4oz cooked, peeled
  prawns (shrimp)
1 garlic clove, crushed
7.5ml/1½ tsp vegetable oil
2 eggs
1 yellow plantain, halved
4 lettuce leaves
2 tomatoes
1 red (bell) pepper, seeded
1 avocado
juice of 1 lemon
1 carrot
200g/7oz can tuna or sardines, in
  brine, drained and flaked
1 fresh green chilli, finely chopped
30ml/2 tbsp chopped spring onions
  (scallions)
salt and ground black pepper

4 Shred the lettuce and arrange on a large serving plate. Slice the tomatoes and red pepper, and peel, stone and slice the avocado, sprinkling it with a little lemon juice. Arrange the vegetables on the plate over the lettuce. Cut the carrot into matchstick-size pieces and arrange over the other vegetables.

5 Add the plantain, eggs, prawns and tuna or sardines. Sprinkle with the remaining lemon juice, scatter the chilli and spring onions on top and season with salt and pepper to taste. Serve as a lunch-time salad or as a delicious side dish.

1 Put the prawns in a bowl, add the crushed garlic and a little seasoning. Heat the oil in a small pan, add the prawns and cook over a low heat for a few minutes. Transfer to a plate to cool.

2 Hard-boil the eggs, and then place them in cold water to cool. Shell the eggs and cut them into slices. Set aside.

3 Boil the plantain in a pan of water for 15 minutes, drain, cool, then peel and slice thickly. Set aside.

COOK'S TIP
To make a complete meal, serve this salad with a meat or fish dish. Vary the ingredients, use any canned fish and a mixture of interesting salad leaves.

Energy 234Kcal/985kJ; Protein 22.1g; Carbohydrate 18g, of which sugars 8.5g; Fat 8.7g, of which saturates 2.1g; Cholesterol 177mg; Calcium 69mg; Fibre 3.3g; Sodium 265mg.

PLANTAIN AND GREEN BANANA SALAD

THE PLANTAINS AND BANANAS CAN BE COOKED IN THEIR SKINS. IF THIS IS DONE, THEY WILL NOT ONLY RETAIN THEIR SOFT TEXTURE, BUT WILL ALSO ABSORB THE DRESSING MORE READILY.

SERVES FOUR

INGREDIENTS

2 firm yellow plantains
3 green bananas
1 garlic clove, crushed
1 red onion
15–30ml/1–2 tbsp chopped fresh
  coriander (cilantro)
45ml/3 tbsp sunflower oil
25ml/1½ tbsp malt vinegar
salt and coarse grain black pepper

1 Slit the plantains and bananas lengthways along their natural ridges, then cut them in half and place in a large pan.

2 Cover the plantains and bananas with water, add a little salt and bring to the boil. Boil gently for 20 minutes, until tender, then remove the plantains and bananas from the water.

3 When the plantains and bananas are cool enough to handle, peel and cut them into medium-size slices.

4 Put the plantain and banana slices into a bowl and add the garlic, tossing gently to mix.

5 Halve the onion and slice it thinly. Add to the bowl with the chopped coriander, oil, vinegar and seasoning. Toss together to mix, then serve as an accompaniment to a main dish.

Energy 256Kcal/1078kJ; Protein 2.3g; Carbohydrate 44.5g, of which sugars 21.7g; Fat 8.9g, of which saturates 1.2g; Cholesterol 0mg; Calcium 31mg; Fibre 2.6g; Sodium 7mg.

BROAD BEAN SALAD <u>AND</u> CARROT SALAD

THESE TWO SALADS ARE FREQUENTLY SERVED TOGETHER. THE FLAVOURS ARE COMPLEMENTARY, AND THE INTENSE GREEN OF THE SHELLED BROAD BEANS PROVIDES A PERFECT CONTRAST TO THE ORANGE OF THE CARROTS. THESE PARTICULAR RECIPES COME FROM MOROCCO, AS IS INDICATED BY THE PRESERVED LEMON IN THE BEAN MIXTURE.

SERVES FOUR

INGREDIENTS

For the broad bean salad
    2kg/4½lb broad (fava) beans
    60–75ml/4–5 tbsp olive oil
    juice of ½ lemon
    2 garlic cloves, finely chopped
    5ml/1 tsp ground cumin
    10ml/2 tsp paprika
    small bunch of coriander (cilantro),
    1 preserved lemon, chopped
    salt and ground black pepper
    handful of black olives, to garnish
For the carrot salad
    450g/1lb carrots, cut into sticks
    30–45ml/2–3 tbsp olive oil
    juice of 1 lemon
    2–3 garlic cloves, crushed
    10ml/2 tsp granulated sugar
    5–10ml/1–2 tsp cumin seeds, roasted
    5ml/1 tsp ground cinnamon
    5ml/1 tsp paprika
    small bunch of coriander (cilantro)
    small bunch of mint

1 To make the broad bean salad, bring a large pan of salted water to the boil. Meanwhile, pod the beans. Put the beans in the pan and boil for about 2 minutes, then drain and refresh the beans under cold running water. Drain. Slip off and discard the thick outer skin.

2 Put the beans in a heavy pan and add the olive oil, lemon juice, garlic, cumin and paprika. Cook the beans gently over a low heat for about 10 minutes, then season to taste with salt and pepper and leave to cool in the pan.

3 Tip the beans into a serving bowl, scraping all the juices from the pan. Chop the coriander and add to the beans with the preserved lemon and garnish with the black olives.

COOK'S TIP
To roast cumin seeds, stir them in a heavy pan over a low heat, until they emit a warm, nutty aroma.

4 To make the carrot salad, steam the carrots over a pan of boiling water for about 15 minutes, until tender. While they are still warm, toss the carrots in a serving bowl with the olive oil, lemon juice, garlic and sugar. Season to taste, then add the cumin seeds, cinnamon and paprika.

5 Finally, chop the coriander and mint, and toss with the carrots. Serve warm or at room temperature.

Energy 299Kcal/1247kJ; Protein 11.1g; Carbohydrate 25.1g, of which sugars 11.4g; Fat 17.8g, of which saturates 2.6g; Cholesterol 0mg; Calcium 136mg; Fibre 11.8g; Sodium 44mg.

ZAHLOUK AND PALE COURGETTE AND CAULIFLOWER SALAD

IN MOROCCO, WHERE THESE RECIPES ORIGINATED, COOKS LIKE TO USE ARGAN OIL FOR SPECIAL DRESSINGS. THIS RARE OIL HAS A REDDISH TINGE AND A RICH, NUTTY FLAVOUR.

SERVES FOUR

INGREDIENTS
For the zahlouk
    3 large aubergines (eggplant)
    3–4 large tomatoes
    5ml/1 tsp granulated sugar
    3–4 garlic cloves, crushed
    60ml/4 tbsp olive oil or argan oil
    juice of 1 lemon
    scant 5ml/1 tsp harissa
    5ml/1 tsp cumin seeds, roasted
      and ground
    small bunch of fresh flat leaf parsley
    salt
For the courgette and cauliflower salad
    60ml/4 tbsp olive oil
    2–3 small courgettes (zucchini),
    1 cauliflower, broken into florets
    juice of 1 lemon
    2–3 garlic cloves, crushed
    small bunch of parsley
    salt and ground black pepper
    5ml/1 tsp paprika, to garnish

1 To make the zahlouk, peel and cube the aubergines and boil in a pan of plenty of salted water for about 15 minutes, until they are very soft. Drain and squeeze out the excess water, then chop and mash them with a fork.

2 Skin and chop the tomatoes. Put the pulped tomatoes in a pan, stir in the sugar, and cook over a gentle heat, until they are reduced to a thick sauce.

3 Add the mashed aubergines. Stir in the garlic, olive or argan oil, lemon juice, harissa and ground cumin. Chop the parsley and add to the aubergine mix, stir until well mixed. Season with salt to taste.

4 To make the courgette and cauliflower salad, thickly slice the courgettes, then heat about half of the olive oil in a heavy pan and brown the courgettes on both sides. Drain on kitchen paper.

5 Meanwhile, steam the cauliflower over a pan of boiling water for 7–10 minutes, until tender. While the cauliflower is still warm, mash it lightly in a bowl and mix in the remaining olive oil, half the lemon juice and the garlic. Add the courgettes. Finely chop the parsley, and add to the salad together with the remaining lemon juice. Season with salt and pepper.

6 Serve the zahlouk at room temperature with plenty of flat bread. Serve the courgette and cauliflower salad sprinkled with paprika.

Energy 302Kcal/1251kJ; Protein 8.3g; Carbohydrate 12.5g, of which sugars 11.5g; Fat 24.7g, of which saturates 3.7g; Cholesterol 0mg; Calcium 139mg; Fibre 8.6g; Sodium 37mg.

KACHUMBALI

THIS RELISH COMES FROM TANZANIA, WHERE IT IS OFTEN SERVED WITH GRILLED MEAT OR FISH. TANZANIA IS ONE OF THE WORLD'S LEADING CHILLI GROWERS, AND THE VARIETY USED HERE SHOULD BE A HOT ONE FOR AN AUTHENTIC FLAVOUR. JALAPEÑO CHILLIES, WHICH ARE AVAILABLE FROM MOST SUPERMARKETS, WORK WELL IN THIS DISH.

SERVES FOUR TO SIX

INGREDIENTS
  2 red onions
  4 tomatoes
  1 fresh green chilli
  ½ cucumber
  1 carrot
  juice of 1 lemon
  salt and ground black pepper

VARIATION
This recipe can be made by very finely chopping the onions, tomatoes, cucumber and carrot. This produces a very moist, sauce-like mixture, which is good served inside pitta breads, and eaten as a salad roll.

1 Slice the onions and tomatoes very thinly and place in a bowl.

2 Peel and slice the cucumber and carrot and add to the onions and tomatoes. Slice the chilli lengthways, discard the seeds, and then chop the flesh very finely.

3 Squeeze the lemon juice over the salad. Season with salt and pepper and toss together to mix. Serve as an accompaniment, salad or relish.

COCONUT RELISH

FOR A COOLER, MORE REFRESHING RELISH, TRY THIS MIXTURE OF COCONUT AND LEMON JUICE. THE SMALL AMOUNT OF CHOPPED CHILLI IS JUST ENOUGH TO MAKE THE TASTEBUDS TINGLE.

MAKES ABOUT 50g/2oz

INGREDIENTS
  50g/2oz fresh or desiccated (dry unsweetened shredded) coconut
  1 fresh red chilli
  10ml/2 tsp lemon juice
  1.5ml/½ tsp salt
  10ml/2 tsp water

1 Grate the fresh coconut and place it in a mixing bowl. If using desiccated coconut, add just enough water to moisten it.

2 Cut the chilli in half and remove the seeds. Chop the flesh into fine slices and then chop the slices into tiny pieces. Use about a 1.5ml/¼ tsp, but more if you enjoy the heat.

3 Add the lemon juice, salt, water and chopped chilli to the coconut. Stir thoroughly to mix.

4 Serve the salad as a relish with cold meats or fish, or as an accompaniment to a main dish.

TOP Energy 50Kcal/211kJ; Protein 1.9g; Carbohydrate 10.1g, of which sugars 8.6g; Fat 0.5g, of which saturates 0.1g; Cholesterol 0mg; Calcium 36mg; Fibre 2.6g; Sodium 17mg.
BOTTOM Energy 303Kcal/1250kJ; Protein 2.9g; Carbohydrate 3.2g, of which sugars 3.2g; Fat 31g, of which saturates 26.7g; Cholesterol 0mg; Calcium 13mg; Fibre 6.8g; Sodium 44mg.

COCONUT CHAPATIS

UNUSUALLY, THE DOUGH FOR THESE CHAPATIS IS TWISTED INTO RINGS BEFORE BEING COOKED ON A GRIDDLE OR HEAVY PAN. COCONUT MILK GIVES THEM A LOVELY FLAVOUR.

MAKES NINE TO TEN

INGREDIENTS
  450g/1lb/4 cups plain
    (all-purpose) flour
  2.5ml/½ tsp salt
  300ml/½ pint/1¼ cups coconut milk
  vegetable oil, for shallow frying

1 Place the flour and salt in a bowl and gradually stir in the coconut milk.

2 Bring the dough together with your hands, then turn it on to a floured surface and knead to form a firm but pliable dough, adding more flour if the dough is on the sticky side.

3 Divide the dough into nine equal-size balls, and roll out each of the balls on a lightly floured surface to form a 21cm/8½in round.

4 Brush the rounds with oil, roll up and twist into a ring, tucking the ends into the middle. Place on a floured board and set aside for 15 minutes.

5 Roll out each of the dough rings to a 5cm/2in round. Brush a heavy frying pan with oil and cook the chapatis for 3–4 minutes on each side, until golden brown. Serve hot as an accompaniment.

MANDAZI

THESE EAST AFRICAN BREADS RESEMBLE DOUGHNUTS. ALTHOUGH THERE ARE SWEETER VERSIONS, THESE SPICY ROUNDS ARE REGARDED AS SAVOURY SNACKS, OR SERVED WITH SOUPS OR STEWS.

MAKES ABOUT FIFTEEN

INGREDIENTS
  4 or 5 cardamom pods
  450g/1lb/4 cups self-raising
    (self-rising) flour
  45ml/3 tbsp caster (superfine) sugar
  5ml/1 tsp baking powder
  1 egg, beaten
  30ml/2 tbsp vegetable oil, plus oil
    for deep-frying
  225ml/7½fl oz/⅞ cup milk or water

1 Slightly crush each of the cardamom pods, shake out the seeds and discard the husks.

2 Grind the cardamom seeds in a small mortar and pestle, then place in a large bowl with the flour, sugar and baking powder. Stir well to mix.

3 Put the egg and oil in a small bowl and beat together, then add to the flour mixture. Mix with your fingers, gradually adding the milk or water to make a dough.

4 Lightly knead the dough until smooth and not sticky when a finger is pushed into it, adding more flour, if necessary. Leave in a warm place for 15 minutes, then roll out to about a 1cm/½in thickness. Cut into 6cm/2½in rounds.

5 Heat the oil in a heavy pan or deep-fryer and deep-fry the mandazis for 4–5 minutes, until golden brown, turning frequently in the oil. Serve.

TOP Energy 179Kcal/762kJ; Protein 4.8g; Carbohydrate 40.8g, of which sugars 2.7g; Fat 0.8g, of which saturates 0.2g; Cholesterol 0mg; Calcium 81mg; Fibre 1.5g; Sodium 44mg.
BOTTOM Energy 149Kcal/631kJ; Protein 3.1g; Carbohydrate 25.9g, of which sugars 3.5g; Fat 4.4g, of which saturates 0.6g; Cholesterol 13mg; Calcium 112mg; Fibre 0.9g; Sodium 152mg.

MOROCCAN BREAD

WARM THIS BREAD IN THE OVEN AND CUT IT INTO THICK SLICES TO SERVE WITH ANY CLASSIC MOROCCAN SAVOURY DISH. IT TASTES GOOD WITH A TAGINE, BUT IS EVEN BETTER WITH A STEW THAT HAS PLENTY OF LIQUID. USE IT TO MOP UP EVERY MORSEL OF SAUCE.

MAKES TWO LOAVES

INGREDIENTS
    275g/10oz/2½ cups strong white
      bread flour
    175g/6oz/1½ cups wholemeal
      (whole-wheat) flour
    10ml/2 tsp salt
    about 250ml/8fl oz/1 cup warm milk
      and water mixed
    10ml/2 tsp sesame seeds
For the yeast starter
    150ml/¼ pint/⅔ cup warm milk and
      water mixed
    5ml/1 tsp granulated sugar
    10ml/2 tsp dried yeast

1 First prepare the yeast. Place the warm milk mixture in a small bowl or jug (pitcher), stir in the sugar and then sprinkle with the yeast. Stir, then set aside in a warm place for about 10 minutes, until the yeast is frothy.

2 In a large bowl, mix together the two flours and salt. Add the yeast mixture and enough warm milk and water to make a fairly soft dough. Knead into a ball and then knead on a floured surface for 10 minutes.

3 Divide the dough into two equal pieces and shape into flattened ball shapes. Place on floured baking trays and press down with your hand to make round breads about 13–15cm/5–6in in diameter.

4 Cover the breads with oiled clear film (plastic wrap) or a clean, damp cloth and set aside in a warm place for 1–1½ hours, until risen. The breads are ready to bake when the dough springs back if gently pressed with a finger.

5 Preheat the oven to 200°C/400°F/Gas 6. Sprinkle the loaves with the sesame seeds and bake in the oven for 12 minutes. Reduce the heat to 150°C/300°F/Gas 2 and continue baking for 20–30 minutes, until they are golden brown and sound hollow when tapped underneath. Serve warm.

Energy 770Kcal/3271kJ; Protein 25g; Carbohydrate 162.8g, of which sugars 3.9g; Fat 6.6g, of which saturates 1g; Cholesterol 0mg; Calcium 260mg; Fibre 12.6g; Sodium 1973mg.

HOLIDAY BREAD

THREE TYPES OF SEEDS — PUMPKIN, SUNFLOWER AND SESAME — ARE USED TO FLAVOUR THIS TASTY BREAD, WHICH IS TRADITIONALLY MADE ON SPECIAL OCCASIONS SUCH AS BIRTHDAYS, WEDDINGS OR RELIGIOUS FESTIVALS. THE LOAVES CAN BE FROZEN, BUT SHOULD ALWAYS BE SERVED WARM.

MAKES TWO LOAVES

INGREDIENTS
    350g/12oz/3 cups strong white
        bread flour
    115g/4oz/1 cup cornmeal
    10ml/2 tsp salt
    150ml/¼ pint/⅔ cup warm milk and
        water mixed
    25ml/1½ tbsp pumpkin seeds
    25ml/1½ tbsp sunflower seeds
    15ml/1 tbsp sesame seeds
For the yeast starter
    150ml/¼ pint/⅔ cup warm water
    5ml/1 tsp granulated sugar
    10ml/2 tsp dried yeast

1 First prepare the yeast. Place the warm water in a small bowl, stir in the sugar and then sprinkle with the yeast. Stir once or twice, then set aside in a warm place for about 10 minutes until the yeast is frothy.

2 In a large bowl, mix together the flour, cornmeal and salt. Add the yeast mixture and enough of the warm milk and water mixture to make a fairly soft dough. Knead the dough into a ball and then knead it on a floured surface for about 5 minutes.

3 Add the seeds and knead them into the dough. Continue kneading for about 5–6 minutes, until the dough is firm and elastic.

4 Divide the dough into two equal pieces and shape into balls, flattening each one to make a frisbee shape. Place on floured baking trays and press down with your hand to make round breads about 13–15cm/5–6in in diameter.

5 Cover with oiled clear film (plastic wrap) or a damp cloth and set aside in a warm place for 1–1½ hours, until risen. The bread is ready to bake when it springs back if gently pressed with a finger.

6 Preheat the oven to 200°C/400°F/ Gas 6 and bake the breads in the oven for 12 minutes. Reduce the oven temperature to 150°C/300°F/Gas 2 and continue baking for 20–30 minutes until the loaves sound hollow when tapped.

VARIATION
You can use poppy seeds instead of sesame seeds.

Energy 999Kcal/4211kJ; Protein 28.2g; Carbohydrate 182.7g, of which sugars 3.1g; Fat 20.4g, of which saturates 2.1g; Cholesterol 0mg; Calcium 325mg; Fibre 8.8g; Sodium 1973mg.

PASTRIES AND DESSERTS

Some of the world's most sumptuous sweet treats are to be found in Middle Eastern pastry shops. Filled with fruit or nuts, then fashioned into elaborate shapes, the pastries emerge from the oven to be coated in syrup or honey. Such delights are not intended to be eaten every day. Family meals usually conclude, as they do in Africa, with fresh fruit. Sherbet is often served, or there may be a fragrant rice pudding. Super-sweet treats like halva and kodafa are saved for special occasions, and are eaten in small portions, with strong coffee or mint tea.

BAKLAVA

THE FILLING FOR THIS FAMOUS MIDDLE EASTERN DESSERT CAN BE WALNUTS, ALMONDS OR PISTACHIOS. THIS VERSION CELEBRATES THE PERSIAN NEW YEAR ON MARCH 21, THE FIRST DAY OF SPRING.

MAKES ABOUT 38-40

INGREDIENTS
350g/12oz/3 cups ground
  pistachio nuts
150g/5oz/1¼ cups icing
  (confectioners') sugar
15ml/1 tbsp ground cardamom
150g/5oz/10 tbsp unsalted
  butter, melted
450g/1lb filo pastry
For the syrup
450g/1lb/2¼ cups granulated sugar
300ml/½ pint/1¼ cups water
30ml/2 tbsp rose water

COOK'S TIP
Use ground hazelnuts or almonds instead
of pistachio nuts.

1 First make the syrup. Place the sugar and water in a pan, bring to the boil, then simmer for 10 minutes, until syrupy. Stir in the rose water and then leave to cool.

2 Mix together the nuts, icing sugar and cardamom. Preheat the oven to 160°C/325°F/Gas 3 and brush a large, rectangular baking tin (pan) with a little melted butter.

3 Taking one sheet of filo pastry at a time, and keeping the remainder covered with a damp cloth, brush the pastry sheet with melted butter and lay on the bottom of the tin. Continue until you have six buttered layers of pastry in the tin. Spread half of the nut mixture over the pastry, pressing it down with a spoon.

4 Take another six sheets of filo pastry, brush with butter and lay over the nut mixture. Sprinkle over the remaining nuts and top with a final layer of six filo sheets, brushed again with butter. Cut the pastry diagonally into small lozenge shapes using a sharp knife. Pour the remaining melted butter over the top.

5 Bake in the oven for 20 minutes, then increase the oven temperature to 200°C/400°F/Gas 6 and bake for a further 15 minutes, until golden and puffed.

6 Remove from the oven and drizzle about three quarters of the syrup over the pastry, reserving the remainder for serving. Arrange the baklava lozenges on a large glass dish and serve with extra syrup.

Energy 1016Kcal/4258kJ; Protein 13.4g; Carbohydrate 128.9g, of which sugars 108.4g; Fat 53.2g, of which saturates 17.4g; Cholesterol 53mg; Calcium 157mg; Fibre 4.3g; Sodium 468mg.

MA'AMOUL

JEWS EAT THESE DATE AND NUT BISCUITS AT PURIM, CHRISTIANS ENJOY THEM AT EASTER AND MUSLIMS SERVE THEM AT IFTAR, THE AFTER-SUNSET MEAL THAT BREAKS THE RAMADAN FAST. THEY ARE MADE IN SPECIAL WOODEN MOULDS, WHICH SEAL THE ROSE-SCENTED PASTRY AROUND THE FILLING.

MAKES THIRTY-FIVE TO FORTY

INGREDIENTS
    450g/1lb/4 cups plain
      (all-purpose) flour
    225g/8oz/1 cup unsalted butter, diced
    45ml/3 tbsp rose water
    60–75ml/4–5 tbsp milk
    icing (confectioners') sugar, for dusting
For the filling
    225g/8oz/1⅓ cups dried dates, stoned
      (pitted) and chopped
    175g/6oz/1 cup walnuts,
      finely chopped
    115g/4oz/⅔ cup blanched
      almonds, chopped
    50g/2oz/⅓ cup pistachio nuts, chopped
    120ml/4fl oz/½ cup water
    115g/4oz/⅔ cup granulated sugar
    10ml/2 tsp ground cinnamon

1 Preheat the oven to 160°C/325°F/ Gas 3. First make the filling. Place the dates, walnuts, almonds, pistachio nuts, water, sugar and cinnamon in a small pan and cook over a low heat, until the dates are soft and the water has been absorbed. Set aside.

2 Place the flour in a bowl and add the butter, working it into the flour with your fingertips. Add the rose water and milk and knead the dough until soft.

3 Take walnut-size pieces of dough. Roll each one into a ball and hollow with your thumb. Pinch the sides.

4 Place a spoonful of date mixture in the hollow then press the dough back over the filling to enclose it, press the edges together to seal.

5 Arrange the pastries on a large baking sheet. Press to flatten them slightly. Make little dents with a fork on the top of the pastries.

6 Bake in the oven for 20 minutes. Do not let them change colour or they will become hard. Cool slightly, and sprinkle with sifted icing sugar.

Energy 186Kcal/775kJ; Protein 3.2g; Carbohydrate 18.4g, of which sugars 8.4g; Fat 11.5g, of which saturates 3.9g; Cholesterol 14mg; Calcium 39mg; Fibre 1.2g; Sodium 49mg.

KAAB EL GHZAL

BETTER KNOWN BY THEIR FRENCH NAME OF CORNES DE GAZELLES — GAZELLE HORNS — THESE CURVED PASTRIES FILLED WITH ORANGE-SCENTED ALMOND PASTE ARE ONE OF MOROCCO'S FAVOURITE SWEET TREATS. THEY ARE TRADITIONALLY SERVED AT WEDDINGS.

MAKES ABOUT SIXTEEN

INGREDIENTS
200g/7oz/1¾ cups plain
  (all-purpose) flour
25g/1oz/2 tbsp butter, melted
about 30ml/2 tbsp orange flower
  water or water
1 large egg yolk, beaten
pinch of salt
icing (confectioners') sugar,
  to serve
For the almond paste
200g/7oz/1 cups
  ground almonds
115g/4oz/1¾ cups icing
  (confectioners') sugar or
  caster (superfine) sugar
30ml/2 tbsp orange flower water
25g/1oz/2 tbsp butter, melted
2 egg yolks, beaten
2.5ml/½ tsp ground cinnamon

1 First make the almond paste. Mix together all the ingredients to make a smooth paste.

2 To make the pastry, mix the flour and a pinch of salt and then stir in the melted butter, orange flower water or water, and about three-quarters of the egg yolk. Stir in enough cold water, little by little, to make a fairly soft dough.

3 Knead the dough for about 10 minutes, until smooth and elastic, then place on a floured surface and roll out as thinly as possible. Cut the dough into long strips about 7.5cm/3in wide.

4 Preheat the oven to 180°C/350°F/ Gas 4. Take small pieces of the almond paste and roll them between your hands into thin "sausages" about 7.5cm/3in long with tapering ends.

5 Place these in a line along one side of the strips of pastry, about 3cm/1¼in apart. Dampen the pastry edges with water and then fold the other half of the strip over the filling and press the edges together firmly to seal.

6 Using a pastry wheel, cut around each "sausage" (as you would with ravioli) to make a crescent shape. Make sure that the edges are firmly pinched together.

7 Prick the crescents with a fork or a needle and place on a buttered baking tray. Brush with the remaining beaten egg yolk and then bake in the oven for 12–16 minutes, until lightly coloured. Remove to a wire rack, cool and then dust with icing sugar. Serve warm or cold.

Energy 163Kcal/682kJ; Protein 4g; Carbohydrate 18.1g, of which sugars 8.2g; Fat 8.8g, of which saturates 1.5g; Cholesterol 16mg; Calcium 53mg; Fibre 1.3g; Sodium 13mg.

BRIOUATES WITH ALMONDS AND DATES

THESE MOROCCAN PASTRIES, MADE WITH FILO OR THE LOCAL EQUIVALENT — OUARKA — ARE A FAVOURITE TREAT. BRIOUATES CAN BE SAVOURY, BUT THESE ARE UNASHAMEDLY SWEET. THE FILLING IS A DATE AND ALMOND PASTE AND THEY ARE COATED IN HONEY AND ORANGE FLOWER WATER.

MAKES ABOUT THIRTY

INGREDIENTS
15ml/1 tbsp sunflower oil
225g/8oz/1⅓ cups blanched almonds
115g/4oz/⅔ cup stoned (pitted)
  dried dates
25g/1oz/2 tbsp butter, softened
5ml/1 tsp ground cinnamon
1.5ml/¼ tsp almond essence (extract)
40g/1½oz/⅓ cup icing
  (confectioners') sugar
30ml/2 tbsp orange flower water or
  rose water
10 sheets of filo pastry
50g/2oz/¼ cup butter, melted
120ml/4fl oz/½ cup clear honey
dates, to serve (optional)

1 Heat the oil in a small pan and fry the almonds for a few minutes until golden, stirring all the time. Drain on kitchen paper to cool, then grind the almonds in a coffee or spice mill. Process the dates in a blender or food processor.

2 Spoon the ground almonds into a mixing bowl or into the blender or food processor with the dates, and blend with the softened butter, cinnamon, almond essence, icing sugar and a little flower water to taste. If the mixture feels stiff, work in extra flower water.

3 Preheat the oven to 180°C/350°F/ Gas 4. Brush a sheet of filo pastry with melted butter and cut into three equal strips, keeping the remaining sheets covered with clear film (plastic wrap) to prevent them drying out.

4 Place a walnut-size piece of almond paste at the bottom of each strip. Fold one corner over the filling to make a triangle and then fold up, in triangles, to make a neat packet.

5 Brush the filo packet again with a little melted butter and set aside. Repeat steps 3 and 4 to make around 30 pastries.

6 While the briouates are cooking, pour the honey and a little orange flower or rose water into a pan and heat very gently. When the pastries are cooked, lower them one by one into the pan and turn them in the honey so that they are thoroughly coated all over.

7 Transfer the briouates to a plate and cool a little before serving, with dates if you wish.

Energy 95Kcal/396kJ; Protein 1.8g; Carbohydrate 7.5g, of which sugars 6g; Fat 6.6g, of which saturates 1.7g; Cholesterol 5mg; Calcium 23mg; Fibre 0.7g; Sodium 17mg.

GHORIBA

CRISP ON THE OUTSIDE, BUT MELTINGLY SOFT IN THE MIDDLE, THESE MOROCCAN ALMOND BISCUITS ARE A POPULAR MID-MORNING SNACK WITH COFFEE OR TEA.

MAKES ABOUT THIRTY

INGREDIENTS
2 egg yolks
1 egg white
200g/7oz/1¾ cups icing
    (confectioners') sugar, plus extra
    for dusting
10ml/2 tsp baking powder
finely grated rind of ½ lemon
a few drops of vanilla
    essence (extract)
about 350g/12oz/3 cups
    ground almonds
sunflower oil, for greasing

VARIATION
Use ground hazelnuts instead of
ground almonds.

1 Preheat the oven to 180°C/350°F/ Gas 4. In a bowl, beat together the egg yolks and egg white with the icing sugar. Add the baking powder, lemon rind and vanilla essence, with enough of the ground almonds to make a stiff paste. Knead the mixture together with your hands. Oil your hands with sunflower oil.

2 Take walnut-size pieces of paste and roll into small balls. Flatten on a board dusted with icing sugar and then place on a greased baking tray about 4cm/1½in apart. Bake for 15 minutes, until golden. Cool on a wire rack.

HONEYCOMB PANCAKES

LIKE DROP SCONES, THESE POPULAR PANCAKES BUBBLE WHEN THE BATTER IS SPOONED INTO A PAN, ACQUIRING A HONEYCOMB TEXTURE. ALSO KNOWN AS BEGHRIR, THEY ARE DELICIOUS WITH BUTTER AND HONEY AND ARE TRADITIONALLY EATEN AFTER SUNSET DURING RAMADAN.

MAKES ABOUT TWELVE

INGREDIENTS
175g/6oz/1½ cups self-raising
    (self-rising) flour
10ml/2 tsp baking powder
30ml/2 tbsp caster (superfine) sugar
1 egg
175ml/6fl oz/¾ cup semi-skimmed
    (low-fat) milk
15ml/1 tbsp rose water or orange
    flower water
15ml/1 tbsp melted butter
sunflower oil, for greasing

COOK'S TIP
Serve these pancakes warm and topped with a knob (pat) of butter on each one. For a breakfast treat, serve with melted butter and a generous helping of real maple syrup.

1 Mix together the flour, baking powder and sugar in a bowl. Add the egg and milk and blend to make a thick batter. Stir in the rose or orange flower water and then beat in the melted butter.

2 Heat a frying pan and brush the surface with a little oil. Pour in a small ladleful of batter, smoothing with the back of a spoon to make a round about 10cm/4in across. Cook for a few minutes until bubbles appear on the surface, then place on a large plate.

3 Cook the remaining pancakes in the same way and place them on the plate in overlapping circles to make a honeycomb pattern. Serve warm.

TOP Energy 102Kcal/426kJ; Protein 2.8g; Carbohydrate 7.8g, of which sugars 7.5g; Fat 6.9g, of which saturates 0.6g; Cholesterol 13mg; Calcium 33mg; Fibre 0.9g; Sodium 5mg.
BOTTOM Energy 82Kcal/346kJ; Protein 2.4g; Carbohydrate 14.6g, of which sugars 3.5g; Fat 1.9g, of which saturates 1g; Cholesterol 19mg; Calcium 42mg; Fibre 0.5g; Sodium 20mg.

ALMOND FINGERS

THIS VERY SIMPLE MIDDLE EASTERN SWEETMEAT IS ALSO POPULAR IN TUNISIA. THE FILO IS ROLLED INTO CIGAR SHAPES, WHICH ARE FILLED WITH A GROUND NUT AND ROSE WATER PASTE.

MAKES FORTY TO FIFTY

INGREDIENTS
200g/7oz/1¾ cups ground almonds
50g/2oz/½ cup ground pistachio nuts
50g/2oz/¼ cup granulated sugar
15ml/1 tbsp rose water
2.5ml/½ tsp ground cinnamon
12 sheets of filo pastry
115g/4oz/½ cup butter, melted
icing (confectioners') sugar,
to decorate

1 Preheat the oven to 160°C/325°F/ Gas 3. Mix together the almonds, pistachio nuts, granulated sugar, rose water and cinnamon for the filling.

2 Cut each sheet of filo pastry into four rectangles. Work with one rectangle at a time, and cover the remaining rectangles with a damp dishtowel to prevent them from drying out.

3 Brush one of the rectangles of filo pastry with a little melted butter and then place a heaped teaspoon of the nut filling in the centre of the pastry.

4 Fold in the sides and roll into a finger or cigar shape. Continue making "cigars" until all the filling and pastry have been used up.

5 Place the fingers on a buttered baking sheet and bake in the oven for 30 minutes, until lightly golden.

6 Transfer to a wire rack to cool and then dust with icing sugar.

COCONUT HALVA

IN EGYPT, THIS SYRUP-SOAKED SWEETMEAT IS CALLED BASBOUSA. TO ACHIEVE THE MOST DELICIOUS STICKINESS, POUR THE COLD SYRUP OVER THE CAKE AS SOON AS IT COMES OUT OF THE OVEN.

SERVES FOUR TO SIX

INGREDIENTS
115g/4oz/½ cup unsalted butter
175g/6oz/generous ¾ cup
granulated sugar
50g/2oz/½ cup plain
(all-purpose) flour
150g/5oz/scant 1 cup semolina
75g/3oz desiccated (dry unsweetened
shredded) coconut
175ml/6fl oz/¾ cup milk
5ml/1 tsp baking powder
5ml/1 tsp vanilla essence (extract)
whole almonds, to decorate
For the syrup
115g/4oz/⅔ cup caster
(superfine) sugar
150ml/¼ pint/⅔ cup water
15ml/1 tbsp lemon juice

1 First make the syrup. Place the sugar, water and lemon juice in a pan, stir to mix and then bring to the boil and simmer for 6–8 minutes, until it thickens. Allow to cool and then chill.

2 Preheat the oven to 180°C/350°F/ Gas 4. Melt the butter in a pan. Add the sugar, flour, semolina, coconut, milk, baking powder and vanilla essence and mix thoroughly.

3 Pour the cake mixture into a greased shallow baking tin (pan), level the surface and then bake in the oven for 30–35 minutes, until the top is golden.

4 Remove the halva from the oven and cut into diamond-shaped lozenges. Pour the cold syrup evenly over the top and decorate with a whole almond placed in the centre of each lozenge. Serve hot or cold.

TOP Energy 71Kcal/294kJ; Protein 1.5g; Carbohydrate 3.2g, of which sugars 1.6g; Fat 5.9g, of which saturates 1.8g; Cholesterol 6mg; Calcium 17mg; Fibre 0.5g; Sodium 25mg.
BOTTOM Energy 807Kcal/3391kJ; Protein 8.3g; Carbohydrate 118g, of which sugars 79.4g; Fat 36.9g, of which saturates 25.5g; Cholesterol 64mg; Calcium 125mg; Fibre 3.8g; Sodium 208mg.

APRICOT PARCELS <u>WITH</u> HONEY GLAZE

THESE PARCELS CAN BE MADE WITH DRIED APRICOTS THAT HAVE BEEN POACHED IN SYRUP BEFORE BEING STUFFED WITH THE ALMOND MIXTURE, BUT FRESH FRUIT IS THE BETTER OPTION. IT HAS A JUICY TARTNESS THAT CUTS THROUGH THE SWEETNESS OF THE HONEY. ROLL THE FILO PARCELS INTO ANY SHAPE, BUT LEAVE THEM OPEN SO THAT FRUIT AND PASTRY BENEFIT FROM THE GLAZE.

SERVES SIX

INGREDIENTS
  200g/7oz/1¾ cups blanched
    almonds, ground
  115g/4oz/⅔ cup granulated sugar
  30–45ml/2–3 tbsp orange flower
    water or rose water
  12 fresh apricots, slit and
    stoned (pitted)
  3–4 sheets of filo pastry, cut into
    12 circles or squares
  30ml/2 tbsp clear honey

1 Preheat the oven to 180°C/350°F/ Gas 4. Using your hands or a blender or food processor, bind the almonds, sugar and orange flower or rose water to a soft paste.

2 Take small walnut-size lumps of the paste and roll them into balls. Press a ball of paste into each slit apricot and gently squeeze the fruit closed.

3 Place a stuffed apricot on a piece of filo pastry, fold up the sides to secure the fruit and twist the ends to form an open boat. Repeat with the remaining apricots and filo pastry.

4 Place the filo parcels in a shallow ovenproof dish and drizzle the honey over them. Bake for 20–25 minutes, until the pastry is crisp and the fruit has browned on top.

5 Serve hot or cold with cream, crème fraîche, or a spoonful of yogurt.

Energy 347Kcal/1455kJ; Protein 9g; Carbohydrate 37.8g, of which sugars 27.4g; Fat 18.9g, of which saturates 1.5g; Cholesterol 0mg; Calcium 120mg; Fibre 4.2g; Sodium 8mg.

M'HANNCHA

THE SNAKE, OR M'HANNCHA TO USE THE ARABIC NAME, IS THE MOST FAMOUS SWEET DISH IN MOROCCO. THE COILED PASTRY LOOKS IMPRESSIVE AND TASTES SUPERB. CRISP, BUTTERY FILO IS FILLED WITH ALMOND PASTE THAT HAS BEEN SPICED WITH CINNAMON AND SCENTED WITH ORANGE FLOWER WATER. SERVE M'HANNCHA AS A DESSERT OR AS AN AFTERNOON TREAT WITH MINT TEA.

SERVES EIGHT TO TEN

INGREDIENTS
  115g/4oz/⅔ cup blanched almonds
  115g/4oz/½ cup butter, softened,
    plus 20g/¾oz for cooking nuts
  300g/11oz/2⅔ cups ground almonds
  50g/2oz/½ cup icing
    (confectioners') sugar
  115g/4oz/⅔ cup caster
    (superfine) sugar
  5–10ml/1–2 tsp ground cinnamon
  15ml/1 tbsp orange flower water
  3–4 sheets of filo pastry
  melted butter, for brushing
  1 egg yolk
  icing (confectioner's sugar) and
    ground cinnamon for the topping

1 Fry the blanched almonds in a little butter until golden brown, then pound them using a pestle and mortar until they resemble coarse breadcrumbs.

2 Place the nuts in a bowl and add the ground almonds, icing sugar, caster sugar, softened butter, cinnamon and orange flower water. Use your hands to form the mixture into a smooth paste. Cover and chill for 30 minutes.

3 Preheat the oven to 180°C/350°F/ Gas 4. Grease a large, round baking tin (pan) or a wide baking sheet.

4 Open out the sheets of filo pastry, keeping them in a pile so they do not dry out, and brush the top one with a little melted butter.

5 Lift one of the filo rolls in both hands and push it together from both ends, like an accordion, to relax the pastry before coiling it in the centre of the tin or baking sheet. Do the same with the other rolls, placing them end to end to form a tight coil like a snake.

6 Take lumps of the almond paste and roll them into fingers. Place them end to end along the long edge of the top sheet of filo, then roll the filo up into a roll the thickness of your thumb, tucking in the ends to stop the filling oozing out.

7 Repeat this with the other sheets of filo, until all the filling is used up.

8 Mix the egg yolk with a little water and brush this over the pastry, then bake in the oven for 30–35 minutes, until crisp and lightly browned.

9 Top the freshly cooked pastry with a liberal sprinkling of icing sugar, and add lines of cinnamon like the spokes of a wheel. Serve at room temperature.

Energy 281Kcal/1168kJ; Protein 4.1g; Carbohydrate 21g, of which sugars 15.8g; Fat 20.6g, of which saturates 8.3g; Cholesterol 56mg; Calcium 56mg; Fibre 1.3g; Sodium 91mg.

EGYPTIAN BREAD AND BUTTER PUDDING

THIS PUDDING IS RATHER ODDLY NAMED, SINCE IT CONTAINS NEITHER BREAD NOR BUTTER. WHAT IT HAS IN COMMON WITH THE CLASSIC ENGLISH DISH IS THE CUSTARD, WHICH IS POURED OVER LAYERS OF FINE PASTRY OR CRACKERS. THE LOCAL NAME IS OMM'ALI, WHICH MEANS "MOTHER OF ALI".

SERVES FOUR

INGREDIENTS
    10–12 sheets of filo pastry
    600ml/1 pint/2½ cups milk
    250ml/8fl oz/1 cup double
      (heavy) cream
    1 egg, beaten
    30ml/2 tbsp rose water
    50g/2oz/½ cup each chopped
      pistachio nuts, almonds and
      hazelnuts
    115g/4oz/¾ cup raisins
    15ml/1 tbsp ground cinnamon
    single (light) cream, to serve

1 Preheat the oven to 160°C/325°F/Gas 3. Lay the filo pastry sheets on top of each other on a baking sheet and bake in the oven for 15–20 minutes until crisp. Remove from the oven and increase the heat to 200°C/400°F/Gas 6.

2 Scald the milk and cream by pouring them into a pan and heating very gently, until hot but not boiling. Slowly add the beaten egg and the rose water. Cook over a low heat, until it thickens, stirring all the time. Remove from the heat.

3 Crumble the pastry using your hands and then spread it in layers with the nuts and raisins in the base of a greased shallow baking dish.

4 Pour the custard mixture evenly over the nut and pastry base and then bake in the oven for 20 minutes, until golden. Sprinkle with cinnamon and serve with single cream.

Energy 575Kcal/2393kJ; Protein 10.1g; Carbohydrate 38.8g, of which sugars 28.9g; Fat 43.3g, of which saturates 23.4g; Cholesterol 95mg; Calcium 255mg; Fibre 1.7g; Sodium 162mg.

ORANGES IN SYRUP

BOTH BITTER AND SWEET ORANGES ARE EXTENSIVELY CULTIVATED IN THE MIDDLE EAST. OF THE SWEET VARIETIES, JAFFA, WHICH ORIGINATED IN ISRAEL, IS PROBABLY THE BEST KNOWN. THIS METHOD OF SERVING THEM, IN SYRUP SCENTED WITH ORANGE BLOSSOM OR ROSE, IS VERY POPULAR.

SERVES FOUR

INGREDIENTS
    4 oranges
    600ml/1 pint/2½ cups water
    350g/12oz/1¾ cups granulated sugar
    30ml/2 tbsp lemon juice
    30ml/2 tbsp orange flower water
       or rose water
    50g/2oz/½ cup chopped
       pistachio nuts, to decorate

1 Peel the oranges with a potato peeler down to the pith.

2 Cut the orange peel into fine strips and then boil in water, changing the water several times to remove the bitterness. Drain and set aside until required.

COOK'S TIP
A perfect dessert to serve after a heavy main course dish. Almonds could be substituted for the pistachio nuts, if you like.

3 Place the water, sugar and lemon juice in a pan. Bring to the boil and add the orange peel. Simmer until the syrup thickens. Stir in the orange flower or rose water, and leave to cool.

4 Completely cut the pith away from the oranges and cut into thick slices. Place in a shallow serving dish and pour over the syrup. Chill for about 1–2 hours. Decorate with pistachio nuts and serve.

Energy 120Kcal/500kJ; Protein 3.6g; Carbohydrate 11.2g, of which sugars 10.9g; Fat 7.1g, of which saturates 0.9g; Cholesterol 0mg; Calcium 70mg; Fibre 2.8g; Sodium 72mg.

FIGS AND PEARS IN HONEY

FRESH FIGS PICKED STRAIGHT FROM THE TREE ARE SO DELICIOUS THAT IT SEEMS ALMOST SACRILEGE TO COOK THEM — UNLESS OF COURSE, YOU TRY THIS SUPERB METHOD.

SERVES FOUR

INGREDIENTS
    1 lemon
    90ml/6 tbsp clear honey
    1 cinnamon stick
    1 cardamom pod
    350ml/12fl oz/1½ cups water
    2 pears
    8 fresh figs, halved

1 Pare the rind from the lemon using a zester or vegetable peeler and cut the rind into very thin strips.

2 Place the lemon rind, honey, cinnamon stick, cardamom pod and the water in a pan and boil, uncovered, for about 10 minutes, until the liquid is reduced by about half.

3 Cut the pears into eighths, discarding the core. Leave the peel on or discard, as preferred. Place in the syrup, add the figs and simmer for about 5 minutes, until the fruit is tender.

4 Transfer the fruit to a serving bowl with a slotted spoon. Cook the liquid until syrupy, discard the cinnamon stick and pour over the figs and pears. Serve.

MOROCCAN-STYLE PLUM PUDDING

THERE'S A STRONG FRENCH INFLUENCE IN MOROCCAN COOKING, AS EVIDENCED BY THIS NORTH AFRICAN VERSION OF THE BATTER PUDDING KNOWN AS CLAFOUTI. GROUND RICE AND FLAKED ALMONDS THICKEN THE MILK MIXTURE, WHICH IS FLAVOURED WITH ORANGE FLOWER WATER.

SERVES FOUR

INGREDIENTS
    450g/1lb fresh plums or other fruit
      (see Variation)
    600ml/1 pint/2½ cups skimmed or
      semi-skimmed (low-fat) milk
    45ml/3 tbsp ground rice
    30–45ml/2–3 tbsp caster
      (superfine) sugar
    75g/3oz/¾ cup flaked almonds
    30ml/2 tbsp orange flower water or
      rose water, to taste
    icing (confectioners') sugar,
      to decorate

1 Preheat the oven to 190°C/375°F/Gas 5. Stone (pit) and halve the plums. Bring the milk to the boil in a pan.

2 Blend the ground rice with 30–45ml/2–3 tbsp cold water, beating well to remove lumps. Pour the hot milk over the rice then pour back into the pan. Simmer over a low heat for 5 minutes, until it thickens, stirring all the time.

3 Add the caster sugar and flaked almonds and cook gently for a further 5 minutes. Stir in the orange flower or rose water and simmer for 2 minutes.

4 Butter a shallow ovenproof dish and pour in the almond milk mixture. Arrange the prepared fruit on top and then bake in the oven for about 25–30 minutes, until the fruit has softened. Dust with sifted icing sugar and serve.

VARIATION
Apricots, cherries or greengages, can also be used for this pudding.

TOP Energy 186Kcal/790kJ; Protein 1.8g; Carbohydrate 45.9g, of which sugars 45.9g; Fat 0.7g, of which saturates 0g; Cholesterol 0mg; Calcium 110mg; Fibre 4.7g; Sodium 30mg.
BOTTOM Energy 308Kcal/1291kJ; Protein 11g; Carbohydrate 38.1g, of which sugars 28.6g; Fat 13.2g, of which saturates 2.4g; Cholesterol 9mg; Calcium 246mg; Fibre 2.4g; Sodium 69mg.

MINTED POMEGRANATE YOGURT
WITH GRAPEFRUIT SALAD

RUBY RED OR SALMON PINK, THE JEWEL-LIKE SEEDS OF THE POMEGRANATE MAKE ANY DESSERT LOOK BEAUTIFUL. HERE THEY ARE STIRRED INTO YOGURT TO MAKE A DELICATE SAUCE FOR A FRESH-TASTING GRAPEFRUIT SALAD. THE FLECKS OF GREEN ARE FINELY CHOPPED FRESH MINT, WHICH COMPLEMENT THE CITRUS FLAVOURS PERFECTLY. SERVE THE COMBINATION FOR BREAKFAST, AS A LIGHT SNACK DURING THE DAY, OR AS A DESSERT AFTER A SPICY MAIN COURSE.

SERVES THREE TO FOUR

INGREDIENTS
    300ml/½ pint/1¼ cups Greek
      (US strained plain) yogurt
    2–3 ripe pomegranates
    small bunch of fresh mint,
      finely chopped
    clear honey or caster (superfine)
      sugar, to taste (optional)
For the grapefruit salad
    2 red grapefruits
    2 pink grapefruits
    1 white grapefruit
    15–30ml/1–2 tbsp orange
      flower water
To decorate
    handful of pomegranate seeds
    fresh mint leaves

1 Put the yogurt in a bowl and beat well. Cut open the pomegranates and scoop out the seeds, removing and discarding all the bitter pith. Fold the pomegranate seeds and chopped mint into the yogurt. Sweeten with a little honey or sugar, if using, then chill until ready to serve.

2 Peel the red, pink and white grapefruits, cutting off and discarding all the pith. Cut between the membranes to remove the segments, holding the fruit over a bowl to catch the juices.

3 Discard the membranes and mix the fruit segments with the reserved juices. Sprinkle with the orange flower water and add a little honey or sugar, if using. Stir gently then decorate with a few pomegranate seeds.

4 Decorate the chilled yogurt with a sprinkling of pomegranate seeds and mint leaves, and serve with the grapefruit salad.

VARIATION
Alternatively, you can use a mixture of oranges and blood oranges, interspersed with thin segments of lemon. Lime segments work well with the grapefruit and mandarins or tangerines could be used too. As the idea is to create a refreshing, scented salad, juicy melons and kiwi fruit would also be ideal.

Energy 188Kcal/784kJ; Protein 8.8g; Carbohydrate 18g, of which sugars 18g; Fat 10.5g, of which saturates 5.2g; Cholesterol 0mg; Calcium 202mg; Fibre 3.6g; Sodium 82mg.

POACHED PEARS IN SCENTED HONEY SYRUP

FRUIT HAS BEEN POACHED IN HONEY SINCE ANCIENT TIMES. THE ROMANS DID IT, AS DID THE PERSIANS, ARABS, MOORS AND OTTOMANS. THE MOROCCANS CONTINUE THE TRADITION TODAY, ADDING A LITTLE ORANGE RIND OR ANISEED, OR EVEN LAVENDER TO GIVE A SUBTLE FLAVOURING. DELICATE AND PRETTY TO LOOK AT, THESE SCENTED PEARS WOULD PROVIDE AN EXQUISITE FINISHING TOUCH TO ANY MIDDLE EASTERN OR NORTH AFRICAN MEAL.

SERVES FOUR

INGREDIENTS
  45ml/3 tbsp clear honey
  juice of 1 lemon
  250ml/8fl oz/1 cup water
  pinch of saffron threads
  1 cinnamon stick
  2–3 dried lavender heads
  4 firm pears

VARIATION
Use whole, peeled nectarines or peaches instead of pears.

1 Heat the honey and lemon juice in a heavy pan that will hold the pears snugly. Stir over a gentle heat until the honey has dissolved. Add the water, saffron threads, cinnamon stick and flowers from 1–2 lavender heads. Bring the mixture to the boil, then reduce the heat and simmer for 5 minutes.

2 Peel the pears, leaving the stalks attached. Add the pears to the pan and simmer for 20 minutes, turning and basting at regular intervals, until they are tender. Leave the pears to cool in the syrup and serve at room temperature, decorated with a few lavender flowers.

Energy 66Kcal/278kJ; Protein 0.5g; Carbohydrate 16.5g, of which sugars 16.5g; Fat 0.2g, of which saturates 0g; Cholesterol 0mg; Calcium 17mg; Fibre 3.3g; Sodium 5mg.

BANANA AND MELON IN ORANGE VANILLA SAUCE

THE INDIAN OCEAN ISLAND OF MADAGASCAR IS A MAJOR PRODUCER OF VANILLA, SO IT IS NOT SURPRISING TO FIND THE SPICE FLAVOURING THIS DESSERT FROM NEIGHBOURING MOZAMBIQUE.

SERVES FOUR

INGREDIENTS
300ml/½ pint/1¼ cups orange juice
1 vanilla pod (bean) or a few drops of
   vanilla essence (extract)
5ml/1 tsp finely grated orange rind
15ml/1 tbsp granulated sugar
4 bananas
1 honeydew melon
30ml/2 tbsp lemon juice

1 Place the orange juice in a small pan with the vanilla pod or vanilla essence, orange rind and sugar and bring gently to the boil.

2 Reduce the heat and simmer gently for 15 minutes, until the sauce is syrupy. Remove from the heat and leave to cool. Once cool, remove and discard the vanilla pod, if using.

3 Peel and roughly chop the bananas and peel, seed and roughly chop the melon. Place the chopped bananas and melon in a large serving bowl and toss with the lemon juice.

COOK'S TIPS
To check whether a melon is ripe, lightly press the area around the centre of the tip of the melon, the surface should give slightly. A ripe melon will also smell pleasantly sweet.

4 Pour the cooled sauce over the fruit and chill in the refrigerator for at least 1 hour before serving.

BANANA MANDAZI

VERSIONS OF THIS MUCH-LOVED DESSERT — BANANA FRITTERS — ARE FOUND THROUGHOUT AFRICA, FROM KENYA TO KWAZULU-NATAL, IN ZAÏRE AND IN THE WEST AND NORTH OF THE CONTINENT.

SERVES FOUR

INGREDIENTS
1 egg
2 ripe bananas, roughly chopped
150ml/¼ pint/⅔ cup milk
2.5ml/½ tsp vanilla essence (extract)
225g/8oz/2 cups self-raising
   (self-rising) flour
5ml/1 tsp baking powder
45ml/3 tbsp caster (superfine) sugar
vegetable oil, for deep-frying

1 Place the egg, bananas, milk, vanilla essence, flour, baking powder and sugar in a blender or food processor.

2 Process to make a smooth batter. It should have a creamy dropping consistency. If it is too thick, add a little extra milk. Set aside for 10 minutes.

3 Heat the oil in a heavy pan or deep-fryer. When hot, carefully place spoonfuls of the mixture in the oil and deep-fry for 3–4 minutes, until golden. Remove with a slotted spoon and drain on kitchen paper. Keep warm while cooking the remaining mandazis, then serve at once.

TOP Energy 158Kcal/662kJ; Protein 2.3g; Carbohydrate 37.9g, of which sugars 35.6g; Fat 0.6g, of which saturates 0.1g; Cholesterol 0mg; Calcium 25mg; Fibre 1.9g; Sodium 48mg.
BOTTOM Energy 387Kcal/1637kJ; Protein 8.5g; Carbohydrate 67.7g, of which sugars 24.7g; Fat 11.1g, of which saturates 1.9g; Cholesterol 50mg; Calcium 258mg; Fibre 2.3g; Sodium 237mg.

CAFÉ GLACÉ

ICED COFFEE IS A POPULAR DRINK IN CAPE TOWN; A SWEET INDULGENCE ON THOSE LATE SPRING DAYS BEFORE THE HEAT OF HIGH SUMMER. THIS IS THE LUXURY VERSION.

SERVES FOUR TO SIX

INGREDIENTS

30–45ml/2–3 tbsp instant coffee
  granules or powder
15ml/1 tbsp granulated sugar
600ml/1 pint/2½ cups milk
475ml/16fl oz/2 cups water
ice cubes and vanilla ice cream
4–6 chocolate flakes, to decorate
8–12 crisp ice cream biscuits
  (cookies) or wafers, to serve

COOK'S TIP
You'll need to provide straws and long spoons for eating this dessert. Adjust the amount of coffee and sugar to suit your taste.

1 Dissolve the coffee in 120ml/4fl oz/ ½ cup of boiling water in a small mixing bowl. Add the sugar and stir well until it dissolves. Chill in the refrigerator for at least 2 hours. Mix together the milk and water in a large jug (pitcher). Add the chilled coffee and stir to mix well.

2 Pour the coffee mixture into long glasses until they are three-quarters full. Add ice cubes and the ice cream to the top of each glass. Decorate with the chocolate flakes and serve with the ice cream biscuits.

SWEET PUDDING

WITH ITS DELICATE FLAVOUR AND SILKY SMOOTH TEXTURE, THIS MILK PUDDING WOULD MAKE THE PERFECT FINALE FOR A MIDDLE EASTERN MEAL. STREW THE PLATE WITH ROSE PETALS, IF YOU LIKE.

SERVES FOUR

INGREDIENTS

50g/2oz/⅓ cup ground rice
45ml/3 tbsp cornflour (cornstarch)
1.2 litres/2 pints/5 cups milk
75g/3oz/scant ½ cup
  granulated sugar
30ml/2 tbsp rose water
50g/2oz/½ cup ground almonds
25g/1oz/¼ cup ground pistachio nuts
ground cinnamon, to decorate
golden (light corn) syrup or clear
  honey, warmed, to serve

1 Blend the ground rice and cornflour to a paste with a little cold milk in a small bowl. Set aside.

2 Bring the remaining milk to the boil in a pan, then add the sugar and simmer gently. Gradually add the ground rice paste to the milk, stirring constantly with a wooden spoon to mix.

3 Simmer the mixture over a very gentle heat for 10–15 minutes, until the mixture has thickened, stirring frequently and being very careful not to burn the bottom of the pan, which would damage the very delicate flavour of the rice.

4 Stir in the rose water and half of the ground almonds and simmer for a further 5 minutes.

5 Cool for a few minutes and then pour the rice mixture into a serving bowl or individual dishes. Sprinkle with the remaining ground almonds and ground pistachio nuts and then decorate with a dusting of ground cinnamon. Serve with warmed syrup or honey.

TOP Energy 87Kcal/370kJ; Protein 5.8g; Carbohydrate 11.2g, of which sugars 11g; Fat 2.6g, of which saturates 1.6g; Cholesterol 9mg; Calcium 188mg; Fibre 0g; Sodium 68mg.
BOTTOM Energy 409Kcal/1724kJ; Protein 14.7g; Carbohydrate 55.6g, of which sugars 34.8g; Fat 15.6g, of which saturates 4.6g; Cholesterol 18mg; Calcium 395mg; Fibre 1.2g; Sodium 235mg.

TROPICAL FRUIT PANCAKES

IN THIS SOUTH AFRICAN DESSERT, PANCAKES ARE FILLED WITH A MIXTURE OF MANGOES, BANANAS, KIWI FRUIT AND ORANGES, MOISTENED WITH A HONEYED CITRUS SYRUP FLAVOURED WITH VAN DER HUM, THE LOCAL BRANDY-BASED TANGERINE LIQUEUR.

SERVES FOUR

INGREDIENTS
    115g/4oz/1 cup self-raising
      (self-rising) flour
    pinch of freshly grated nutmeg
    15ml/1 tbsp caster (superfine) sugar
    1 egg
    300ml/½ pint/1¼ cups milk
    15ml/1 tbsp melted butter or
      margarine, plus extra for frying
    15ml/1 tbsp fine desiccated
      (dry unsweetened shredded)
      coconut (optional)
    whipped fresh cream, to serve
For the filling
    225g/8oz prepared ripe, firm mango
    2 bananas
    2 kiwi fruit
    1 large orange
    15ml/1 tbsp lemon juice
    30ml/2 tbsp orange juice
    15ml/1 tbsp clear honey
    30–45ml/2–3 tbsp orange liqueur
      (optional)

1 Sift the flour, nutmeg and caster sugar into a large bowl, add the egg and most of the milk and beat with a wooden spoon to make a thick, smooth batter.

2 Add the remaining milk, melted butter or margarine, and the coconut, if using, and continue beating until the batter is smooth and of a fairly thin, dropping consistency.

3 Melt a little butter or margarine in a large non-stick frying pan.

4 Swirl the hot fat round the pan then pour in a little batter to cover the base. Fry until golden, then toss or turn with a spatula. Repeat with the remaining mixture to make about eight pancakes.

5 Dice the mango, roughly chop the bananas and slice the kiwi fruit. Cut away the peel and pith from the orange and cut into segments.

6 Place the fruit in a bowl. Mix together the lemon and orange juices, honey and orange liqueur, if using, then pour over the fruit. Fold a pancake in half and spoon a little of the fruit in the centre, Fold the corners over. Serve with whipped cream.

Energy 303Kcal/1285kJ; Protein 8.5g; Carbohydrate 56.5g, of which sugars 34g; Fat 6.5g, of which saturates 3.3g; Cholesterol 60mg; Calcium 239mg; Fibre 4.1g; Sodium 182mg.

SPICED NUTTY BANANAS

THIS BAKED BANANA DESSERT FROM CENTRAL AFRICA COULDN'T BE SIMPLER. THE NUTTY CRUST
CONTRASTS BEAUTIFULLY WITH THE CREAMY BANANA BENEATH, AND THE RUM SAUCE IS DELICIOUS.

SERVES THREE

INGREDIENTS

　6 ripe, but firm, bananas
　30ml/2 tbsp chopped unsalted
　　cashew nuts
　30ml/2 tbsp chopped unsalted
　　peanuts
　30ml/2 tbsp desiccated (dry
　　unsweetened shredded) coconut
　7.5–15ml/½–1 tbsp demerara
　　(raw) sugar
　5ml/1 tsp ground cinnamon
　2.5ml/½ tsp freshly grated nutmeg
　150ml/¼ pint/⅔ cup orange juice
　60ml/4 tbsp rum
　15g/½oz/1 tbsp butter or margarine
　double (heavy) cream, to serve

1 Preheat the oven to 200°C/400°F/
Gas 6. Slice the bananas and place them
in a greased, shallow ovenproof dish.

2 Mix together the cashew nuts,
peanuts, coconut, sugar, cinnamon
and nutmeg in a small bowl.

3 Pour the orange juice and rum over
the bananas, then sprinkle the nut and
sugar mixture over the top.

4 Dot the top with butter or margarine,
then bake in the oven for 15–20
minutes, until the bananas are golden
and the sauce is bubbly. Serve with
double cream.

COOK'S TIPS
Freshly grated nutmeg makes all the
difference to this dish. More rum can be
added, if preferred. Chopped mixed nuts
can be used instead of peanuts.

Energy 455Kcal/1902kJ; Protein 7.7g; Carbohydrate 51.5g, of which sugars 45.3g; Fat 20.6g, of which saturates 10g; Cholesterol 11mg; Calcium 29mg; Fibre 4.4g; Sodium 69mg.

PAPAYA AND MANGO WITH MANGO CREAM

MAKE THE MOST OF MANGOES WHEN THEY ARE IN SEASON BY MIXING THEM WITH PAPAYAS AND TOSSING THEM IN AN APRICOT SAUCE. A CHILLED MANGO CREAM IS THE PERFECT TOPPING.

SERVES FOUR

INGREDIENTS

2 large ripe mangoes
300ml/½ pint/1¼ cups extra thick
    double (heavy) cream
8 ready-to-eat dried apricots, halved
150ml/¼ pint/⅔ cup orange juice
    or water
1 ripe papaya

1 Take one thick slice from one of the mangoes and, while still on the skin, slash the flesh with a sharp knife in a criss-cross pattern to make cubes.

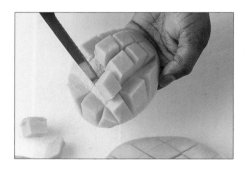

2 Turn the piece of mango inside-out and cut away the cubed flesh from the skin. Place the flesh in a bowl, mash with a fork to a pulp, then add the cream and mix together. Spoon into a freezer-proof container, cover and freeze for about 1–1½ hours, until half frozen.

3 Put the apricots and orange juice or water in a small pan. Bring to the boil, then simmer gently until the apricots are soft, adding a little juice or water, if necessary, to keep moist. Remove the pan from the heat and set aside to cool.

4 Peel, stone (pit) and chop or dice the remaining mango as before and place in a bowl. Cut the papaya in half, remove and discard the seeds and peel. Dice the flesh and add to the mango.

5 Pour the apricot sauce over the fruit and gently toss together so the fruit is well coated.

6 Stir the semi-frozen mango cream a few times until it is spoonable but not soft. Serve the fruit topped with the mango cream.

COOK'S TIP
Mangoes vary tremendously in size. If you can only find small ones, buy three instead of two to use in this dessert.

Energy 462Kcal/1914kJ; Protein 2.6g; Carbohydrate 23g, of which sugars 22.8g; Fat 40.6g, of which saturates 25.1g; Cholesterol 103mg; Calcium 67mg; Fibre 3.6g; Sodium 26mg.

FRESH PINEAPPLE WITH COCONUT

IN THOSE PARTS OF AFRICA WHERE PINEAPPLES ARE GROWN, THE FRUIT AND THE FRESHLY PRESSED JUICE ARE SOLD AT ROADSIDE STALLS. THIS RECIPE CELEBRATES THE FRUIT'S FANTASTIC FLAVOUR.

SERVES FOUR

INGREDIENTS

   1 fresh pineapple, peeled
   slivers of fresh coconut
   300ml/½ pint/1¼ cups
     pineapple juice
   60ml/4 tbsp coconut liqueur
   2.5cm/1in piece of preserved stem
     ginger, plus 45ml/3 tbsp of
     the syrup

1 Slice the pineapple, arrange in a serving dish and scatter the coconut slivers on top.

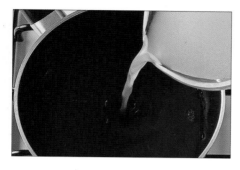

2 Place the pineapple juice and coconut liqueur in a pan and heat gently.

3 Thinly slice the preserved stem ginger and add to the pan together with the ginger syrup. Bring just to the boil and then simmer gently, until the liquid is slightly reduced and the sauce is fairly thick.

4 Pour the sauce over the pineapple and coconut, leave to cool, then chill in the refrigerator before serving.

VARIATION
If fresh coconut is not available, then use desiccated (dry unsweetened shredded) coconut instead.

Energy 175Kcal/744kJ; Protein 1.2g; Carbohydrate 31.9g, of which sugars 31.9g; Fat 2g, of which saturates 1.3g; Cholesterol 0mg; Calcium 43mg; Fibre 2.8g; Sodium 12mg.

FRAGRANT RICE

THIS RICE PUDDING RECIPE COMES FROM NORTH AFRICA, WHERE IT IS SERVED WITH A SPRINKLING OF CHOPPED DATES AND NUTS. THE FRAGRANT MIXTURE IS ALSO USED AS A FILLING FOR PASTRIES.

SERVES FOUR

INGREDIENTS
  75g/3oz/scant ½ cup short grain rice
  about 900ml/1½ pints/3¾ cups milk
  30ml/2 tbsp ground rice
  50g/2oz/¼ cup caster
    (superfine) sugar
  40g/1½oz/⅓ cup ground almonds
  5ml/1 tsp vanilla essence (extract)
  2.5ml/½ tsp almond essence (extract)
  a little orange flower water (optional)
  30ml/2 tbsp chopped dried
    stoned (pitted) dates
  30ml/2 tbsp pistachio nuts,
    finely chopped
  30ml/2 tbsp flaked almonds, toasted

1 Place the rice in a pan with 750ml/ 1¼ pints/3 cups of the milk and heat gently until simmering. Cook, uncovered, over a very low heat for 30–40 minutes, until the rice is completely tender, stirring frequently and adding more milk, if necessary.

2 Blend the ground rice with the remaining milk and stir into the rice pudding. Slowly bring back to the boil and cook for 1 minute.

COOK'S TIP
Orange flower water is used in surprisingly large quantities in Moroccan sweets and pastries. However, unless you are partial to the strongly perfumed flavour, add it very sparingly, taste, then add more as required.

3 Stir in the sugar, ground almonds, vanilla and almond essences and orange flower water, if using, and cook until the pudding is thick and creamy.

4 Pour into serving bowls and sprinkle with the chopped dates, pistachio nuts and almonds.

ORANGE AND DATE SALAD

FRESH DATES ARE BEST FOR THIS FRAGRANT SALAD. IT IS POPULAR THROUGHOUT THE ARAB WORLD, AND CAN BE SERVED AS A DESSERT OR AS AN ACCOMPANIMENT TO ROASTED MEATS.

SERVES FOUR TO SIX

INGREDIENTS
  6 oranges
  15–30ml/1–2 tbsp orange flower
    water or rose water (optional)
  lemon juice (optional)
  115g/4oz/⅔ cup stoned dates
    (see Cook's Tip)
  50g/2oz/⅓ cup pistachio nuts
  icing (confectioners') sugar,
    to taste
  a few whole blanched almonds

COOK'S TIP
Use fresh dates, if you can find them, although dried dates are delicious in this salad, too.

1 Peel the oranges with a sharp knife, removing all the pith, and cut into segments, catching the juices in a bowl. Place the orange segments in a serving dish.

2 Stir in the juice from the bowl together with a little orange flower or rose water, if using, and sharpen with lemon juice, if liked.

3 Chop the dates and pistachio nuts and sprinkle over the salad with a little sifted icing sugar. Chill in the refrigerator for 1 hour.

4 Just before serving, sprinkle over the toasted almonds and a little extra icing sugar and serve.

TOP Energy 343Kcal/1437kJ; Protein 14.3g; Carbohydrate 32.5g, of which sugars 16.8g; Fat 17.9g, of which saturates 3.8g; Cholesterol 13mg; Calcium 327mg; Fibre 2.1g; Sodium 140mg.
BOTTOM Energy 156Kcal/655kJ; Protein 4.4g; Carbohydrate 19.9g, of which sugars 19.6g; Fat 7.1g, of which saturates 0.9g; Cholesterol 0mg; Calcium 101mg; Fibre 4g; Sodium 76mg.

SWEET COUSCOUS WITH ROSE-SCENTED FRUIT COMPOTE

ALTHOUGH COUSCOUS IS BEST KNOWN FOR ITS SAVOURY ROLE, IT IS ALSO EATEN AS A DESSERT OR AS A NOURISHING BREAKFAST DISH. THIS SWEET, NUTRITIOUS MIXTURE TASTES GREAT WITH A DRIED FRUIT COMPOTE. MAKE THE COMPOTE A FEW DAYS AHEAD, SO THAT THE FLAVOURS CAN MINGLE, AND SERVE IT WARM, WITH THE FRESHLY COOKED SWEET COUSCOUS. THE MILK MIXTURE, WHICH IS POURED OVER JUST BEFORE THE DISH IS TAKEN TO THE TABLE, MAKES IT LOVELY AND CREAMY.

SERVES SIX

INGREDIENTS
    300ml/½ pint/1¼ cups water
    225g/8oz/1⅓ cups couscous
    50g/2oz/scant ⅓ cup raisins
    50g/2oz/¼ cup butter
    50g/2oz/¼ cup granulated sugar
    120ml/4fl oz/½ cup milk
    120ml/4fl oz/½ cup double
      (heavy) cream
For the fruit compote
    225g/8oz/1 cup dried apricots
    225g/8oz/1 cup stoned (pitted)
      prunes
    115g/4oz/¾ cup sultanas
      (golden raisins)
    115g/4oz/⅔ cup blanched almonds
    175g/6oz/generous ¾ cup
      granulated sugar
    30ml/2 tbsp rose water
    1 cinnamon stick

1 Prepare the fruit compote a couple of days in advance. Put the dried fruit and almonds in a bowl and pour in just enough water to cover. Gently stir in the sugar and rose water, and add the cinnamon stick. Cover and leave the fruit and nuts to soak for 48 hours, during which time the water and sugar will form a lovely golden-coloured syrup.

2 To make the couscous, bring the water to the boil in a pan. Stir in the couscous and raisins, and cook gently for 1–2 minutes, until the water has been absorbed. Remove the pan from the heat, cover tightly and leave the couscous to steam for 10–15 minutes. Meanwhile, poach the compote over a gentle heat until warmed through.

COOK'S TIPS
The couscous can be served on its own, drizzled with clear or warmed honey instead of with the dried fruit compote. The compote is also delicious served chilled on its own or with yogurt.

3 Tip the couscous into a bowl and separate the grains with your fingertips. Melt the butter and pour it over the couscous. Sprinkle the sugar over the top then, using your fingertips, rub the butter and sugar into the couscous. Divide the mixture between six bowls.

4 Heat the milk and cream together in a small, heavy pan until they are just about to boil, then pour the mixture over the couscous. Serve immediately, with the dried fruit compote.

Energy 661Kcal/2771kJ; Protein 9.4g; Carbohydrate 95.6g, of which sugars 75.9g; Fat 29.3g, of which saturates 12.1g; Cholesterol 46mg; Calcium 143mg; Fibre 4.8g; Sodium 82mg.

MINT TEA

IN MOROCCO, WHERE IT IS THE NATIONAL DRINK, MINT TEA IS KNOWN AS ATAY BI NAHNA. THE MINT LEAVES ARE LEFT TO INFUSE IN THE SWEET BREW SO THAT THE FLAVOUR IS PRONOUNCED. IN OTHER MIDDLE EASTERN LANDS, SUCH AS LEBANON, THE MINT IS ADDED ONLY WHEN SERVING. MINT TEA IS ENJOYED THROUGHOUT THE DAY. IT QUENCHES THE THIRST, EASES A SOCIAL OCCASION, WELCOMES A GUEST AND IS AN ESSENTIAL PART OF THE BARGAINING PROCESS WHEN MAKING A MAJOR PURCHASE.

SERVES TWO

INGREDIENTS
10ml/2 tsp Chinese gunpowder green tea
small bunch of fresh mint leaves
granulated sugar, to taste

1 Put the tea in a small tea pot and fill with boiling water. Add the mint leaves and leave it to infuse (steep) for 2–3 minutes.

2 Stir in sugar to taste and pour into tea glasses or cups to serve.

COOK'S TIPS
At feasts and on special occasions, the making of mint tea can be an elaborate ceremony: the best green tea is chosen and only fresh spearmint (*Mentha spicata*), of which a well-known cultivar called Moroccan is used. A fine silver-plated, bulbous-shaped teapot is selected for brewing and the heavily sweetened tea is poured rhythmically into fine glasses. For an additional flounce of ceremony, a fresh, fragrant orange blossom or jasmine flower may be floated in each glass. In winter, wormwood is sometimes added for extra warmth, and infusions flavoured with aniseed or verbena are quite common.

Energy 20Kcal/86kJ; Protein 0.2g; Carbohydrate 5.2g, of which sugars 5.2g; Fat 0g, of which saturates 0g; Cholesterol 0mg; Calcium 3mg; Fibre 0g; Sodium 1mg.

INDEX